28844

D0437473

EXPOSITION

OF

ECCLESIASTES

By

H. C. LEUPOLD, D. D.

Professor of Old Testament Exegesis
Capital University Seminary, Columbus, Ohio

BAKER BOOK HOUSE
Grand Rapids, Michigan

TO
MY DEAR CHILDREN

HERBERT	ELSIE
FERN	RUSSELL

FOREWORD

There is one book of the Old Testament that is written particularly to furnish guidance and counsel for God's people in evil days and times of depression. Its counsel is as timely now as it was when the book was written, for this old world has changed but little except for the dress in which it is clad.

This book is Ecclesiastes.

But unfortunately, it is so little understood that few of its interpreters and readers seem to have recognized that it has a living message that meets the special problems also of our age.

It is a book which the church may put into the hands of her afflicted and bewildered children with the suggestion: "Here is divine counsel for evil days."

It is with these thoughts in mind that we are offering this Exposition, that we might render a service to those who seek to guide their footsteps by the light of the Word. We hope to make a part of the treasures of this blessed book accessible to the church.

We have, therefore, set forth the material of this Exposition in such a manner that we believe even the intelligent layman who knows nothing of Hebrew can easily gather the substance of the interpretation.

One glance will suffice to convince the exacting student that we have gone quite exhaustively into the exegetical problems of the book.

Also the pastor who may not profit from an examination of the original language will find that our Exposition aims to meet his needs.

THE AUTHOR.

ABBREVIATIONS

BDB—Hebrew and English Lexicon of the Old Testament, by Francis Brown, S. R. Driver and C. A. Briggs, 1907.

Buhl—Hebräisches Handwörterbuch, Gesenius, edited by Frants Buhl, Leipzig, 1905.

KS—Lehrgebäude der hebräischen Sprache, II Syntax, 1897, by Eduard König.

KW—Hebräisches und aramäisches Wörterbuch zum Alten Testament, 1922, by Eduard König.

GK—Gesenius-Kautzsch, Hebr. Grammatik, 271 Edition, 1902.

EXPOSITION OF ECCLESIASTES

INTRODUCTION

1. Name

The name by which this book is commonly known in English is Ecclesiastes. This is nothing more than a transliteration of the name that the Greek translators gave to it in seeking a Greek equivalent for the Hebrew title and so reveals nothing of the character of the work as does the original name. What the Hebrew name implied was rendered in a very acceptable fashion by *Luther*, who gave the book the title, *Der Prediger*, which means, The Preacher, the secondary title found in our English version. The Hebrew name of the book is Koheleth (pronounced Ko-háy-leth). This is derived from the Hebrew root *kahal*, which, though it is not used in the Kal, signifies "to assemble as a congregation," and the corresponding noun *kahal* means a "congregation." He, however, who assembles a congregation does it for the purpose of addressing it, and so the term rightly designates the "Preacher." The feminine ending of this Kal participle designates the office, as similar official titles have feminine endings in the Hebrew.

This correct interpretation of the name of the book was recognized and explained already by Jerome and is now quite commonly accepted. To have the term carry meanings such as "gatherer" or "collector," viz., of proverbs and sentences, has no solid foundation, nor does it agree with the nature of the book. So also Ginsburg's interpretation fails to satisfy, namely, "an assembler of scattered people into the more immediate presence of God; a gatherer of those afar off unto God."

2. Author and Time of Composition

The book has the name Koheleth because it claims
to have been written by Koheleth. The opening statement reads: "The words of Koheleth." The author designates himself in this way again in 1:12 and 12:9.
Interesting is the passage 7:27, in that it uses the
feminine form of the verb with this same noun as its
subject, indicating that the author may also be conceived as a kind of personification, let us say, of wisdom.

The rest of 1:1 reads: "The son of David, king in
Jerusalem." These words are in apposition with the
name Koheleth. It is this statement, together with the
thoughts of the first two chapters, which gave rise to
the view that, like Proverbs and the Song of Solomon,
the book, too, was of Solomonic authorship. This is the
view of the matter as it has been traditionally held:
after Solomon had strayed from Jehovah and His ways
and had plunged into idolatry he toward the close of
his life recovered himself in true repentance, and in
testimony both of his repentance and of the wisdom
that he had gathered as to the worth and the value of
all earthly possessions he wrote this book, which so
strongly stresses the vanity of all earthly things.

This same approach had been developed somewhat
differently by the Jews who, with various modifications
of the tale, related that, because of his idolatry and the
dissatisfaction of the people with his rule toward the
end of his life, Solomon was compelled to relinquish
his throne and wandered about among his people, pay-
ing the price of his folly and telling his sad tale. He is
then said to have recovered his spiritual balance. Having been obliged to relinquish his throne, he could very
appropriately say: "I *was* king over Israel in Jerusalem," 1:12. One cannot avoid having the feeling that
this tale was devised in order to furnish an explanation
for the past tense in this quotation.

Only the last days of Solomon were deemed a suitable time for the writing of this book, for the whole tone, especially of Chapter 2, is that of a man who has lived long and tried out the true value of earthly goods to the utmost, as indeed the writer claims that he did, and so, after a lifetime of earnest experimentation, arrives at this result.

Several serious weaknesses of this explanation, however, at once challenge attention. A rather extensive substructure has to be developed to carry the heavy superstructure. The substructure is the fiction of the repentance of Solomon. On the subject of this repentance the historical books of the Scriptures are strangely silent. Any man, reading what the books of the Kings report on the matter, would, without a doubt, conclude that, since his defection from the Lord is the last fact recorded concerning him, this sin was the last item to be reported. For his repentance, had it actually occurred, would certainly have been a matter of such great moment as to make the writer's silence with regard to it entirely unpardonable, especially when a comparatively full account of his life is being offered, as is certainly the case in Kings.

In addition to the silence of the historical books there is the silence of this very book of Ecclesiastes. For, without a doubt, the author does not speak as a man who had once lapsed from grace and was by God's mercy restored. The book might even, if that were the case, raise a doubt as to the genuineness of his repentance inasmuch as it nowhere makes reference to it. The book as a whole is sometimes regarded as proof of the author's repentance in that it is claimed that only a man who had come back to the Lord could have written so valuable a book. But the flaw in the argument, aside from its begging the question, is the fact that we search in vain for even the slightest indication that the author ever had experienced a notable repentance to record.

But this is not all. There are certain statements in the book which cannot be harmonized with the assumption that Solomon wrote it. There are complaints about corrupt officials and corrupt practices of men in high station. With reference to this fact we may very aptly cite the words of Jahn, quoted by *Keil* (*Einleitung*): "Solomon could not have complained so bitterly of oppression, of unrighteousness on the part of judicial authorities, of the elevation of fools and slaves to positions of dignity, and of disabilities laid upon the rich and the prominent, without writing a satire upon himself." A strange picture of Israel's sufferings and oppressions is unrolled before our eyes. Kings are found to be very tyrannical and debauched. Unrighteousness prevailed, and uprightness and true piety were trodden underfoot. At almost every turn something indicates that "the times are out of joint."

But what the Scriptures report concerning Solomon's reign is the very opposite of such a gloomy situation. In I Kings 4:20 we read: "Judah and Israel were many as the sand which is by the sea in multitude, eating and drinking and making merry," and verse 25: "Judah and Israel dwelt safely, every man under his vine and under his fig tree, from Dan even unto Beer-Sheba, *all the days of Solomon.*" This is not a report concerning a temporary prosperity which prevailed during Solomon's reign. In view of this statement the complaints brought by Jeroboam about taxes must appear as exaggerated, and they certainly cannot invalidate the account of verse 25, which is strong and all-inclusive. Israel never saw better days than those it experienced under David and Solomon.

Over against the weaknesses of this position—which position many feel they must take in faithfulness to the very Scriptures themselves—are to be placed the *positive arguments* from the Scriptures themselves, which indicate that the book as such gives a far different answer to the question, "Who was the author?"

First of all, there are the positive statements of the book itself, the chief of which we quoted before, 1:1: "The words of the Preacher, the son of David, king in Jerusalem." Neither here nor elsewhere in the book is the name of Solomon mentioned. Besides, "king in Jerusalem," is a title that is nowhere else used in the Scriptures with reference to Solomon. The Septuagint translators sensed the inadequacy of the heading from this point of view and felt constrained to add the words "of Israel" after the word "king." But if it be objected that only Solomon could be meant by the statement of verse 1, especially in view of the activities listed in Chapter 2, we answer: "This is correct in a sense, but still the words are so chosen as to induce us to feel that it is not the historical Solomon who is meant." We shall explain this more fully in a moment.

Of far greater weight is the argument that the condition in which the people addressed find themselves agrees most closely with the condition of the people after the return from the Exile, particularly with the time of Malachi. We shall specify a few items at once. Outwardly Israel is depressed, deprived of its civil liberty, suffering from grievous misrule and much injustice, enduring all the indignities which the enemies of God's people ought to have suffered, and, apparently, living on without hope of a propitious future. All power is in the hands of cruel and greedy oppressors.

Spiritually Israel stands on a low level. The fine repentance manifested in the period immediately after the return from the Exile is a thing of the past. Gloom and hopelessness have filled the hearts of many. And they expect too much from material resources and advantages. The spirit of finding fault with God's leadings is coming to the forefront. A spirit of disputatiousness over against those who would set them right is becoming manifest. Work-righteousness and externalism are sadly in evidence. And, above all, spiritual despair and blank hopelessness have seized upon the minds of those who constitute the better element spiritually. A comparison of the following passages, even before we examine the book in detail, will show the correctness of this claim: cf. 7:10 with Mal. 2:17; 3: 13-15; Neh. 1:3; Ezra 4:5; Neh. 9:36 f.; Ps. 123:3 f.; especially cf. Eccles. 8:9 with Neh. 5:15; cf. Eccles. 5:1, 5, 6 with Mal. 1:8, 14.

To this may be added, from another point of view, the effective description of *Ginsburg*: "But we submit that the state of oppression, violence, and misery depicted in this book cannot be reconciled with the reign of Solomon, and is therefore against the Solomonic authorship of it. Palestine, the inheritance of the Lord, was then groaning under the oppression of satraps and presented such a scene of injustice and violence, that death was thought preferable to life, and not to have been born at all was deemed still better (4:1-4; 5:7); Asiatic despotism, which permits no will to its subjects, was rampant (8:1-4), filling the 'holy places' with wicked officials (8:10), suddenly raising servants to posts of honor, and hurling the great from their lofty positions (10:5-7); this tyranny, with its numerous spies, had penetrated into the privacy of families to such a fearful extent, that it actually became dangerous to give utterance to one's thoughts in the secrecy of home (10:20); wickedness and crime were perpetrated with perfect impunity, so much so, that people were thereby encouraged to commit heinous sins, and were led to deny the moral government of God (8:10 f.) and to neglect their duties to the Creator (5:1-5)."*

One counterargument may be met at once. It is the argument that Malachi and Ecclesiastes cannot be con-

---

*Ginsburg, Christian D., *Coheleth, Commonly Called the Book of Ecclesiastes*, London: Longman, Green, Longman, and Roberts, 1861, p. 250.

temporary books because Malachi writes in a pure Hebrew style whereas Ecclesiastes is strongly tinged with Aramaisms and evidences of a decided change in the language which tends toward many departures from pure Hebrew. This argument does not impress us as being particularly convincing. It proceeds on the assumption that in a given age the literary style of writers as to type of language employed must be quite uniform.

A very simple and natural assumption *could* readily explain this difference in style. Consider a man who has steeped himself in the writings of the past that are couched in the purest classical Hebrew and has, perhaps, largely had his contacts with men of a similar kind, who may even have still spoken a pure Hebrew, and you have an author who may have written like Malachi, especially since he may have consciously sought to pattern his style after the purest Hebrew models. Assume, on the other hand, the case of a man who has, perhaps, not lived so assiduously in the very style of the sacred writings of the past and has besides dwelt among those whose Hebrew was more rapidly undergoing modifications along the line of adopting Aramaic patterns of expression, and you have the style of Ecclesiastes. For that matter, even the living in a different locality might almost have been sufficient to account for the stylistic differences between these two books. It is a mechanical, artificial, and unhistorical assumption that contemporary authors must use distinctly similar styles.

A third strong argument belongs here. It is the argument from language. The language of Ecclesiastes is distinctly late in character, dating from the period after the Exile. It is very true that altogether too much emphasis has in some instances been placed on this argument in connection with the problem of fixing the date of other Biblical books. But here, for the nonce, it is entirely in place. He that has read the Aramaic portions of Ezra and Daniel and compared them with the language of Ecclesiastes must admit a close affinity between them. In his commentary *Delitzsch* has a useful list of late words that Ecclesiastes uses (p. 190-201, English edition) ; likewise *Volck* in Strack and Zoeckler's commentary (p. 106-108) ; also *Koenig, Einleitung* (p. 432).

Let these items be mentioned in addition to the distinctly late words of Aramaic and Persian origin: the use of *she* for *'asher,* which had by this time almost crowded the latter form aside; the almost entire cessation of the use of imperfects with *waw conversive;* the use of the personal pronoun as a separate subject with a verb having the pronominal suffix ending, and this not for emphasis; the more frequent use of participles and conjunctions, etc.

Who, then, was the author, and what did the claim in 1:1 mean when it referred to the "son of David, king in Jerusalem"? We shall have to content ourselves with the fact that, as the book repeatedly claims, the author is Koheleth, the Preacher, who in sections of this book impersonates Solomon. Some interpreters have an aversion to the idea of accepting this literary figure, for they fear that such acceptance would sanction, directly or indirectly, some form of deceit. But mark well, we do not for a moment suggest that Koheleth tried to lead anyone to believe that he was actually Solomon. There is no "pious fraud"; there could not be, in the very nature of the case. Writing almost 600 years after Solomon's time, the author, speaking as though he were Solomon, would not be attempting to deceive anybody. On reading his book everyone recognized that he was attempting to communicate wisdom that Solomon might have accumulated. Men knew the Preacher and his reputation (12:9 f.). The use of such a literary device is as harmless as when Tennyson writes the poem *Sir Galahad,* and begins: "My good blade carves the casques of men." To claim that the use of such a literary figure involves something in the nature of deceit or forgery does not further the cause of truth. We shall have to content ourselves with the fact that the author is anonymous.

Besides, it should be noticed that the figure of having the author speak in the person of the wise king Solomon extends only through the first two chapters of this book. The figure has by that time served its purpose and is quietly dropped. After reading from Chapter 3 to the end of the book no one would surmise for a moment that Solomon might have written this portion. So we shall have to designate the author simply as Koheleth.

It was felt at quite an early date that one would not dare to ascribe the book to Solomon without hesitation. The *Talmud* has the notice that Ecclesiastes is one of the four books that come to us from Hezekiah and his college of scribes. That, of course, needs to involve no more than that this group acted as collectors of extant literary remains. *Luther* makes several statements under this head. In his *Table Talk* he drops the remark that the author of the book may have lived at the time of the Maccabees and may have been Sirach. But in the Introduction to the book (written in 1524) he ascribes the book to later redactors, who put Solomon's thoughts into the form in which we now have them, and says: "To tell the truth, this book was not written by Solomon himself with his own hand, but the words heard from his mouth by others were finally arranged by the learned men, as we now have them." In his lectures on the book (published in 1532) he lets Solomon be the speaker but supposes that several of those that were present at the time these sentiments were uttered proceeded very shortly to commit them to writing. In any case, Luther recognized the existence of a problem but never arrived at a positive conclusion.

Hugo Grotius (1644) was the first interpreter who definitely advanced the idea that the book is not to be ascribed to Solomon. Since his time his contention has been received more and more widely, even by very conservative scholars. At the present time there are but few interpreters who do not accept it.

Of these few, *Taylor Lewis,* the translator of Zoeckler's comments on the book, in Schaff's American edition of *Lange's Commentary,* stands out. However, his arguments in support of his contention carry little force. A careful reading of them leaves the impression that he fails to meet the issue squarely.

Another valiant contender for authorship by Solomon is *Rupprecht* in his *Einleitung.** Though in all things else of a Biblical critical nature Rupprecht is a very safe guide, a valiant contender for sound views on Old Testament problems, this is one instance where he has failed to convince us though he gives as able a statement of the case as we know. For example, he claims that a tone of world-weariness may characterize the utterances of men in good days even as a similar tone is found creeping into the works of classical Roman writers of the Augustan period. However, the parallel does not fit inasmuch as the writer of our book does not actually use the tone of a world-weary man. Furthermore, the passage alluded to above, I Kings 4:25, forbids putting the days of Solomon on a par with the effete Augustan age. In Chapter 2 especially the writer speaks about carefully conducted experiments which yield definite results. In the rest of the book he speaks of very concrete ills that surround him and his contemporaries. Not for a mo-

---

*Rupprecht, Eduard, *Einleitung in das Alte Testament*, Gütersloh, C. Bertelsman, 1898.

ment do we find him living in the midst of a *thriving* people, lamenting over the vanity of things. He is surrounded by a *suffering* people.

3. The Purpose of the Book

In determining what purpose this book is to serve we should emphasize particularly the following facts. The book is written primarily for the godly in Israel. They are the only ones, as usual, who would give attention to a book such as this. Since the times are evil and the godly suffer much, this is primarily a book of comfort. It shows God's people how to meet their difficult problems. *Cox* is right in claiming that this is "one of the most consolatory and inspiriting Scriptures." It is for this reason that the second half of the book gives counsel and comfort for evil days exclusively. Many of the efforts to expound this book suffer from the defect of not having discovered this basic truth about the book.

The way is prepared for such comfort by the first part of the book, which beautifully illustrates the second major purpose of the book. By teaching with tremendous emphasis the vanity of all earthly things the author first disillusions his hearers. For men will have at least some expectation of the comfort and the solace that are to be derived from the possession of earthly goods. As long as they are thus minded they are preparing the way for added sorrows. Especially in evil times men should stake no hope on earthly goods and treasures. The best service that can be rendered a man is to divorce him from the things of this world as completely as possible. We call that disillusionment. The author aims to achieve such an end as thoroughly as possible. Men who know the vanity of all things are well prepared for the trials of depressing times.

In addition to these two major purposes of the book, which run parallel with the two halves of this book, there is a subsidiary purpose, we believe, which takes account of the danger which godly men run of falling into the sins of a certain age. This is the purpose of *warning*. Certain sins are the besetting sins of an age. The ungodly may not be persuaded to break with them. The godly will heed instruction. Therefore we have the author's warnings against formalism, discontent, attempting to solve what lies beyond our ken, looking with longing at what is thought to have been a desirable past, and the like.

Therefore, we believe, the following three words correctly summarize the purpose of the book: comfort, disillusionment, and warning. A still more accurate formulation of the purpose could be stated thus: to counsel and to comfort troubled saints.

This positive statement of the case ought to help us to arrive at a correct estimate of the many and widely divergent pronouncements on the purpose of the book that we are apt to encounter. For there are few Biblical books with regard to whose purpose there is a greater lack of unanimity. Men either try to fit the book into Solomon's age and so miss the mark, or else, by positing a very late date, they fail to harmonize the book with its times and the requirements of such times. A good bit of confusion is caused by the attempt, so commonly made by the critically-minded, to assign a date that is far later than the external and the internal evidence warrants. To a very large extent, an unscriptural approach has led commentators to misjudge the purpose of the book.

Some interpreters employ the terms theoretical and practical and claim that a proper statement of the case requires that we insist upon a fair balance of the theoretical and the practical elements in the book. We can accept such a claim with certain modifications. In evil times, such as those that obtained when the book originated, men are not given to idle theorizing. Men need solid practical help. So, whatever seems to savor of theory in this book is theory only for the purpose of affording direct and practical counsel and comfort for men whose souls are being sorely tried.

From this point of view, as well as from the standpoint of faith in inspiration, we regard as unsatisfactory all claims that would make of Ecclesiastes "the breviary of the most modern materialism and extreme licentiousness" (*Hartman*). Never was a book misunderstood more sadly than was Ecclesiastes when this was stated as its purpose; or even the following: *Heine* classed it as the "Song of Skepticism" (*Das Hohelied der Skepsis*).

When the reader is struggling to find a solution of the purpose of the book he may find that the following opinion has a strong appeal, namely, that this book is the record of an earnest thinker's struggles with his many problems: he wrestles with them, states them frankly and honestly; and finally arrives at certain conclusions that he feels justified in holding. A better view of the work as a whole shows the author to be an inspired agent of God who is speaking throughout with that certainty and freedom from doubt which should mark a man in whom God's Spirit dwells—this does not involve a mechanical theory of inspiration. In no instance is the author skeptical or troubled by doubt. His position is firm, and his views are so eminently sound that he can, by his divinely given message, stabilize those who will give heed to his words.

Quite unsatisfactory is the claim that this book has as its theme, "All is vanity." Such a view is not permissible since the author himself clearly sets forth his theme in 12:13: "Fear God and keep His commandments." Though the Scriptures nowhere else give so emphatic proof of the vanity of all things as they do in this book, this proof is only a means to an end, namely, to persuade men not to have undue confidence in worldly treasures. "All is vanity" is, indeed, the keynote of the *first* half of the book.

Another very common statement of the purpose of the book is that it "sets before us the search for the *summum bonum*" (the highest good). Though the author of the interpretation of this book in the *Expositor's Bible,* following the lead of many others, in his day made the claim: "As for the design of this book no one now doubts that it sets before us" this quest, a very serious objection must be made to this view. God's people are not searching after the *summum bonum.* They have it. They cannot be God's people and still have any doubt as to whether God is the highest good or not. They do not have to engage in a search after the Highest Good. It is the very essence of faith to have it. Least of all do inspired writers venture upon such a quest. Besides, if the book be rightly interpreted, there is nothing in it that leads one to this view. The philosophical approach has suggested thoughts such as these, and revealed truth is diametrically opposed to the philosophical quest after truth, at least in this one instance.

A few of the remaining formulations of the chief thought or purpose of the book may yet be mentioned. *Oehler* speaks the truth but does not say enough when he maintains: "The standpoint of the book can briefly be said to be that of resignation."* Incidentally, yes. It seeks to inculcate resignation, but a resignation coupled with a clear and intelligent faith.

Those interpreters who label this a "philosophical didactic poem" may be said to be correct if the word "philosophic" is hedged about with sufficient restrictions so as to rule out all possibility of the solution of man's major problems by the use of his own reason without divine guidance.

----

*Oehler, Gust. Fr., *Theologie des Alten Testaments,* Stuttgart, Steinkopf, 1882, (p. 881).

There is no doubt about the fact that much confusion has prevailed in regard to this book. In addition to the serious misinterpretation of the general purpose and of many individual passages, a good bit of the difficulty no doubt arose from the fact that the author looks at different sides of the questions he posits. As a result he makes claims that, unless they be rightly understood, seem to be opposites. He speaks of the value of wisdom, yet he seems to contend that the acquisition of wisdom is of no profit. He seems to counsel extreme soberness, yet he advocates being of a merry heart. These *and many others* that could be mentioned are paradoxes that are no less serious than are those of life itself. A fair interpretation will, however, see that the author is entirely just in his claims and justified in his conclusions.

4. Style

Because of uncertainty in arriving at a satisfactory view of the book's purpose, conflicting claims in regard to the style of the book have also been voiced. Some have found the style excessively harsh, or have seen the author multiplying devices in a labored attempt to state clearly the problems he is toiling to solve. Others speak of the apt and marvelously skillful style. The latter claim is the one we share as our exposition will demonstrate. The author's thoughts are expressed with amazing exactitude. New constructions are employed. Participles are handled with a deftness that challenges our admiration. On the whole, his style is a very adequate vehicle for expressing his very helpful counsel.

Since some of the features of this style were not sufficiently understood, and many writers were quite at sea as to what the author sought to achieve, the translations offered are unfortunately often so defective as to lead readers far from an adequate comprehension of the author's immediate purpose and to cause much unnecessary bewilderment. The translation that we offer, though occasionally devoid of literary elegance, is sufficiently helpful to relieve at least the major difficulties. It has also given serious attention to many of the modern versions.

Another problem on which we must say a word is the literary form: Is the book poetry or prose? Again commentators are divided into two almost equal camps. Dependable men like *Hertzberg* and long before him *Zoeckler* established poetical form almost throughout the book. Equally sober men like *Delitzsch* and *Koenig* failed to detect sufficient evidence to cast their vote for poetical structure. The attitude of the Jewish scholars, who provided the accents that are still used also in the poetical books, should bear some weight with us. They failed to class Ecclesiastes among the poetical books and to provide it with a corresponding set of accents. *Pfeiffer* summarizes the position of the majority when he writes: "On the whole, Ecclesiastes is written in prose, except 1:2-8, 15, 18; 2:14a; 3:2-8; 4:5f.; 5:3 (Heb. 5:2) ; 6:7; 7:1-11; 8:1, 5; 9:7f., 17f.; 10:1-3, 6-20; 11:1, 3a, 4, 6a, 7, 9f.; 12:1-8."*

The situation may, then, be stated about as follows: we have in this book a rhythmical prose which repeatedly soars to the level of poetic form with parallelism and like ornamentations. I have, for my part, not investigated this problem with sufficient thoroughness to do more than just to record an impression. Since the question is a moot one, those commentators who presume to make textual emendations in order to bring the text into harmony with a particular theory of meter or the like that they happen to hold are dealing presumptuously with the text and deserve to have all such efforts of theirs viewed with suspicion. This criticism applies to much of that which is offered in

---

*Pfeiffer, Robert H., *Introduction to the Old Testament,* New York: Harper and Brothers (1941), p. 724.

the margin of the Kittel text of the Hebrew Bible as material bearing on textual criticism. We have, therefore, refrained from trying to give a semblance of poetic form to our translation. By its arrangement of the text the Kittel Hebrew Bible suggests that perhaps half of the book is regarded as poetic in structure.

5. The Integrity of the Book and the Text

Much could be said on this score. It is sufficient for our purpose to indicate that criticism has used its customary approach in trying not so much to interpret the book as to make it fit into a preconceived scheme of things.

Siegfried, as extreme a critic as has assailed the book, (and why should Biblical books have to be assailed?) claims to have discovered successive authors, who built each man on his predecessor, interpolating to their heart's content or according to their particular theological bias, men whom he designates as Q1, Q2, Q3, Q4, and Q5. He then claims to have discovered two redactors and three epilogists. This extreme position has been satisfactorily refuted by the claim that the successive authors could have far more readily written a new and original work than to have tried to make a work with which they disagreed convey their thoughts by alterations and interpolations superimposed.

The more moderate critics make use of their usual freedom in seeking to improve the Masoretic text by frequent conjectures. Since this cannot be regarded as a safe exegetical procedure, we can do nothing other than to reject it as being too greatly conditioned by the subjective wishes of the critics.

The fact remains that we have in this book, as ordinarily, a good Hebrew text, which may, as sound exegetical criticism develops a truly scientific method in this field, perhaps be improved in a few minor details. Though the versions on this book, too, have been subjected to a minute analysis, their study has thus far apparently yielded nothing to overthrow our confidence in the integrity of the Hebrew text of the book.

6. Outline

Also under this head the widest divergence of opinion obtains. Some interpreters have despaired of tracing any consecutive thought throughout the book. They will admit the occasional sequence of parts and a more or less loose relation of these parts to one another and content themselves with letting the book ramble along.

Other commentators find two, three, four, seven, twelve, and thirteen major parts and an equal diversity of themes. *Galling* breaks up the whole into thirty-seven (!) parts, each of which he calls a *Sentenz*— parts practically unconnected with one another.

One scheme of division that has sober scholars to support it may, according to its chief exponents, be labelled the Vaihinger-Keil outline. However, even this seems to be so unclear that even after careful study one finds great difficulty in retaining the elaborate statement of parts in mind.

We believe that the Outline which we have appended is true to the contents of the book and, as to its major parts, sufficiently clear to be retained in mind without too much effort. The strictest logic might want to object, e.g., to II, D., the insertion of an *exhortation* in the demonstration of the Vanity of All Things, but we believe that the practical purpose of the book makes such an insertion quite proper without breaking up the orderly development of thought.

After elaborating this outline independently we were struck by the fact that it is closely akin to the outline offered by *W. J. Deane* in the *Pulpit Commentary*, which we had not previously examined. We believe, however, that this effort of Deane's could have been improved upon if, instead of numbering eleven "sections" in the first half and eighteen in the second, he had sought to relate them more closely to one another and to study how these sections readily group themselves under convenient heads. He would thus have secured a more clearly articulated outline.

Outline

I. PROLOGUE: "All Is Vanity" (1:1-11)

II. THE VANITY OF ALL THINGS (1:12-6:12)

    A. *First Group of Things Whose Vanity Is Demonstrated* (1:12-2:23)

        1. The vanity of human striving after wisdom (1:12-18)

        2. The vanity of human mirth (sensuous enjoyment) (2:1-11).

        3. The vanity of human wisdom as such (2:12-17)

        4. The vanity of human labor (2:18-23)

    B. *General Principles That Show that Such Vanity Is a Logical Necessity* (2:24-3:22)

        1. Real enjoyment in all things depends on a higher source than man (2:24-26)

        2. For God is the Absolute Ruler over His people (3:1-15)

        3. Even perversion of justice must serve His sovereign purpose (3:16-22)

    C. *Another Group of Things by Which Vanity Is Demonstrated* (4)

        1. By the sad lot of the oppressed (4:1-3)

        2. By the futility of earthly endeavor (4:4-6)

        3. By the futility of the acquisition of riches (4:7-12)

        4. By the vanity of high station (4:13-16)

D. *An Inserted Exhortation—against the Danger of Becoming Vain in Worship* (5:1-9)
1. Warning against formalism (5:1-7)
2. Comfort in the face of oppression (5:8, 9)

E. *The Third Group of Things by Which Vanity Is Demonstrated* (5:10-6:12)
1. The vanity of riches (5:10-20)
   a) As being unable to satisfy (5:10-12)
   b) As being a harm to man (5:13-17)
   c) Brief exhortation to enjoy the gifts God permits (5:18-20)
2. The vanity of possessing goods that cannot be enjoyed (6:1-6)
3. Why a man cannot be satisfied with riches (6:7-9)
4. Why it is useless for a man to strive for riches (6:10-12)

III. COUNSEL FOR DAYS OF SUFFERING (7:1-12:7)

A. *The Value of Suffering* (7:1-10)
1. Its value by way of comparison (7:1-4)
2. The value of the rebuke of the wise in times of suffering (7:5-7)
3. The value of patient endurance of suffering (7:8-10)

B. *The Value of Wisdom at Such Times* (7:11-29)
1. Wisdom, a fine regulative in days of suffering (7:11-14)
2. Wisdom, the golden mean (7:15-18)
3. The self-restraint of wisdom in the face of humiliation (7:19-22)
4. The difficulty of attaining unto true wisdom (7:23-29)

C. *Problems on Which Wisdom Throws Light* (8:1-10:20)

  1. Submission to the heavenly King (8:1-8)

  2. The oppression of the righteous (8:9-13)

  3. The inability to fathom God's doings (8:14-17)

  4. The similar fate of the godly and the ungodly—no cause for pessimism and inaction (9:1-10)

  5. The higher destiny controlling the final outcome (9:11, 12)

  6. Wisdom still the greatest of Israel's resources (9:13-18)

  7. The ultimate readjustment of disturbing discrepancies in God's government (10:1-11)

      a) Folly will bear its usual fruit (1-4)

      b) The discrepancy—Israel's humiliation (5-7)

      c) The ultimate failure of great worldly enterprises through lack of wisdom (8-11)

  8. A correct estimate of the rulers of the time (10:12-20)

      a) The vanity of the endeavors of foolish rulers (12-15)

      b) Their reprehensible debauchery (16-20)

D. *Exhortation to Benevolence and Cheerful Activity* (11:1-8)

E. *Exhortation to Youth to Enjoy the Days of Youth* (11:9-12:7)

IV. EPILOGUE (12:8-14)

  1. The author's authentication of himself (8-11)

  2. The author's recommendation of his message (12-14)

7. The Outstanding Theological Thought

We do not intend to go into great detail on this point. The study of the exposition of the book itself will best reveal what this work embodies. To gain a summary view, it will be best briefly to review the Outline (Number 6 above). It will then become apparent that nowhere is the doctrine of the vanity of all things taught with greater emphasis and applied more consistently than in this book. Yet not one bit of exaggeration is to be detected in this emphatic portrayal.

It is at this point that we ought to point very distinctly to the use of the phrase "under the sun," a characteristic phrase of Koheleth's. Few interpreters have understood it rightly; hardly any have applied it consistently. In it lies the corrective for the extravagant views that Koheleth seems to utter. It must always be borne in mind that by the use of this phrase the author rules out all higher values and spiritual realities and employs only the resources and gifts that *this* world offers. The use of this phrase is equivalent to drawing a horizontal line between earthly and heavenly realities and leaving out of consideration all that is above this line, that is to say, all higher values. To such a course of procedure no man need object, for that is a course that men who are in trouble and out of it very commonly follow, behaving as though the heavenly realities and spiritual treasures were entirely inaccessible.

In the second chief part there is a great wealth of counsel for days of suffering. This fact makes this book one that should be most assiduously put to use in the days of trouble and depression. It has an undying message for such times, a fact which very few commentators stress. It touches most intimately those problems which stir men to the very depth of their being in evil days. In this connection it shows the value of true wisdom; it reconciles apparent discrepancies in God's government of the world as we observe it; it counsels humble submission under God's almighty hand; it points to the readjustments that a final judgment brings; and it teaches the lesson of *faith* with a most delightful emphasis by the manner in which it treats all these subjects.

In vindication of the good author and his valuable book we must reject certain misconceptions and rather serious criticisms that have been laid to the charge of this book. These belong under this caption, for certainly Koheleth's theology would have been sadly deficient if any single one of these charges had any substantial foundation.

Such serious charges as the following are raised against Koheleth. He is accused of having no belief in a hereafter. This charge is based particularly on 3:21. This passage, rightly construed, teaches the very opposite and gives indication of a well-founded belief in a hereafter. Some interpreters see the doubt, as they call it, of 3:21 resolved into faith by the time 12:7 is reached. Though it does justice to 12:7, such a view is still unsatisfactory.

All the passages that resemble 4:2 or 6:8 are regarded an indication of a deep-seated pessimism on Koheleth's part. However, he has surrounded all these statements with so many safeguards that they are not only not dangerous but are true to the very letter and convey a deep Scriptural conception of the vanity of this world and what it has to offer.

Then all passages like 2:24 and 3:12, 13 are taken either as evidence of reaction against dull despair or as indications of Epicureanism on the author's part. They are neither. A careful examination of them, according to their meaning and the connection in which they appear, will demonstrate that all these passages are among the most sober and useful bits of counsel that was ever given to mortal man. We need never feel that we have to offer apologies for the so-called low level of Koheleth's conception of these and similar problems. He is a true man of God who is offering invaluable counsel.

Equally untenable is the charge of fatalism, based on statements such as 7:13, or the charge of advocacy of the ethics of expediency, based on 7:16-18. Compare the exposition on these passages.

Besides, a suggestion which is otherwise in a general way applicable to the so-called wisdom literature of the Scriptures (Job, Proverbs, Ecclesiastes, and some Psalms) that the distinctively *Israelitish* element recedes more into the background over against that which is distinctively *human* (*Volck*) is not entirely apropos in reference to this book. Some commentators have erased the distinctive Israelitish features and are thus able to advance this claim. For one thing, note what emphasis is laid on wisdom as Israel's prerogative and the value of possessing it in evil days (9:13-18).

Even statements such as: "Those attributes of the divine being that throb with life and warmth (*lebenswarm*) are missing" (*Hertzberg*) in this book must be accepted with reservations. They do not point to a limited conception of the deity on the author's part but to the fact that he found it necessary to stress certain divine attributes in order to carry through his purpose. To draw conclusions from his silence would be unfair to him.

It is, however, one of the unique features of this book that it uses only the general divine name that designates merely the deity, viz., *Elohim*, and not the specific name that designates the faithful God of covenant and promise, *Jehovah*. The reason for this may be found in the fact that for many faith had to be reconstructed from the bottom up. Not the advanced knowledge of God that ripened faith has is what the author stresses. Simple basic attributes and concepts

such as are set forth are covered by the general term
God—*Elohim.*

In a negative way it may be claimed that this
book gives prominence to the Messianic element in
revelation in that it shows how with the measure of
revelation that it had before the Christ came Israel
was sore beset in faith and required special counsel to
enable it to weather the hard shocks that assailed
faith—a situation which is entirely relieved by the
coming of the Christ of God. This point of view is
specially stressed by *Vilmar* in his *Collegium Biblicum.*

8. The Relation of Koheleth to Greek and Babylonian Thought

Following a tendency that is rather customary in
critical circles, the effort is made to derive the material
of Ecclesiastes, in part at least, from extra-Israelitish
sources. One school of critics makes Koheleth a borrower from Greek philosophers. Another school sends
him to Babylonian or even Egyptian thinkers. The
ground has been rather thoroughly canvassed by
scholars. The attempts to identify Koheleth with Greek
thought suffer chiefly from the contradictory nature
of the rival claims. In one case they send our author
to Heraclitus, in another to the Stoics and not to
Heraclitus, in another to Epicurus and to neither of
the two before mentioned. No scholar can point to anything definite. The claimants were and are at war
among themselves. Their straining to make a point
is only too evident. We feel that *Delitzsch* was correct
in saying: "Not a trace of Greek influence" in Koheleth.

Somewhat more serious are the attempts to make
Koheleth a borrower from Babylonia. An unbiased
examination of individual passages, however, can convince any investigator that, even where a formal re-
semblance seems to obtain, the contrast in spirit between any two so-called parallel passages is telling.

Light is not borrowed from darkness. See by way of illustration the outstanding case treated in connection with 9:9.

The same is true in relation to Egyptian influence. With reference to this *Galling* admits "direct or indirect parallels" in some instances, pointing particularly to 1:12; 8:1; 8:10. But he adds very wisely that "in no case is it permissible to postulate an acquaintance with the literature apparently involved," that is to say, "acquaintance with the original language" of these documents.* *Galling* points to one remote possibility as far as the influence of Phoenician materials is concerned in reference to the familiar expression *tachath hashshemesh*, "under the sun." In Phoenician inscriptions of the fifth century (*Albright* seems to date this instance in the third century; see below) one instance of the use of the phrase has been found, which he claims may in itself reflect Greek influence . . . but he rightly claims that Koheleth may have already found the expression current in Hebrew.

Albright, referring first of all to archaeological sources, says: "As might be expected from its date [3rd cent. B. C.] the book remains without appreciable elucidation from archaeological sources." Mentioning that in both Egypt and Mesopotamia writings have been discovered in which a "similar fatalism is inculcated," he hastens to remark that none of these "remotely approaches the latter's [Koheleth's] high standard of piety." We do not agree with him as to the late date of the book, nor as to the charge of belief in some kind of fatalism. But another remark of his is helpful when he says: "In Eccl. 11:2 we find the numerical ladder 'seven-eight' which is quite common in Ugaritic literature, as well as in Hittite texts . . .

---

*Galling, Kurt, *Handbuch zum Alten Testament*, (Eissfeldt) Tübingen, F. C. B. Mohr (Paul Siebeck), 1940 (p. 49).

over a millennium earlier."* Albright apparently implies that such a "numerical ladder" was a common
literary device that was used by many nations of
antiquity.

9. Exegetical Literature

The following commentaries, which are for the
most part quite readily accessible to the average student, have distinct value.

Luther, *Auslegung des Predigers Salomo*, Exposition of Ecclesiastes printed 1532. St. Louis edition,
Vol. V, 1372ff. This work still has distinct value inasmuch as Luther understood that this book seeks to
inculcate a cheerful use of God's gifts, not monastic
abstinence.

Reynolds, Edward, *A Commentary on the Book of
Ecclesiastes*, London, 1811. This work reflects the trend
of interpretation that was popularly current in Eng-
land somewhat more than a century ago.

Hengstenberg, E. W., *Commentary on Ecclesiastes*,
in *Clark's Foreign Theological Library*, Edinburgh,
English edition translated by D. W. Simon (1869).
Still the most valuable commentary that we have been
able to secure. Unfortunately the prejudice against
Hengstenberg's solid, conservative scholarship has
prevented many from discovering a position that is
far in advance of their own and of the latest works on
this Biblical book.

Zoeckler, in Lange's *Homiletisches Bibelwerk, Der
Prediger Salomo*, Bielefeld and Leipzig, 1869, English
edition in Schaff's edition of Lange, Scribner's, 1870,
translated by Taylor Lewis. A very solid and thorough
work, still one of the best. Zoeckler is one of the ablest

---

*Albright, W. F. in the *Old Testament Commentary* (the
article, "The Old Testament and Archaeology") Alleman and
Flack: The Muhlenberg Press, 1948 (p. 160).

and best advocates of the Solomonic authorship of this book.

Delitzsch, Franz, *Commentary on Ecclesiastes*, in the famous Keil and Delitzsch *Commentary*, English edition in *Clark's Foreign Theological Library*, Edinburgh, 1877, translated by M. G. Easton. Still in many respects a most admirable work. Its thorough scholarship makes certain portions particularly useful. Unfortunately the critical approach has in a number of instances thrown Delitzsch out of sympathy with Koheleth and led him to make severe criticisms and wrong estimates of his position.

Bradley, George Granville, *Lectures on Ecclesiastes*, Oxford, 1885. An attempt to popularize the book of the Preacher, but too many concessions are made to a rather liberal approach.

Volck, Wilhelm, *Der Prediger Salomo*, in Strack and Zoeckler's *Commentary*, Noerdlingen, (Beck) 1889. Though it is somewhat brief, this volume still deserves to rank as an able work of the moderately conservative type.

Deane, W. J., *Ecclesiastes*, in the *Pulpit Commentary*, edited by Spence, Funk and Wagnalls, New York, 1913. A constructive work of some merit.

Cox, Samuel, *The Book of Ecclesiastes*, in the *Expositor's Bible*, A. C. Armstrong, New York, 1903. Intended for the lay reader also, this work summarizes results and is not a commentary in the usual sense. Though it is not extremely critical it fails very signally to catch the author's point of view and is extremely misleading.

Fausset, A. R., in the *Commentary, Critical and Explanatory* on the whole Bible by Jamieson, Fausset, and Brown, Doran, New York, (no date, an American reprint). A fair work for the lay reader though it clings too tenaciously to traditional opinions.

Wildeboer, D. G., *Der Prediger, Kurzer Hand-kommentar*, Freiburg, Leipzig, Tuebingen, 1898. Very brief. Strongly critical.

Siegfried, C., *Goettinger Handkommentar*, 1898. Extremely critical.

Barton, G. A., *The Book of Ecclesiastes, a Critical and Exegetical Commentary* (the *International Critical Commentary*) Scribner's, New York, 1909. A very scholarly and exhaustive work that advocates the critical position, though it is somewhat less extreme than is Siegfried's commentary.

Jastrow, M., *A Gentle Cynic, being a Translation of the Book of Koheleth, stripped of Later Additions, also its Origin, Growth, and Interpretation*, Lippincott Co., Philadelphia, 1919. As the title indicates, this is an attempt, by accepting as valid and final the results of a certain school of critics, to arrive at the original Koheleth and to interpret it for the laity in particular. Such efforts seldom yield anything satisfactory. About one fifth of the current text is discarded.

Williams, A. Lukyn, *Ecclesiastes* (*Cambridge Bible for Schools and Colleges*), Cambridge, 1922. Very helpful and moderately conservative, though somewhat brief.

Hertzberg, H. W., *Der Prediger* (*Sellin's Commentary*), Leipzig, 1932. One of the latest and best of modern works. Its position is moderately critical. Strange to say, in a rather complete bibliography Hengstenberg's *Commentary* is not even listed.

Galling, Kurt, *Prediger Salomo* (*Eissfeldt's Commentary*) Tuebingen, F. C. B. Mohr, 1940. The Hebrew text is radically revised in this work, chiefly on the basis of conjectures. As a result nothing rests on a sure foundation though clever translations often result from such a treatment of the text.

Aalders, G. Ch., *Het Boek de Prediker*, Kampen, 1948. This recent Dutch commentary has many helpful and constructive approaches and is characterized by a conservative spirit.

The textbooks on Introduction to the Old Testament supply some useful material, e.g., Keil, Deinzer, Raven, Koenig, Driver, Brewer, Knopf, Pfeiffer, Young; also the briefer commentaries such as the *Old Testament Commentary,* by Alleman and Flack, and the *Abingdon Commentary.* Also the articles in encyclopedias like Vaihinger in *Herzog,* Beecher in the *International Standard Bible Encyclopedia.*

Also the *Midrash Rabba on Ecclesiastes,* translated by A. Cohen, London, Soncino Press, 1939.

Also MacDonald, Duncan Black, *Hebrew Literary Genius,* Princeton University Press, 1933, Chap. XIV. The author is a strong exponent of the idea that the word *hebhel* ("vanity") emphasizes "transitoriness."

Also *Journal of Biblical Literature,* vols. 46, 49, 50, and 53.

Also *Religion in Life,* 1950 (spring number).

Also Ginsberg, H. Louis, *Studies in Koheleth,* New York, The Jewish Theological Seminary, 1950. In addition to other minor studies the author developes especially the theory that "Koheleth wrote in Aramaic." His arguments are, however, so finespun as to make it difficult to accept them.

CHAPTER I

I. The Prologue, 1:1-11.

(1) The words of Koheleth, the son of David, king in Jerusalem. (2) Vanity of vanities, says Koheleth, vanity of vanities, nothing but vanity! (3) What does a man get in all his toil in which he toils under the sun? (4) One generation is always going, and another is always coming, but the earth stands forever. (5) The sun rises, and the sun sets, eagerly hastening to its place where it regularly rises. (6) Going to the south and turning about to the north, the wind keeps on perpetually changing its direction; but the wind turns again to its rounds. (7) All the streams flow to the sea, but the sea does not fill up. To the place where the streams flow, there they keep on flowing. (8) All things are tiresome, so much so that man cannot express it. The eye does not get its fill of seeing, nor is the ear filled with hearing. (9) That which has been is that which will be, and that which has been done is that which will be done, and there is nothing new at all under the sun. (10) If there be a thing of which men say: "See this; it is new"—long ago it existed already in the olden times which were before us. (11) Men do not remember the former things, and also the things to come will not be remembered by them that shall come later still.

The words of Koheleth, the son of David, king in Jerusalem.

This is the equivalent of the title page in a modern book which gives the title of the book, its author, and some measure of identification of its author.

With most of the conservative exegetes we hold that this is rather a literary device than a literal statement of fact (see the Introduction under the heading "Authorship").

The title the author gives himself is "Koheleth," which is commonly accepted to mean the "Preacher," as A.V. and A.R.V. indicate by the subtitle of the book, and as *Luther* indicated by the exclusive use of the title *Der Prediger*—all of whom follow the lead of the Septuagint, which suggested this meaning with its title Ecclesiastes.

The Hebrew root *kahal*, which is involved, signifies to gather in a public assembly. The feminine form of the participle used here signifies an office (see *GK*, 122 r), a type of form which begins to appear after the Exile (cf. *sophéreth*, Neh. 7:57, and *pokhéreth*, Ezra 2:57). So the title would rightly seem to signify one who calls or addresses a public assembly. This was also the opinion of *Jerome*, who said: "By this term a man is designated who assembles a group, that is, a congregation; one whom we should call a preacher (*concionatorem*)." — Such feminine nouns, passing over from the abstract usage to the concrete, could also come to designate a masculine as is the case here; cf. *KS*, 251.

Other suggested translations are based too much on incidental aspects and have little solid ground in fact, such as "great orator" or "great collector," viz., of men's thought and sayings or "debater," and the like. "Collector of sentences" (*BDB*) is not too well established; see *König, Einleitung*.

Though the rest of the title, "son of David, king in Jerusalem," does not specifically mention Solomon it yet plainly has him in mind. And it surely merits repeating at this point that basically many of the thoughts expressed and developed may originally have been offered in writings of Solomon that were still extant at the time when Koheleth wrote, or were at least extant in tradition. So, in order to avoid even the semblance of plagiarism, the writer gives credit where credit is due.

The claim that this heading or title page cannot have been penned by the author of the book but must be ascribed to some editor surely goes beyond the facts of the case. Any man, having written a book such as this, might well write the name of the book and the name of the author at the head of it in a perfectly objective fashion. To postulate that he must write in the first person, as the author does in 1:12, is rather arbitrary. On the other hand, it would be equally arbitrary to claim that the available evidence compels belief in the idea that v. 1 was written by Koheleth. The decision has to be: either possibility would be equally reasonable.

The expression used as an apposition, "king in Jerusalem," is found nowhere in the Scriptures with reference to Solomon, neither is the other expression that is used in v. 12, "king over Israel." To this we may add the fact that personified Wisdom is found speaking to men in a kindred book—Proverbs—especially in the first eight chapters, and especially in Chapter 8, as well as in the New Testament (see Matt. 11:19). Furthermore, if this book is to be regarded as a confession of the penitent Solomon and as evidence of his repentance, we should, indeed, have reason to expect to find quite a different train of thought running through the book, and also some specific statement of his sin or at least of his repentance. In the reference that he makes to his former life in 1:12 ff. and 2:1 ff. he plainly assures us that, in tasting to the full of all that the world has to offer, he did not dismiss wisdom but passed through all the delights that this earth had to offer while he held fast to the hand of wisdom. Such a statement is that of a man who has no particular need for repentance, in the sense of a complete reversal of his direction. We offer this in addition to the material presented in the Introduction under the section, "Author and Time of Composition."

In v. 2 the author states a subtheme of his book, not the major theme. For in the second half of the book this thought of the vanity of all things is practically lost sight of till it unexpectedly reappears in 12:8.

The reason the author makes such an issue of the vanity of all things becomes clearer if one considers the time and the circumstances under which the book was written. It was a season when the fortunes of Israel stood at low ebb; men in Israel were discouraged and disappointed; faith burned with a dim light. One reason for this spiritual and physical depression was the fact that men had expected too much from purely earthly values. If a man assesses the worth of earthly things rightly he will not expect too much of them, and consequently when they fail him, he will not be unduly disappointed, cf. the Introduction, "Outstanding Theological Thoughts." So Koheleth may be said to be trying to disabuse men's minds of their unwarranted trust in earthly things so as to condition his contemporaries the better for inevitable disappointments in the sorry times in which they lived. Were men disappointed in those evil days? It was because they had not fully learned to appreciate beforehand what a vain thing the world at large is. The Preacher will help them to make good the oversight by giving the most comprehensive proof of this thesis that has yet been furnished. He that rightly absorbs it all will need no disillusionment in regard to what the natural world offers. His estimate of the world will be entirely correct. See similar sentiments in Ps. 90:3-10; 102:24-26; 35:5 f.; Gen. 5:29; 47:9.

The exact force of the word "vanity" (used thirty-one times in the book—*BDB*) must be ascertained most carefully. We have retained the traditional rendering "vanity of vanities," but this was done only because it

is the least objectionable of the available translations.
The word "vanity," *hebhel,* really means a "vapor" or
"breath," something like the breath that condenses as
we exhale into the cold winter air, condenses and dis-
appears at once. Now the point is, shall *hebhel* be translated "transitoriness" or "vanity"? Does it refer to
that which is fleeting or to that which is utterly futile?
The latter connotation is the one usually associated
with the English term "vanity" in connections such as
these.

It is our conviction that *hebhel* connotes primarily
that which is fleeting and transitory and also suggests
the partial futility of human effort. Certainly, to construe the verse in such a way as to make it mean practically that life is futile and utterly empty would mean
to put a pessimistic meaning into the term that is not
warranted by facts. This word emphasizes rather how
evanescent earthly things are, how swiftly they pass
away, and how little they offer while one has them.
All this is rather fully covered by *KW* with the three
words *Flüchtiges, Kraftloses, Nichtiges.*

Furthermore, it should be noted that in this verse
we have a Hebrew superlative—"vanity of vanities"
(cf. Song of Songs). It is even repeated for that matter
(see *KS* 309 h). It would, therefore, be closer to the
English idiom if we were to translate rather freely:
"Oh, how utterly transitory, how utterly transitory
are all things! This is the Preacher's first contention."

Besides, a careful evaluation of v. 3 must go hand
in hand with the correct consideration of v. 2. For v. 2
is to be understood in the light of the thought that is
added by v. 3: "What does a man get in all his toil
in which he toils under the sun?" The answer is obviously not: "He gets nothing." But the answer surely
is: "He does get precious little." Pressing these statements unduly leads interpreters to ascribe to Koheleth
the doctrine of the futility of life. In the light of the

rest of the book such a claim would do the author a
grave injustice. The author is not at this point offering the "Song of Songs of Pessimism" (*H. Heine*) but,
as we might justly expect of a Scriptural book, a strong
statement of sober fact, that fact, namely, which is
recorded in Rom. 8:20, "The creature was made subject to vanity," and whose beginning is recorded in
Gen. 3 in the fall of mankind and the resultant curse
upon the world. This is a truth to which already our
first parents gave utterance when they called a son of
theirs "Abel," (Hebrew: *hebhel*) that is to say,
"vanity." James says (4:14) : "For what is your life?
It is even a vapor," (Greek: *'atmis*) the term used by
Aquila for *hebhel*.

Nor is there anything particularly pessimistic about
the statement of this verse. It does not disregard certain other Scriptural facts such as that God made the
world very good. For between the first creation and the
present situation stands the calamity of the fall into
sin, an event which brought in its train the most tragic
consequences for mankind and for the world in which
man lives. Nothing is truer than the fact that our
natural life, our ordinary human existence with all
that it has to offer apart from God, is absolutely vain,
useless, and unsatisfactory.

It is here that the very important expression "under
the sun" must be carefully evaluated, for the correct
appreciation of this phrase is one of the major safeguards of the message of the entire book. Not without
reason does it occur so often—twenty-five times, that
is, the phrase itself apart from certain equivalents of it.
By misunderstanding the basic import of the phrase
many commentators have imputed very harsh asser-
tions to Koheleth. (Compare in the Introduction the
section, "The Outstanding Theological Thoughts").
Each time the phrase occurs it is as though the author
had said, "Let us for the sake of argument momentarily

rule out the higher things." If one follows his suggestion one obviously has earthly things pure and simple
to reckon with; nothing more. Is a statement like v. 3
hard to understand in this light? Obviously not; for
one might paraphrase it thus: Certainly a man gets
very little out of his toil in which he toils as long as
he busies himself exclusively with earthly things. In
that sense, surely, v. 2 is absolutely true!

The proper evaluation of this phrase removes a number of difficulties of interpretation. Time and again the
author presents what would normally have been regarded as a very extreme utterance, if not rank heresy.
But the presence of the little phrase "under the sun"
always says in effect, "What I claim is true if one deals
with purely earthly values." And the attentive reader
will at once have to admit that the author has stated
something that a man must subscribe to. This is obvious from a few samples, which we list by way of
anticipation, such as 2:18, 22; 4:1; 5:13 ff; 6:1-6.

Galling is entirely correct when he reminds us at
this point that here as elsewhere Koheleth is dealing
with man as such when he asks: "What does a man
get . . .?" Every son of Adam, be he Jew or Gentile,
must have the same feeling of not achieving anything
substantial if he immerses himself in things n the
purely mundane level. So *Barton* speaks quite in the
spirit of these two verses when he asserts that "all" in
v. 2 ("all is vanity") does not refer to the universe
but to all the activities of life. Verse 3 imperatively demands this interpretation because of its contiguity with
v. 2. Otherwise v. 2 would almost offer the monstrous
doctrine of the utter uselessness of the whole created
universe—a very bad case of *Weltschmerz*, to say the
least.

In the orginal "gain" (*yithron*) is really a noun
meaning practically that which is left over when a
given transaction is completed—"surplusage" as some

translate it. (The *mah,* "what," the interrogative pronoun, is practically used as an adjective; cf. *KS* 69). The answer that has now been given to the question of v. 3 could be formulated somewhat as follows: "If a man thus busies himself with earthly values alone, what he has left in the end is practically nothing."

Leaving for the present the various forms of human activity, the author goes on to show how man, the actor on the stage, is actually set against the background of things of this earth, which corroborate the point just made, that all purely earthly things are so very transitory. These earthly things are in a perpetual flux, in a continual round of activity, which keeps them practically running around in circles. Koheleth enumerates the following as contributing to the general atmosphere of the evanescent: successive generations coming upon the scene; the sun running its course; the wind making its circuits; the streams flowing to the sea: all of them phenomena so many and varied that the eye keeps viewing them endlessly.

Quite obviously the writer does not mean that this is the only point of view from which nature may be considered. He, no doubt, accepted as readily as did any Old Testament man of God the sentiment expressed by Ps. 19, "The heavens declare the glory of God, and the firmament showeth His handiwork." Furthermore, it would never have occurred to him to deny the excellent adaptation of created things to the purpose for which they were created. But he says, in effect: There is another aspect of things that we observe round about us: they reflect and illustrate the transitory character of the earth apart from God. He is not unduly critical; he merely sees the many aspects from which this world may be viewed.

This is true especially if we translate v. 4: "One generation is always going, and another is always coming"—participles in the Hebrew, expressing actions that go on continually; *KS* 239d. How true! But does that observation produce any further results? It is actually a continual round of things, a running around and around, if heavenly values are going to be left out of consideration. True, "the earth stands forever," but in this connection that means nothing more than that the earth is the permanent ground on which this coming and this going of generations actually take place.

The connection being what it is, there cannot be an assertion here about the eternal duration of the earth, for the expression "forever" (*le'olam*) is frequently very relative in its meaning and here signifies little more than "a good long while." One need not, therefore, fear that this verse contradicts Ps. 102:25f.— "Generation" (*dor*) being the new and important issue in the thought development, though a noun here stands first in the sentence (*KS* 339i).

There is, of course, as the fathers since Jerome have observed, something tragic about having man, the noble creature derived from the earth, continually pass away while the "earth," the crude material from which he is made, continues (*Hertzberg*).

This continual appearing of new generations on the face of the earth does seem to illustrate rather forcefully man's transitoriness. One generation is always in process of dying off while its successor is in process of coming on the scene. This does not mean that the author holds a cyclic interpretation of history, but it does mean that he has observed how transitory man seems to be.

That same apparently futile round of things is obvious in the case of the sun (v. 5), which between rising and setting seems to "pant" (*sha'aph*) along its course, for it seems as though it had much ground to cover to get back to its point of rising. But the process as such makes it appear that there is nothing stable about the sun. Day after day it gets back "to the place where it regularly rises."

This round of motion serves as a type of the existence all things that she shines upon must lead, for the illustration is built on the assumption that the uniformity of pattern of the things in the world will result in a background of life which is of the same kind as is human life itself. In her activity, which in itself is mechanical repetition of a ceaseless striving, the sun is in this regard a type and symbol of human life (*Hengstenberg*). Apart from this connection it would hardly do to use the sun merely as a figure of the vanity of life and of things in general. For the sun is at the same time a powerful instrument of good in promoting and maintaining growth and appears regularly in the Scriptures as an object for which God is to be praised. Those things in regard to which she comes under consideration here are clearly specified in the text: the ceaseless round of rising, setting, and hastening back to the starting point.

Coming to the wind (v. 6), we may make a similar observation concerning it. This time the participles are put first in the sentence and we are more than half-way through the verse before we discover that the wind is being discussed. Only south and north are mentioned, but the intermediate points of the compass are plainly included. And the end of the matter is: the wind is always turning back to the circuits or rounds that have been planned for it. The only constant thing about the wind is its changing. This idle round of movement is typical of all earthly existence and shows the world, animate as well as inanimate, to be subject to the same law of transitoriness or fluctuation. Note that the root *sabhabh* appears four times.

Or take the streams (v. 7), rather the typical "wadis" of the Holy Land that are waterless the greater part of the year. As far as the stream as a stream is concerned, it keeps up the same apparently transitory round of things. The wadi keeps running to the sea, and although that seems to get it nowhere it persists in running to the sea. So the whole of the physical background of life provides a backdrop that agrees with life itself if you leave out the spiritual realities. Both are very transitory in all their aspects, to say the least.

The thought of v. 7 is not: First the streams empty into the sea and then return to their streambeds by way of the clouds and the rains; but: First they empty into the sea, and then they empty into the sea again. By what means they manage to get back from the sea is of no moment, nor shall we endeavor to determine what laws of physics the author believed in, as far as this subject is concerned. The unwearied sameness of the procedure is alone being considered as a procedure that is in harmony with the general course that the world runs. Other aspects of the case are not under consideration such as that as a part of this process waters are drawn from the sea into the clouds, thence to be dropped as showers upon the earth, and presently to find their way into the streambeds. — On *mekom* with *schwa*, see *GK* 130 c.

In fact, this ceaseless round of things can prove very tiresome (v. 8), so much so that man cannot even express how tiresome life is when viewed from this angle. True, there are other angles of life, but this one, considered alone, is very prominent. The eye cannot even see it all, and the ear cannot hear it all — this dreary aspect of life on the purely earthly level. This verse is not trying to say how apparently insatiable the eye and the ear are. That would bring a matter under discussion that has nothing to do with the subject in hand.

Nor do some of the renderings of this verse that are offered help the situation. An example is A. R. V.m:

"All words are feeble." In this connection these words may not be translated thus. Or to insist that the adjective *yeghe'im* means "tired" or "weary," as it usually does in Hebrew, is quite inadequate. That would yield another inappropriate thought: This old world is getting pretty well tired out. That would be a half-sentimental notion, for the correctness of which no proof can be offered. One could, perhaps, translate: "All things toil; man cannot tell how much."

Considering the general run of futile things (v. 9), the author asserts that there is a sameness about it which marks it in all its parts. "That which has been is that which will be; and that which has been done is that which will be done" — (correlative sentences, *KS* 382c). All things — and that covers much ground — and all actions — and that covers equally much ground — bear the stamp of monotonous sameness so that the final conclusion from this point of view is: "And there is nothing new at all under the sun." — *Kol* ("all") is here used as it is in Judg. 13:14 and Ps. 143:2.

This brings a new angle of the case to the fore, which seems to call for a little more investigation. Does there not appear from time to time something that may be called new? No, says v. 10; this apparent fact is to be explained as follows: "If there be a thing of which men say: 'See this; it is new,' — long ago it existed already in the olden times which were before us." (On the indefinite use of "men" in the expression "men say" as expressed by the third person singular, see *KS* 324d). The explanation is, therefore, that the thing which is claimed to be new, indeed appeared on the scene before, only it was long ago in a previous generation. — "Long ago" (*kebhar*) is one of the favorite words of the author, see 2:16, 3:15; 4:2; 6:10; 9:6f.

As soon as we arrive at this point we see that this is exactly what v. 11 is trying to say. For it has for

a long time been a matter of dispute whether the words
ri'shonim and *'acharonim* mean "former generations"
and "later generations" or "former things" and "later
things," since the words could have either meaning. If
the word "things" is supplied in both cases, the verse
ties in intimately with v. 10. A thing was, perhaps,
called new, though it had appeared before, "because
men do not remember the former things, and also the
things to come will not be remembered by them that
come still later." In other words, man's memory is
pretty short. We have forgotten much of what went
before or have never bothered to hand it on to the next
generation. And much of what we see transpiring now
will after the same pattern be lost to the generations
to come. Things are, therefore, occasionally referred to
as being new because we do not remember how they
appeared earlier in history.

If we were to construe this verse (11) as referring
to former and later "generations," something would
be introduced into the discussion which is not half as
pertinent as v. 11 is according to our approach, which
makes it the explanation of v. 10. A literal translation
of the verse, supplying "generations" after "former"
and "later," could yield the same result, for it would
read: "There is no remembrance to the former generations," etc. This means: Former generations did not
remember things; and coming generations also will
not remember the things that shall come later.

To speak of this thought as a "resigned assertion"
(*eine resignierte Behauptung*) as *Hertzberg* does fails
to do justice to it. It simply records a fact of common
observation.

So, then, all that has been said is not an unhappy
lament of a disappointed soul which has been dealt
some rough blows by life. Nor does it stem from a
chronic pessimist. All that needs to be borne in mind is
the basic declaration of v. 3. If you consider purely

earthly values, what is your work? What do you
achieve? What is life? Merely a dreary part of a ceaseless round, which keeps going on all about us in nature,
in the coming of generations, in the sun, the winds,
the streams, and in all things. Your own activity is
futile; the world appears equally futile. All this is, of
course, an indirect way of saying: Do not rule out
or eliminate the higher values; then everything takes
on a different outlook, including your daily task wherein you toil.

II. THE VANITY OF ALL THINGS (1:12-6:12)

A. The First Group of Things Whose Vanity Is Demonstrated (1:12-2:23)

1. The vanity of human striving after wisdom (1:12-18)

(12) **I, Koheleth, was king over Israel in Jerusalem, and I set my mind upon searching out and
exploring by wisdom all that is done under the
heavens. (13) A sorry task it is which God has given
the sons of men to toil at. (14) I looked at all the
works that are done under the sun, and behold
everything is vanity and striving for wind. (15) That
which is crooked cannot be made straight, and that
which is lacking cannot be counted. (16) I said to
myself thus: Look, I have become great and have
increased in wisdom above all that were before me
over Jerusalem; and my mind has acquired wisdom
and knowledge in abundance. (17) For I applied
my mind to the acquisition of wisdom and knowledge
and madness and folly. And I found out that this,
too, is a striving after wind. (18) For where there
is much wisdom there is much vexation, and if a
man gets more knowledge he also gets more sorrow.**

The whole background of our life has transitoriness
bordering on futility stamped upon its face, if higher
values are left behind (v. 2-11).

The author goes on to explore the matter further
by considering successive areas into which man has ven-
tured in his self-sufficient quest. In each case his
experience has been the same. Here (v. 12-18) the
acquisition of purely earthly wisdom is under consideration.

Israel had a wisdom of a higher sort as her richly
developed Wisdom Literature (e.g., Job and Proverbs)
indicates. Wisdom was certainly a prized possession
in the age of Solomon. It lent more lustre to the name
of that king than any of his other achievements did.
His wisdom was the factor that brought the Queen of
Sheba to his court. Wisdom was the chief item in the
promise that God gave him to provide whatsoever he
might ask (I Kings 3:12).

Since the age after the Exile found itself stripped
of all such glories it would naturally look back with
deep longing to the glorious days of this great king.
But since man is only too strongly inclined to engage
in an independent search after the truth, leaving out
God and the higher elements that grow out of revelation, it is quite proper to show to what such a quest
would lead. That truth the author effectively demonstrates. Whether Israel's spiritual leaders had by this
time had much contact with Greek philosophy and its
claims may always remain a moot question. But certainly, Koheleth's findings may be said to furnish an
answer to those people who need guidance along
this line.

Verse 12. Koheleth for a moment impersonates
Solomon and describes an experiment that he attempted.
Solomon's own investigation along the line of what
the quest of wisdom arrives at when it leaves heavenly
values out of consideration run along the line of what
is indicated in v. 13-18. Koheleth impersonates Solomon,
as we said, and lets the experiment develop. That
some such perfectly legitimate impersonation is being

used appears in the initial statement, "I, Koheleth, was king over Israel in Jerusalem." Solomon would hardly have used the past tense at a time when he was still king unless his own kingdom and reign were in process of ending in an almost total collapse. Nor can this difficulty be removed by pointing to the fact that the verb involved may well mean "become." "I, Koheleth, became king." The issue is not what he became but rather whether his position enabled him to conduct his experiment effectively. His *being* king made that possible, not his becoming king. To stake the Solomonic authorship of the book on this verse and on 1:1 involves one in the countless difficulties that we have pointed out in the Introduction. This verse must rather be interpreted in harmony with the clear and unmistakable facts enumerated.

Verse 13. Koheleth describes Solomon's experiment by saying that there was a carefully made resolve of his that lay at the root of it all: "I set my mind upon searching." In the Hebrew "heart" (*lebh*) commonly signifies the mental faculties, therefore we may translate it "mind" here and in many similar passages that follow. The meaning of the verse is not that he, Koheleth, investigated *everything*. Since in the process of the description of what he did the author in vv. 16-19 mentions the *acquisition of wisdom* as his major concern, the experiment must be said to center rather about the noble endeavor of *getting wisdom*. The ideas expressed in vv. 13-15 should be subordinated to that major purpose. Then the sequence of thought runs about as follows: In the quest of wisdom I left no area untouched; I busied myself with everything. ("Search" means to investigate the roots of a matter; "explore" to explore a subject on all sides — *Barton*). Again, it has been suggested that the statements employed do not imply the extensive gathering of data but a careful analysis of existing facts.

It must at once be added, however, (13b) that such
a quest is a "sorry task" or as some commentators
prefer to express it "an ill business" hard and difficult
"to toil at," an undertaking which is enough to drive
almost any man to despair. But why say that *"God"*
has given this undertaking to "the sons of men to toil
at" when Solomon chooses the quest deliberately? It
seems that Koheleth phrases the thought in this manner
because he wants to indicate that all "the sons of
men" (really only a plural of "men" — *KS* 254g) even
if they know not God, feel a deep compulsion or inner
urge to discover the truth. God has put that urge into
their heart. But they are at the same time caught in
the difficulty that the task that God has laid upon them
by the very fact that they are human beings fails to
yield the desired result. It is hard, difficult, unreward-
ing; it is bad business. You strive after high objectives,
but your quest fails to produce satisfactory results.

Or, to state the outcome almost at once as the author
does in v. 14, the net result of the study of all things
that are done "under the heavens" (almost the same
as "under the sun") done, I say, in the pursuit of
wisdom are "vanity and striving for wind." *Luther*
calls this *Haschen nach Wind.* As *KS* indicates (80)
re'uth almost equals an adjective like "mere." No
matter how thoroughly a man investigates, how broad
the area is that is taken in hand, it is found to be a
rather fruitless endeavor.

Verse 15 shows more particularly how v. 14 is
meant and is not merely the statement of a universal
truth to the effect that "that which is crooked cannot
be made straight, and that which is lacking cannot be
counted." In other words, the claim is not a sweeping
assertion: "Things cannot be changed," but it rather
ties up v. 15 with what precedes. By engaging in a
comprehensive quest for wisdom you soon begin to
realize that you are achieving nothing, you are

straightening out none of the many things that have been crooked; and, in fact, many things are lacking and ought to be supplied, but they are so many that a man cannot even count "that which is lacking."

Beginning with v. 16 and continuing through v. 17 the same result is stated in words that Koheleth said to himself. They constitute his summary reflections on his project. They amount to this: I did succeed in becoming a great man and so had access to resources that others did not have; and besides I grew in wisdom above all that had ever been before me over the people of God, in fact, by honest mental effort I added to the natural capacities that God had given me, acquiring "wisdom and knowledge in abundance." Or, stating the case a little more fully (the conjunction *we* may here be translated "namely" or "for") I really set for myself a double task, not only to understand one side of the matter but both. And by getting mastery of both into the picture I was surely able to maintain a better balance of judgment, for I aimed at the acquisition of wisdom and knowledge on the one hand and of folly and madness on the other. The quest for the sum total of earthly values in the realm of intellectual effort was, therefore, not taken lightly but was carried through with a thoroughness that was worthy of so noble an experiment.

The pronoun "I" (*'ani*) which is here expressed, is not used emphatically. It rather represents more distinctly the suffix that was already expressed in the affirmative and indicates a point in the development of the language where the force of the subject contained in the verb form was felt less distinctly. See also 1:16; 2:1, 11-15, 18, 20, 25; 3:17f.; 4:1, 4, 7; 5:17; 7:25; 8:15; 9:16; cf. *KS* 18.

Who can assert with finality that such projects must have been quite foreign to the thinking of Solomon? It is reasonable to assume that behind the

literary device employed (the author's impersonation
of Solomon) there was an actual substratum of fact,
namely, Solomon once engaged in this venture, but it
was Koheleth who wrote it up in his own way at a much
later date and with a certain freedom of expression and
also in a style which is not quite that of Solomon but
is a late type of Hebrew because Koheleth wrote in a
different literary age.

The upshot of it all was, as it had to be because it
was limited to the things "done under the heavens," "I
found out that this, too, is a striving after wind," in
other words, a pursuit that yields precious little of
lasting value. The closest analogy to the experiment
here described would in our day be an honest attempt
to solve all problems and to attain to all knowledge by
the processes of rational thinking. It would be the
philosopher's attempt to probe into the depth of
matters by his unaided and unenlightened reason apart
from any disclosures of truth that God has granted to
man. If anyone is candid with himself and with others
he must admit that such efforts produce very meagre
results and could without undue harshness be aptly
termed "a striving after wind." But the point that the
author makes is not quite this observation. It was not
so much that his search for wisdom was not yielding
wisdom. It was another practical consideration.

That consideration was, first of all: "For where
there is much wisdom, there is much vexation"; and if
a man gets more knowledge he also gets more "sorrow"
(*makh'obh*) v. 18. Just to look at one side of wisdom
for a moment will show how true this observation is.
There is always a large element of "knowledge" in
wisdom. So here this increase of knowledge, which is
mentioned in the parallel member of the verse, leads
a man to find out many disturbing things that may
militate strongly against his peace of mind. Had he
let well enough alone and not engaged in the quest after

wisdom he would have been spared all this "vexation" or irritation (*ka'as*). To get at the root of a practical understanding of things, helpful as it may be, always carries this unpleasant feature with it. And as long as higher values are left aside, the unpleasantness of the experience is bound to be much accentuated. "Sorrow," too, grows out of getting "more knowledge," for much of the growth in knowledge brings with it a deeper insight into the many things that are wrong and out of gear in this world. It is, however, from this angle primarily that the quest after wisdom is designated "a striving after wind."

Viewed thus, we wonder how interpreters can arrive at conclusions such as: "The burden of the verse is *blessed is ignorance!*" (*Barton*). Better is the German proverb, *Viel Wissen macht Kopfweh.* The author has merely stated in his own unique way what all men are ready to admit on the basis of their own observation. Nor is there any reason to reduce the last saying to the level of a schoolboy's maxim, something like, "By pain and whippings we grow in knowledge," which result *Galling* arrives at by holding too insistently to the basic meaning of *makh'obh*, "physical pain," and by dropping all thinking on the subject to too low a level.

The first form of v. 17, *wa'ettenah*, offers one of the few examples of the classical use of the *waw consecutive*, which is fading out of use at this time —*KS* 200b — an indication of the late composition of the book.

2. *The vanity of mirth* (sensuous enjoyment) 2:
1-11

(1) I said to myself: "Come, now, I will put you
to the test with mirth and enjoy good things." But
this also was vanity. (2) Of laughter I said, it is
utterly mad; and of mirth, what is it accomplishing?
(3) I sought in my mind to nourish my flesh with
wine—my mind was still keeping control by means
of wisdom—and to lay hold on folly, until I should
see what good there is for the sons of men in that
which they do under heaven during the appointed
number of days of their life. (4) I undertook great
projects; I built houses for myself; I planted vineyards for myself. (5) I made for myself gardens and
parks and planted in them all manner of fruit trees.
(6) I made for myself pools of waler with which to
irrigate a forest where the trees grew. (7) I acquired
menservants and maidservants; also such as were
born in my own house did I have. I also had great
possessions, cattle and flocks, more than all they that
had been before me in Jerusalem. (8) I gathered for
myself also silver and gold and treasures such as
kings have and such as come from provinces; I
secured for myself men-singers and women-singers
and the luxuries of the children of men, concubines
very many. (9) So I became exceedingly great above
all that preceded me in Jerusalem; also my wisdom
stayed with me. (10) Nothing that my eyes desired
did I deny them, nor did I refuse my mind any gaiety;
for my mind found joy because of all my labor, and
this was my portion from all my toil. (11) But when
I looked on all the works that my hands had

wrought, and on the toil it had cost me to achieve it, lo, all was vanity and striving for wind, and there was no profit under the sun.

A new field and its possibilities are investigated— the joys that man can find for the delight of his senses. For in seasons of need, want, and lowly condition men will look upon the various forms of pleasure that the children of men know and will consider their own position as particularly unfortunate just because such pleasures are denied them. No era of Israel's history was richer in possibilities for various pleasures, and no person in a better position to make the most·of them than Solomon. His evaluation of such joys is here submitted.

We cannot deny that Solomon may have made some such tests. Koheleth has written them up in a somewhat free fashion, not being too careful to make every detail exactly as Solomon would have written it. For he is not trying to delude his readers into believing that he was Solomon. That is why he can write v. 7 and v. 9 (cf. 1:16) about those that had ruled before him in Jerusalem, a clear case of falling out of the role for a moment.

Koheleth resolves to try the experiment of determining just what real satisfaction sensuous enjoyment can yield. By the term "sensuous" we do not refer to that which is grossly sensual in the reprehensible sense of the word but merely to that which delights the senses without being necessarily sinful. He "says in his heart," an expression which means "he resolves" or "he says to himself." The imperatives that state the self-exhortation to engage in the experiment are feminine forms (*lekhah* and *'anassekah*) and are, therefore, no doubt addressed to the soul (see Ps. 16:2). The difficulty of getting a good equivalent for *simchah* is obvious. We used two terms, "mirth" and "gaiety." These translations show that harmless amusements and

delights are meant—things that can make a person
glad—as the verb root *samach* clearly shows. The
parallel expression used ("enjoy good things") points
in the same direction. This expression, though literally
to be translated "to look upon the good," is well covered
by "to enjoy good." Besides, the passage must be considered as a whole (v. 1-11) and so the items listed in
v. 4-9 show what things the writer thinks of when he
uses the term "mirth." Not a bad English equivalent
would perhaps be the colloquial expression, "He had
lots of *fun* in making this experiment."

It is a style of writing that is frequently employed
by Hebrew authors that, even before a matter is given
in a more detailed description, the outcome of it all is
indicated. This is also done here in v. 1b and 2. The
first half of the verdict is: "But this also was vanity."
We could paraphrase this typical sentence: "I found
no lasting values in this attempt." Verse 2 certainly
expresses this thought at greater length. Some features
of the experiment would lead the experimenter to gaiety
or "laughter"; others would involve simple enjoyment
or "mirth." But of the one he had to say that it was
"utterly mad," and with regard to the other ask, "What
is it accomplishing?" Lest this conclusion be thought
of as being too drastic and the thinking of some sadly
disillusioned fellow, it should be noted here that Koheleth has again limited himself to purely earthly values.
It is true that v. 1 and v. 2 do not say so; but v. 3 brings
the phrase that necessitates this limitation, viz., "under
heaven." A similar proverbial expression is the familiar: "The loud laugh betrays the empty head," or,
Am vielen Lachen erkennt man den Narren.

One angle of the experiment with mirth is dwelt
upon a little more at length. It is the well-reasoned use
of wine. The case as such demands a more detailed
statement lest the author lay himself open to misunderstanding. For he proposes to use wine, not as a de-

bauchee, but as a connoisseur. "I sought in my mind" could be paraphrased, "I conceived of the project." In several of these cases, like v. 1, "I said to myself," and here, "I sought in my mind," and v. 15, "I said to myself," the Hebrew has the word "heart" for "myself" or "mind." The term "heart" indicates largely the center of mental processes (*Denkwerkstätte,* KW).

"To nourish my flesh with wine" should be taken as a reference to a consumption of wine which enables a man to get the highest possible enjoyment by a careful use of it, so that appetite is sharpened, enjoyment enhanced, and the finest bouquets sampled and enjoyed. Approximating or falling into drunkenness is plainly not under consideration. The very thought of such crude extravagance is barred by the expression, "my mind was still keeping control by means of wisdom." In other words, here was a carefully controlled experiment.

The expression "to lay hold on folly" as describing the next step of the experiment is difficult to evaluate. It can hardly be the continuation of the experiment with wine. The term *sikhluth* must be "folly" in the neutral sense (as *Williams* observes) and might, therefore, include all those harmless and enjoyable forms of nonsense that are known. If it is viewed in this light, the two sides of mirth considered thus far — wine and folly — must be regarded as constituting the lowest level on which the experiment operated. Koheleth wanted to be sure to try them out until he "should see what good there is for the sons of men in that which they do under heaven during the appointed number of the days of their life." This way of stating it admits that the last two areas of mirth mentioned are not very substantial, for they are brief as is every man's life.

The author now lists a number of tests of mirth which are poured in a bigger mould. This experiment is worthy of a great man although we believe that these verses (4-9) stand under the shadow of v. 3, which confined the field of investigation to things "under heaven." Here, then, are substantial earthly projects, undertaken, let us say, without God in mind but merely as an attempt to see how much enjoyment they can give. Practically all the items mentioned are known to have been undertaken by Solomon. They are all "great projects." The repetition of the little dative of interest *li*, that is, "for myself," shows that the projects are not thought of as being in any sense humanitarian or philanthropic. They are not for the good of man or for the good of the realm but rather to afford the author of them personal satisfaction. That agrees with the approach that we claim lay imbedded in v. 3.

"Houses" and "vineyards" are mentioned first as being typical of the great works projected. All Bible readers know that the greatest of all the building operations undertaken by Solomon was the construction of the Temple at Jerusalem. It would, however, have been quite improper to mention that in this connection, for it was undertaken with some measure of divine mandate and in completion of the great plans for which David had provided much of the needed material. It was, moreover, a public building erected for the common good. But other royal residences that were completed after the Temple may well be thought of. See I Kings 7:10-12; 9:19. As for the vineyards, they are not mentioned in the historical books but are referred to in the Song of Solomon (8:11). David's vineyards, of which we read in I Chron. 27:27, must also have passed into Solomon's hands.

The author next mentions (v. 5) horticultural experiments. Regarding this activity of his no notice is preserved in the records available. It is not unreasonable to suppose that some kind of oral tradition with reference to a venture of this sort may have been current. In any case, this may be thought of as a thoroughly worthy enterprise, such as kings should

engage in. If we compare Deut. 11:10, it would appear
that in Mosaic times gardens were kept for the cultivation of practical vegetables although in the earliest
mention of one (Gen. 2:8) it is clearly regarded as a
place where vegetables and trees and every form of
vegetation grew. The "parks" here mentioned have
trees as their chief feature, as here stated, and "fruit
trees" in particular. The word employed for parks
(*pardesim*) gave rise to a Greek word παραδεῖσος, "para-
dise," which is also the Persian original for this word.

Again (v. 6) a major project, which is closely
linked with the preceding one, is described. It had to
do with the matter of irrigation. Song 7:4 may contain
a reference to pools that Solomon built at Heshbon. In
any case, the "pools of Solomon" that lie near Beth-
lehem must be a product of the Roman times at the
earliest, though there may have been some project of
Solomon's at this point at an earlier date. But, as
Hertzberg suggests, "forests where the trees grew"
may be merely a more elaborate statement for "parks"
(v. 5). In that case the pools would have provided
water for the parks. "Forests where trees were
reared" (A.R.V.) should be rejected as a translation,
for the verb employed cannot be limited to young trees
springing up from the ground. By retaining the emphasis of the dative of interest ("for myself") which,
by the way, is repeated eight times, we are to regard
this project, not as undertaken particularly for the
common good, but for the personal satisfaction of
the king.

A big establishment requires many servants. The
writer brings these into the picture as being worthy
of mention. They were slaves of both sexes as well as
such who had been born in his own house, such as
Abraham also had (Gen. 17:27). These were especially
prized for their inbred loyalty. Since for the main-
tenance of such a household and also for the occasional

purpose of sacrifice (see I Kings 8:63), much cattle was required, the king did not fail to make proper provision for acquiring all these animals. And if the reference to I Kings is properly evaluated, the correctness of the following statement will be obvious, "above all that were before me at Jerusalem."

With a certain modest haste the enumeration draws to a close lest it weary the reader by a too extended consideration of the individual features of the experiment. The following items are merely mentioned without being elaborated extensively. There were first the gold and the silver, which constituted the chief glory of that age for some (cf. II Chron. 1:15; 9:27; I Kings 10:27; 9:28; 10:11, 14, 22). For the treasures named were surely such as were worthy of "kings" and such as would have come from subjugated "provinces," for to such the reference is here being made rather than to districts into which Solomon had divided his realm.

"Singers" to provide music must have been deemed one of the rarest pleasures that a royal court could afford, to judge by the remarks of Barzillai on the occasion of David's return after the rebellion of his son (II Sam. 19:31) — The above translation takes *ta'anugoth* in the sense of delights of love, referring to the "pleasures of love" — *BDB* — that Solomon's harem afforded. Fortunately, this phase of the matter is briefly disposed of.

The expression *shiddah weshiddoth* is rendered "concubines very many" after A.R.V. although it has been extremely difficult to translate from days of old. The Greek translators rendered it "pourers of wine," a rendering that borders on the trivial. Luther and A.V. preferred the somewhat harmless "musical instruments." But the fact remains that the expression seems to be parallel with "delights of the children of men," and as to form is apparently related to the Assyrian *shadadu*, meaning "love." All of which is not out of harmony with I Kings 11:1-3. In fact, if the whole experiment has any relevance to the facts of the life of Solomon, his sensualism would also have to receive consideration.

The next statement (v. 9) may be regarded as a summary: "So I became exceedingly great above all that preceded me in Jerusalem." There is no doubt about it that none of Israel's kings could ever cope with Solomon for splendor and greatness. But it does seem that the statement, "also my wisdom stayed with me," must be limited to the earlier part of his reign. His wisdom did control all his ventures until his wives led him astray (I Kings 11:4ff). It is quite in keeping with the Scriptural record to hold that wisdom animated the king prior to his lapse from grace. — The expression "I became exceedingly great" has an unusual force in the Hebrew: "I was great, and I added."

To assure us that the experiment has been carried on in a thoroughgoing manner so that later no one might be able to charge him with not having been sufficiently thorough in making the test of such delights, the author assures us that he spared nothing, denied himself nothing.

So this verse is still in the nature of a summary. It says in effect: Whatever occurred to me as possibly entering into the experiment I undertook. And, while the various projects were being put to the test one by one, there was at least some pleasure in the doing of them. And that was, in fact, what led the author to move from one experiment to the other as he says: "For my mind found joy because of all my labor, and this was my portion from all my toil." The projecting of the plans was a pleasure. The plans were so interesting that the interest they created was his reward. At least this much must be affirmed. If even the excitement of the novelty of the experiments had held no interest for their author, he would have been a very

blase personality. But this pleasure lasted only as long
as the project was being taken in hand, and the novelty
of it had not yet worn off.

But the backward look on all that was undertaken
was extremely disappointing. Here it is (v. 11) : "But
when I looked . . . all was vanity and striving for
wind." The familiar versions (*Luther,* A. V., and
A.R.V.) regard this verse as the next step in the
process by using an initial "then." The summary
character of the verse is, perhaps, made a little more
distinct by making the initial conjunction adversative
("but") and subordinating the first clause ("when I
looked"). — By this time the claim heard before (1:3)
certainly takes on a stronger meaning: "there was no
profit under the sun." Purely earthly values have a
queer tendency to let one down and thoroughly dis-
appoint one.

3. The vanity of wisdom as such (2:12-17)

(12) **So I turned about to regard wisdom in
relation to madness and folly; for what will the man
do that comes after the king? That which men have
done long ago. (13) And I observed that there is
an advantage of wisdom over folly even as there is
an advantage of light over darkness. (14) As far as
the wise man is concerned, his eyes are in his head,
but the fool walks along in the dark. Yet I recognized, even I, that one lot befalls both. (15) So I
said to myself: "As it befalls the fool, so shall it also
befall me; and why then was I wise overmuch?"
Then I said to myself: "Also this is vanity." (16)
For men do not remember either the wise man or
the fool for any length of time inasmuch as in the
days to come both will have been long forgotten.
How the wise and the fool die alike! (17) Therefore
I was disgusted with life; because everything which
is done under the sun seemed wrong to me; for
everything is vanity and striving for wind.**

"I turned" implies the taking up of a new subject. Strictly speaking, it is not an entirely new subject to investigate the actual value of wisdom, cf. 1:12ff. Nevertheless, the subject has so many angles, and the previous argumentation may not have fully convinced the gainsayers. Besides, Koheleth is definitely turning from the previous subject. Therefore, from another point of view the same conclusion is reached.

The method is again employed of interpreting a thing by reference to its opposite. "Wisdom" is thought of "in relation to madness and folly" as some commentators construe the phrase. The causal clause may lead an interpreter astray if he draws the subject matter of 2:18ff into the argument as *Hengstenberg* does. In any case, to let the thought turn to the successor of the king and to what manner of man he might be, is in no wise prepared for and also confuses the issue. The clause "for what," etc., is merely an explanation as to why the king undertook the investigation. He realized what men generally might do, men who come after him or any investigator in particular who might take up the same issue: that, namely, which they have always done, i.e., not deal with the matter exhaustively and bring it to a clean-cut issue as *he* proposes to do. For Solomon thought problems through to a final conclusion.

Expositors usually have almost insuperable difficulties with the reference to the man that comes after the king. Either corruption of the text or else utter incongruity of the subject matter is claimed. We believe that the approach we have used solves the difficulty adequately.

The writer is going to arrive at the conclusion that purely earthly wisdom is also vanity. But he must concede that, even generally speaking, wisdom has some advantages. He states these in vv. 13f. So the statement of the case may be said to run somewhat like this: though it must be conceded that wisdom has its uses, even this remarkable treasure falls under the general condemnation of vanity if it is viewed as dealing with purely earthly values.

Koheleth would be disqualifying everything in the Scriptures that comes under the head of wisdom literature (Job and Proverbs in particular) were he to make such a sweeping assertion as: "Wisdom is utter vanity from every point of view." Therefore he voices the basic claim, "There is an advantage of wisdom over folly," and adds the emphatic comparison, "even as there is an advantage of light over darkness." This comparison is strong. The author is not one of those who call "evil good, and good evil, that put darkness for light and light for darkness," Isa. 5:20.

He fortifies this approach still more (v. 14) lest he be misunderstood. He is, of course, thinking of true wisdom on the higher level, and he says of the one who has this gift that "his eyes are in his head." On the other hand, "the fool walks along in the dark." Having stated the case thus, he ought not to be in the same class with those who make rash and unwarranted claims.

He now states the other side of the matter (14b), the indictment. The new angle of the case that should give a man pause is that he can by his own observation verify the fact that, as far as these two men are concerned, "one lot befalls both." When Koheleth inserts parenthetically "even I," his purpose seems to be to assert that others have made a similar observation. He now arrives at the same insight. — The use of *gam* before *'ani* is adversative and may rightly be regarded as one of the typical words in Koheleth's vocabulary when he wishes to raise an objection to a view that is currently held (see also *BDB*). We have with care avoided translating *miqreh* "fate." Fate is some dark, mysterious power beyond God's reach and above His control, and so is a purely heathen concept. "Lot"

avoids this connotation. As v. 16 indicates, the lot
under consideration is death.

But, as v. 15 shows, in the conclusion Koheleth has
formulated on the matter it is the mere fact of dying
that is thought of. Not, how men die, but that they
die. Death is the great leveller. The reader might have
expected that God would take cognizance of the fact
that the one man had cultivated wisdom and would
exempt him from tasting of death. Nothing of the
sort — "as it befalls the fool, so shall it also befall
me." So what was the use of striving strenuously to
achieve wisdom? That statement, we believe, is a good
paraphrase of the text, "Why, then, was I wise overmuch?" Not that the man overdid it, but that he tried
to excel others in the thing he reflects on. And so the
usual conclusion, "Also this is vanity."

Some interpreters draw the conclusion, "The
strange fatalistic conception of God that Koheleth
has begins to appear here" (*Hertzberg*). Only those
readers find fatalism here who insert it into the argument. If God does not seem to value one's quest for
wisdom but lets one die as the fool dies, does that not
show that wisdom did not help and, therefore, was in
vain? As far as this angle of the case is concerned,
the logic is cogent, and the conclusion is correct. But
that is not fatalism.

Another pertinent observation that follows much the
same line of thought may be added (v. 16). Not only are
the wise man and the fool doomed to die, but they will
both be alike forgotten. It would seem quite proper to
have the fool forgotten and the wise man remembered.
But that is not how the case turns out; "for men do
not remember either the wise man or the fool for any
length of time, inasmuch as in days to come both will
have been forgotten." Koheleth would have that
thought included in the idea, "How the wise and the
fool die alike."

Concerning this statement it should be noted that there are many points of similarity between the two men in their death. It may come to both suddenly. It may arrive when important things seem to clamor for completion. It may be by accident. It may be accompanied by much pain or protracted sickness. It may come under distressing circumstances. It may cause untold grief to those who are nearest to him who is called away. As to the outward form and the attendant circumstances, no man can draw any exact conclusion as to whether he that dies governed himself by wisdom or not.

There is too much truth in this observation to allow us to brush it aside. Whether a man likes it or not, that is the way things are. There may be a few qualifying remarks that could be added, let us say in the spirit of Prov. 1:7 or Ps. 112:6, to bring out several additional angles that bear upon the case. Surely, we do not here have a polemic against Prov. 10:7. But the original observation must be admitted to be true.

The conclusion that is now drawn from the preceding statements is worded in somewhat strong terms: "Therefore I was disgusted with life; because everything that is done under the sun seemed wrong to me; for everything is vanity and striving for wind." It is only fair to say that not every man's reaction would necessarily be quite as strong as is this one, and so the statement may be said to have something of a subjective and autobiographical element in it and need not be regarded as normative for all. Not every man must feel exactly the same way when he regards the facts involved. He may feel that it ought not to be so. He may not like it. He is under no compulsion to be "disgusted with life." (This translation "disgusted" may be more in keeping with our idiom than the literal "I hated life"). Koheleth, carrying his experiment on with some zest, feels a very strong reaction setting in. At least all readers must agree that from this point of view "all is vanity and striving for wind."

Two further observations may be appended. One is that, in view of the facts here set forth, most people might be quite ready to share in the second conclusion here drawn, "Everything which is done under the sun seemed wrong." This statement certainly voices the utter confusion that we have all felt is reigning on earth.

The other is — and this is vastly more important in evaluating everything here said — the author pointedly reminds us that he had only the purely earthly values in mind, for he adds the now familiar phrase "under the sun" — "everything which is done under the sun seemed wrong to me," and we must remember that he is bringing to a conclusion his examination into the value of *wisdom*, begun in v. 12. That is why we made this approach normative for the understanding of the entire section.

4. **The vanity of labor** (in view of the uncertainty with reference to one's successor) 2:18-23

(18) **Also I was disgusted with all my toil wherein I had toiled under the sun, that I must leave it to the man that shall come after me. (19) For who can tell whether he will be a wise man or a fool? Yet he shall have control of all that I toiled over and wherein I have dealt wisely under the sun. This, too, is vanity. (20) So I began to give myself up to despair over all the toil wherein I toiled under the sun. (21) For here is a man who has toiled in his work with wisdom, knowledge, and efficiency, yet his portion shall be given to one who has not toiled for it. This, too, is vanity and a great evil. (22) For what does a man get for all his toil and for the striving of his mind wherein he toils under the sun? (23) For all his days he has sorrows and vexation in his occupation. Even at night his mind cannot rest. This too, then, is vanity.**

There are reasons for regarding one's work as one of the finest blessings of life. Witness the attitude of the man who is about to be declared superannuated. But. from other points of view also one's daily work comes under the condemnation of being "vanity," especially if such work confines itself to earthly pursuits and ambitions and leaves out of consideration spiritual and heavenly values. It is this latter kind of work that Koheleth is now considering, for in the section before us the phrase "under the sun" appears three times (v. 18, 20, 22).

But even in this area the thought is pointed up a bit more sharply in that the author reflects, not on work as such, but upon a factor that is often to be met with in connection with work, and that is the question, "What will the man who comes after me and takes over my work do with the things I have labored so hard to achieve?" Although it cannot be claimed that the successor always fails to conserve what his predecessor achieved or, for that matter, even ruins it, yet only too often some such outcome is to be observed. There is some propriety about thinking of Solomon's own case. He may have had some justified misgivings about Rehoboam.

Koheleth begins with one of those repetitions that he loves: "I was disgusted with all my toil." But he at once sharply points up the one angle from which he is viewing his work and calling, for that is practically what "toil wherein I have toiled" means in this instance. That one point, as indicated above, is "that I must leave it to the man that shall come after me." One might well say that his daily work and his calling are values that are for a time entrusted to his care like so many other earthly possessions. Then the job passes over into the next man's hands — "I must leave it." And one never has a guaranty (v. 19) whether the successor will be "a wise man or a fool." Time will tell. "Yet he shall have control of all that I toiled over and

wherein I have dealt wisely under the sun" (*yishlet,*
"have full control," is aptly rendered by the Greek
translator ἐξουσιάζεται.) After the conscientious worker,
great or small, may come a thoroughly shiftless man.

It must surely be one of life's bitter disappointments
to see the work which one loved and over which one
toiled disintegrate in such a case. But we should not
forget the above-noted "under the sun." Leave out
higher values, and this is almost invariably the result
sooner or later. Consequently v. 20 is quite in place
here as expressing a man's feelings: "So I began to
give myself up to despair over all the toil wherein I
toiled under the sun." ("I began to give myself" is
literally, "I turned about to cause my heart to despair";
our rendering simplifies, but not unduly).

To make our point unmistakably clear we should
add that such a conclusion can never be reached except
in quite a relative sense and only under unusual circumstances in the case of a man who is committed to
toiling for the truly higher values — God's Word and
Christ's gospel — though God knows that such work
is not without its disappointments at times.

Koheleth would yet make plain what he says by
indicating (v. 21) that he has not conducted his experiment on a trivial level. He is not thinking of a man
who has no heart for his work but rather of one "who
has toiled in his work with wisdom, knowledge, and
efficiency." The full force of these three terms may be
caught by phrasing the matter thus: constructive wisdom, comprehensive knowledge, and skillful workman-
ship. One might expect such toil to be a reason for a
hopeful outlook. But only too often "his portion shall
be given to one who has not toiled for it." Perhaps
no nation witnessed this type of succession of men in
jobs as did our own country, where earlier generations
in pioneer days obviously had to toil hard, and succeed-
ing generations too often did not appreciate what had

been wrought and made little effort to conserve it. Such experiences teach us in their own way that "this, too, is vanity and a great evil."

For if one looks at the future — and a man does well to think in terms of achieving something lasting and worth while for the future — the Preacher feels he must state the issue thus: "What does a man get for all his toil and for the striving of his mind wherein he toils under the sun?" (v. 22). If one sees one's work disintegrate under the hand of incompetent persons who follow one, surely that is ground enough for a remark such as, "What's the use?"

Summing up this aspect of the case, Koheleth says: "For all his days he has sorrows, and vexation is his occupation. Even at night his mind cannot rest." (*BDB* renders the second clause: "His task is sheer vexation.") This would seem to apply only after a man begins to reflect on who and what his successor shall be and to see reasons for believing that this successor will not measure up to expectations. The disappointment gnaws at one's heart, and day and night the vexatious thought is present. Very properly, then, comes the old refrain that in view of this situation "this, too, is vanity."

Grammatical Notes

v. 2. The infinitive *sechoq* is obviously treated as a noun (*KS* 24lk).

v. 5. *Bahem,* "in them," has a masculine suffix though the suffix refers the *gannoth,* which is feminine (*KS* 14).

v. 6. The same situation obtains — *mehem* has the masculine suffix referring to *berechoth,* "pools."

v. 8. *Shiddah weshiddoth* is one of those cases in which the singular is joined to the plural of the same noun and is used to signify "very many" (*KS* 74).

v. 14. *Hechakham* stands prominently in the emphatic position. It is a nominative absolute (*KS* 341h).

v. 16. In the construction *zikhron lechakham* the *le* serves as a substitute for the construct relationship (*KS* 336z).

v. 21. The repetition *'adham . . . 'adham* equals "the one . . . the other." (*KS.* 34).

v. 22. The use of the verb *hawah* here indicates that its original meaning "to fall" has not yet been entirely lost (*KS.* 326h).

B. General Principles That Show that Such Vanity Is a Logical Necessity (2:24-3:22)

1. Real enjoyment in all things depends on a higher source than man (2:24-26)

(24) **It is not a good thing inherent in man that he is able to eat and drink and get satisfaction in his toil. This, too, have I seen that such a thing is entirely from the hand of God. (25) For who can eat, and who can have enjoyment apart from Him? (26) For to the man who is good in His sight He gives wisdom and knowledge and joy, but to the sinner He gives the vexation of gathering and heaping up in order to give to the man that is good in God's sight. This, too, is vanity and striving for wind.**

Koheleth has thus far been demonstrating the vanity of things by the most direct method. He has given a practical demonstration by showing what the seemingly most enjoyable things really amount to when they are put to a practical and an exhaustive test. He now follows something that is akin to the deductive method. Some general principles are stated, not by way of giving conclusions that are drawn from previous data, but by way of showing that the same conclusions have to be drawn from certain commonly accepted general principles.

For the first time Koheleth reaches beyond the level
of the things under the sun and, leaving the strict division between things "under the sun" and higher
spiritual values to be found in the things that are
above, indicates that on the higher level there is a
source of true joy. But the case is first stated negatively: The ability to enable him to have true enjoyment does not lie in man. Verse 24 calls for a simpler
translation than that of our versions, viz., "It is not
a good thing inherent in man that he is able to eat
and drink, etc."

Translated thus, v. 24 agrees with v. 25 (properly
translated) as well as with v. 26, and one point is
common to all. In justification of our translation of
v. 24 observe that the positive and not the comparative is used in the Hebrew. Literally, "It is not a good
thing in man," *'en tobh ba'adham*. Again, the imperfect often expresses ability; therefore *sheyyo'khel*,
"that he can eat."

The matter is quite simple. A somewhat similar
phrase is used in 3:12 and 8:15, where the translation
may be, "There is nothing *better*, etc." But that does
not imply that the same translation is proper here.
There is no particle following in this passage as there
is in those other passages to suggest a comparison and
to prescribe that *tobh* ("good") be translated as a
comparative. *Hertzberg* resorts to a device which shows
the grammatical difficulty of all who interpret as he
does by inserting the *min* comparative after the word
tobh. — The versions inserted *la*, "for," in a number
of cases. — Our translation must be maintained in
the face of the almost universal trend of the familiar
versions and in the face of comments like *Ginsburg's*,
"But against these renderings [like ours] is to be
urged that they are contrary to the scope of the whole
argument." The fact of the matter is that only this

rendering of v. 24 is in harmony with vv. 25 and 26 as well as with what immediately follows in Chapter 3.

The thought of this passage is, true enjoyment is possible, but it does not lie within man's power to bestow it upon himself. Man is not the fountain of good. Such good is for the present defined as "eating and drinking and getting satisfaction." Even that does not lie within man's power to bestow upon himself. Such a definition does not indicate a low level of appreciation of what may be called good. The choice of good things mentioned is motivated by the preceding thoughts which had dealt with the problem of enjoying good in the things of earth. One may take this passage to mean: Even things on this low level cannot be enjoyed unless God so grants. What the author seeks to indicate is merely this, that even the simplest forms of enjoyment cannot be made to yield satisfaction by man himself. Eating and drinking and "getting satisfaction" in such things come from a higher source, namely, "from the hand of God." He can make a man realize that food and drink are a divine gift and can put man in a position where he deeply appreciates them as divine gifts and so has deeper satisfaction, or, as the Hebrew states it, "His soul seeth good."

Note our translation of v. 25: "For who can eat, and who can have enjoyment apart from Him?" Observe how this differs from the wording of the familiar versions. Even the King James and the A.R.V. translate *yo'khel* "can eat." According to a parallel *chush* can also mean "have enjoyment" (*BDB*). Our rendering necessitates the reading *mimménnu*. This is also the reading found in certain manuscripts (at least eight) and the Septuagint and the Syriac and Jerome. So we have a thought that is in perfect harmony with the preceding. But it is reduced to a general principle by the verb "have enjoyment." No enjoyment of any kind is possible "apart from Him." *Chuts mimménnu* is a strong compound preposition that is found in later usage only and is found only here in the Scriptures.

To round out this part of the thought it is essential that there be some indication as to the basis on which God does allot enjoyment when it pleases Him to do so. The next verse (26) indicates what that basis is.

God's gifts are very often conditioned by man's attitude. When they are set before the judgment of God, some are found to be "good." They please Him. Not absolute perfection is meant; the word "good" gains its meaning from the contrasted word "sinners" (*chote'*). The "good" are here then the ones who are not habitual sinners. To them God grants "wisdom and knowledge." But this is not the type that is described previously, where "wisdom and knowledge" are "vanity." For since "joy" is at once appended, the terms must apply to a wisdom and a knowledge which enable a man to derive joy from the things of life.

However, to the man who lives in sin (*chote'*— participle for continuing action) He gives "the vexation of gathering and heaping up" goods and treasures (these objects must be understood). God disposes of what the wicked gather in such a way that they themselves may be said to give it to him to whom God pleases to have it given. Surely, such an experience of the sinners is "vanity and striving for wind."

CHAPTER III

2. For God is the Absolute Ruler over His people (3:1-15)

(1) For everything there is a season and a specific time for every affair under the heavens. (2) A time to bring forth and a time to die; A time to plant and a time for uprooting that which is planted; (3) A time to slay and a time to heal; A time to tear down and a time to build; (4) A time to weep and a time to laugh; A time to mourn and a time to dance; (5) A time to scatter stones and a time to gather stones; A time to embrace and a time to refrain from embracing; (6) A time to seek and a time to lose; A time to keep and a time to throw away; (7) A time to rip and a time to sew; A time to keep still and a time to speak; (8) A time to love and a time to hate; A time for war and a time for peace. (9) What profit has the active man in the thing in which he toils? (10) I have seen the work that God has given the children of men to occupy themselves with. (11) He does everything beautifully at its proper time; He also has given eternity into men's hearts; only that man cannot find the work that God does from beginning to end. (12) For I recognized that among men there is nothing better than to be cheerful and to get good during one's life. (13) And also that any man should eat and drink and enjoy things in all his toil, that is a gift of God. (14) For I recognized that whatever God does will be forever. It is not possible to add to it or take away from it. And this God does that man may stand in awe of Him. (15) Whatsoever is has

been long ago; and that which is to be has been long ago; and God seeks out him who is persecuted.

The last thought that had been suggested at the close of Chapter 2 is now developed in its broadest application. It had been intimated that no man can give himself any enjoyment unless God wills it. The sovereign rule of God is now unfolded in its broadest aspects, not with the purpose of developing this truth as such, but for the purpose of affording comfort in a twofold way. In the first place, if the manifold activities of men are controlled by God's plans, then the present calamities of Israel did not befall His people without His predetermined will and counsel. Already that thought takes the sting out of adversity for men who trust God. In the second place, it behooves afflicted persons to put their hope in the deliverance which God will bring about in His own good time, for the times of all constructive work among God's people depend on God's appointment.

The fact that Israel's lot is being viewed as a sorely depressed and miserable one appears from v. 15, where those that are "driven away" (literally, "pursued") are thought of as "sought out by God"; and again in v. 16, where perversion of justice grievously disturbs those who suffer from it; and lastly in v. 18, where we find that men are being put to the test by God. Such being Israel's lot, the remnant of the people are apparently in need of comfort and of guidance. Both are offered by the Scripture before us.

Two other modes of approach seem unsatisfactory. We certainly do not here have only the practical observation that all things are to be done at their proper time, or as *Alleman* says: "The most apparent application of these verses is the lesson of timeliness." For true as it may be that all things should be carefully timed by man, and necessary as it may be to select the proper time for all our undertakings, yet some of the things mentioned by way of illustration cannot in any way be governed and ordered by men. Especially the first mentioned come under this head, for "bringing forth" and "dying" are surely not to be wisely timed by us. Besides, such counsel would serve little purpose in the book at this point. The book is speaking on the subject of the vanity of things; that is being demonstrated. Besides, such a self-evident truth as, "There is a proper time for all work we do," does not call for such extensive proof.

It should also be noted that, if the passage intended to teach that there is a proper time for doing all things, some such direct application should have been made somewhere. But nowhere do the thoughts that follow after the series of pairs of things for which there is a time make this application. Nowhere are the readers told directly or indirectly, before or after the long series, "Now be sure you time your action wisely so that it coincides with the right time." Besides, nowhere is the slightest hint given as to how to determine the right time.

The commentators who have noted this fact then operate with the idea that the God of this passage is the hidden God, and only the hidden God (*Der Gott, dem Koheleth gegenuebersteht, ist der verborgene Gott, nur der verborgene — Galling*). Or they drop to a still lower level as is indicated by the *Abingdon Bible Commentary* which has the surprising heading, "Hopelessness of struggle against an Arbitrary God" — *Geo. L. Robinson.*

Furthermore, if the idea to be expressed were that for all *human* activity there is a proper time, that would hardly motivate the author's giving fourteen pairs of examples. A few instances would have sufficed. Hardly any one of the writers who favor this approach seems to have noticed that fact. They, therefore, usually have very little, if anything, to say about the forms of activity that are mentioned, whereas the interpretation we follow has quite a bit to say about their meaning and their applicability.

There is still another consideration, perhaps the clearest of all, that shows that this approach is right, for v. 11, spoken in obvious reference to vv. 1-8, says that *God* "does everything beautifully at its proper time." That thought would be out of place if the whole passage were to say: *"Man* should see to it that he does everything at its proper time."

Nor can we be entirely satisfied with the type of interpretation which suggests that, since all types of endeavor can be carried through successfully only if the sovereign will of God has determined that they shall succeed, therefore man should make sure that he has chosen such a time. Also from that point of view — for some application of the general principle made with reference to man's conduct seems implied and not merely an abstract declaration of God's sovereignty — from this point of view, we say, the opening words present difficulties. For the reference to the time of dying can hardly be a suggestion for a man to arrange his dying with reference to God's appointed time.

It follows from these considerations that the different types of activity mentioned in vv. 2-8 are to be conceived exclusively as forms of *divine* activity — there is a proper time for *God* to do things. Since, then, the time for all things has been determined, everything rests on God's will and good pleasure, both the time when such a work is to be carried through as well as the carrying through itself.

Furthermore, purely earthly relationships are not being examined, neither is God's activity and control with reference to them, but rather the control and the governance of the *church.* For thus, Jerome indicates, this passage was from days of old interpreted by the Jews in the Targum. He says: "The Hebrews understood everything which is written about the opposite kinds of action and the proper time for them, up to the point where he says 'a time for war and a time for peace' as referring to *Israel*." A long list of commentators has been reluctant to follow *Hengstenberg* when he again strongly stressed this approach till at the present time *Hertzberg*, though timidly, returns to it.

It can also be demonstrated that all these activities for which it is said that there is a special time are elsewhere in the Scriptures spoken of as forms of activity which God at some time or another has engaged in either for the correction or for the deliverance of the church.

Since, therefore, in evil days those persons who love the church sigh and pine for her deliverance, here there is a Scripture passage which, if interpreted according to the analogy of Scripture, yields the comforting and the instructive thought: God has His times and His seasons; the grievous seasons of suffering are terminated when God's time has arrived; the seasons of refreshing, however, break in upon the church when God's good time has arrived. There is a time for both.

There is no thought, therefore, in the passage of a dark fate, which with its blind and irrevocable decrees controls all events, binding, perhaps, even the hands of God.

At the same time those who know God cannot help but associate with these utterances the thought that it is always God's love that determines Him to institute corrections and always also to hasten the seasons when He displays His favor.

Lastly, this suggestion also, of necessity, grows out of the unfolding of the thought: If it depends on God and His predetermined counsel what shall be done and what not, it is quite in vain for man to hope by his efforts to stem the tide of adversity or to hasten the

day of mercy. A sober restraint is imposed upon man
by the salutary consideration that God rules with
sovereign will and wisdom. Man can thus learn to surrender to a guidance that will prevail whether man
consents or not, which is yet a guidance that can in
every case be trusted absolutely.

The general principle is enunciated first: (v. 1)
"For everything there is a season and a specific time
for every affair under heaven."

Here a truth is emphasized that is also stated elsewhere in the Scriptures. See Ps. 102:13, "a set time to
favor Zion"; or Ps. 75:2, "When I shall find the set
time, I will judge uprightly." Or again, in reference to
Jesus' being taken captive, "No man laid hand on Him,
because His hour was not yet come." Or again, apart
from the set time that God determines, the sovereign
rule of God is indicated in Deut. 32:39: "See now that
I, even I, am He, and there is no god with Me: I kill
and make alive; I wound and heal, and there is none
that can deliver out of My hand."

LXX has the verse read: τοῖς πᾶσιν ὁ χρόνος, καὶ καιρὸς
τῷ παντὶ πράγματι ὑπὸ τὸν οὐρανόν. The following rendering
might then also be given: "For everything there is a
suitable time (BDB) and a particular season (*Zeit-
punkt* — KW) for every business (*Barton*) under the
sun." — *Zemān* is a late word. The late use of *chephets*
appears here, viz., "affair," "matter." *Luther* rendered
'*eth*, "time," *Stunde*, "hour," which is very much to
the point.

Twenty-eight times the word "time" is used. Fourteen pairs of opposites are employed in an effort to
cover the widest possible range and thus practically
every aspect of human life. Life in its beginning and
its end is first mentioned, and to indicate the constructive approach of the entire passage, the first term used
is one of constructive achievement and the last one is
the word "peace." Old prescriptions as to the manner

of arranging the passage in Hebrew Bibles have led to the unusual style of printing the two opposites in two parallel columns as we still find it in the Hebrew Bibles.

Some commentators translate the first infinitive *laledheth* as a passive, "to be born." There is no instance in the Hebrew Bible in which an active form of this verb is used in a passive sense. Of doubtful value as an example of an active infinitive being translated as a passive is Jer. 25:34: "For the days of your slaughter *litboach* are fully come." Similarly in Hos. 9:11, the infinitive *ledah* is used in an active sense. For if the days appointed for their slaughter are fully come (*māle'û*), the agents of the slaughter need only be thought of, and the propriety of the use of the active infinitive is clear. Here as always the verb *ledheth* means "to bring forth." LXX has τοῦ τεκεῖν. Not things that God permits to happen to us are under consideration as fixed by a kind of determinism, but rather works that God does or permits to come upon the church. Zion has appointed times when she may bring forth and so be prosperous and increase. Such thoughts are to be found elsewhere in the Scriptures in reference to Zion. Isa. 54:1, "Sing, thou barren, thou that didst not bear." Again, 66:7, "Before she travailed she brought forth, before her pain came she was delivered of a man-child" (cf. v. 8, "Zion travaileth").

There are, then, seasons when God grants His church the ability to bring forth children. At such times she grows though it may cost her the travail of grievous birth throes. On the other hand, there will be seasons of death for the church when God chastises her because of her sins. "Death" (*muth*) does not always signify extinction of existence. In the Scriptures a season of death is frequently synonymous with very severe affliction whereby God has brought someone low. So Ps. 85:6, "Wilt Thou not quicken us again that Thy people may rejoice in Thee?" God's people must have been conceived of as being dead, else no quickening would be possible. Likewise Ps. 71:20, "Thou who hast showed us many and sore troubles, wilt quicken us again, and wilt bring us up again from the depths of the earth." So Hos. 6:2, "After two days He will revive us: on the third day He will raise us up." Ezek. 37, the vision of the valley of the dry bones, is an amplified use of the same thought in a figure. Deut. 32:39 remains the basic passage: "I kill, and I make alive."

Grievous as a situation may be, there is, we note, comfort in this general observation. If seasons of grievous affliction rest upon the church, God has determined them in His sovereign wisdom. He is not ignorant of the state of His people. On the other hand, He also has seasons of "bringing forth," to which His own people will anxiously look forward. The thought might be stated thus: There is a periodicity about the things that happen to the Zion of God that helps us to understand her state and to know in how far the hand of God is involved in what transpires.

Furthermore, if the work of the church is regarded from the common aspect of a work of planting, it is to be borne in mind that God has seasons when He pleases to let planting be done and again seasons when He desires to have the work of uprooting be done. Again, no man can alter God's wise purposes by endeavors of his own, for God's purpose reigns supreme. Passages indicating this point of view in regard to "planting" are Ps. 80:8, "Thou broughtest a vine out of Egypt, Thou didst drive out the nations and plantedst it." Ps. 44:2, "Them [Israel] Thou didst plant." On "plucking up," cf. Ps. 80:12, "Why hast Thou broken down its walls, so that all they that pass by the way do pluck it?" (also v. 13). Those people who were living through a season that was characterized mostly by "plucking up" can at least discern from this that "there is a divinity that shapes our ends."

God's corrective dealings with men have become so rigorous that they must (v. 3) be designated as slaying (lit., "murder," *harogh*). This same verb is used in reference to God's severe dealings with His people in Ps. 78:31, 34, He "slew the fattest of them" and, "When He slew them, then they inquired after Him." See also Jer. 12:3. The gracious work of "healing" in reference to His people is referred to in the famous passage, Exod. 15:26, "I am the Lord that healeth thee." A similar setting over against each other of these two forms of activity on God's part is found in Deut. 32:39, "I kill, and I make alive; I wound, and I heal," and also in Hos. 6:1, "He hath torn, and He will heal us; He hath smitten, and He will bind us up."

It must be admitted that the analogy of the Scriptures in regard to these words points with an emphasis that cannot be ignored to forms of divine activity in behalf of His people. To interpret after this manner is not an unwarranted "spiritualizing" of the text but the very type of interpretation that penetrates into the depth of the matter.

The second half of the verse reads: "A time to break down and a time to build." The familiar figure comes to mind where the breaking down (*parats*) of the walls of God's vineyard is referred to in Isa. 5:5 and Ps. 89:40, the verb used here being used in both those passages. This was the verb that was employed by the sacred writer in referring to the desolate state of the walls of Jerusalem after the return of the captives (Neh. 2:13). So, too, the verb "to build up" (*bānāh*) is used in the Scriptures of spiritual reconstruction. In Jer. 24:6 this must be the case, for the promise at once (v. 7) speaks of giving a "new heart." Jer. 42:10, no doubt, has the same force. In Ps. 51:18, "build Thou the walls of Jerusalem," spoken by David in the days when the walls of stone stood intact, the reference is to the repairing of the spiritual damage done by the grievous sin committed by the king. Cf. also Ps. 102:13, 14.

Again, (v. 4) if our interpretation is to be in harmony with what we have thus far found, this cannot be a reference to mere weeping of tears but must be a reference to spiritual grief over sin and its effects, for we find the same verb used in Luke 6:21, "Blessed are ye that weep," and in John 16:20, "Ye shall weep and lament." In connection with "mourn" we involuntarily think of the second beatitude (Matt. 5:4), which again refers to more than external grief. In connection with the "skipping about" (*rekodh*), which does not strictly mean "dance," we think of David's joy as he danced before the ark. The thought still remains: It is God who gives us occasion for these varied activities, and He does it when it pleases *Him*.

The list is made intentionally long, for it is the writer's intention to drive home with emphasis the thought that the many sides of life are under the control of God's omnipotent rule, especially all spiritual activities that affect the church. The general principle upon which the casting away of stones (v. 5) proceeds is stated in Mark 13:2, namely, when a portion of the church grows as corrupt as Israel had grown in Christ's time. A parallel to the thought of "embracing" is found in Jer. 13:11, where God says: "As a girdle cleaveth to the loins of a man, so have I caused to cleave to Me the whole house of Israel." But, as the earlier part of the chapter indicates, in Jeremiah's day the time had come to put Israel away, i.e., "to refrain from embracing." The situation of the writer of Psalm 42 was one where he was shut off from communion with God. Kindred thoughts are expressed in Prov. 4:8 and 5:20.

It is not necessary to seek for many parallels to establish our point of view and our particular mode of interpretation. The analogy has been very close. Note in addition that the verb "cast off" (v. 6) is used in reference to Israel in II Kings 13:23 and Jer. 7:15. Since Ps. 71 is a prayer of the whole people Israel, v. 9 of that Psalm belongs here.

To the many forms that God's favor and His disfavor may have these relatively new thoughts are added. On the one hand it may, in God's wisdom, be a time when He rends His people (v. 7) as a man may rend a garment in wrath. Only when it pleases God will such damage be repaired. Or again there may be a time, providentially ordained, when it is proper for God to maintain a stony silence when His people call upon Him. When such a season is ended, it may please God again "to speak." But when He speaks, it is He who speaks with the result that "it is done; He commands and it stands fast." As is done throughout this section, a word of reproof is paired with a word of hope and promise. For just as assuredly as the hard words of divine chastisement have now gone into effect with reference to Israel, so the words that connote God's favor shall be powerfully fulfilled when God's good time has come. This thought, of course, reaches back to v. 2 and governs this entire passage.

A clear illustration of how, under the providence of God, hate may give place to love (v. 8) is found in Ps. 105:25, where Egypt's hatred of Israel is attributed to God's working, which may be contrasted with Exod. 11:3, where, due to God's causation, Israel enjoys great favor in the eyes of the Egyptians. The periodicity of God's working is thereby beautifully illustrated. It served a divine purpose for Israel's good to have Egypt hate her. How else could Israel have been made ready to follow God's guidance out of the land? When God's purpose for Israel was fully ripe, and His people were asked to leave, God bestowed favor upon His people in order to enrich the impoverished nation. Compare besides Ps. 106:46; II Kings 25:27; Isa. 60:16; 49:23; 57:19.

Just as manifold as these various activities of God's favor and His disfavor may be as they are here enumerated by twenty-eight verbs, just so manifold are the types of dealing God has with His people. This thought also flows from the passage, and the disconsolate Israelite is bidden to remember how varied God's modes of working are to restore and to heal His people. But the chief feature of the comfort offered in the passage lies in this, that for every time and season of correction there comes at its expiration a season of refreshing. But — and this has the greatest emphasis — *God is the absolute Ruler of His people.*

Verse 9 attaches itself intimately to the preceding series of activities — "What profit has the active man in the thing in which he toils?" for these activities have been described as being under the absolute and final control of God. For if it rests with God what is to be done for His church and His people in special seasons, why should a man endeavor to exercise control, or why should he deem it to be incumbent upon him to rectify all the ills to which the church of God may be subjected at any given time? Proper activity in the area of one's calling is highly commended elsewhere in the Scriptures. But to try to be active and to exercise control in the area where God is in control, profits one nothing. There man surely has no profit of his toil; he should leave the issues with God. — *Yithron* is one of the Preacher's characteristic words; it means "the outcome," "that which is left," "profit."

Verse 10. Since man is seldom so fully conscious of the truth of the matter as he ought to be and usually presumes, though with much good intention, to steer things aright in troubled days, man has much toil as a result. That this is a matter of common observation is very evident ("I have seen"). At the same time this "toil" of man is *given him by God* that he might exercise himself fruitlessly therein and so come to the proper understanding of his own limitations and of God's supreme control. For after having engaged in this useless attempt at improvement he emerges — if he will suffer God to teach him — a wiser and a better man. So the statement of the verse that God has given to man such toil that he might exercise himself therein is perfectly correct.

It is obvious that especially the last two verses furnish striking examples of the fact that every statement must be evaluated according to the connection in which it appears. Strange meanings could be extracted from vv. 9 and 10 if they were dissociated from what precedes and what follows.

Though man travails over insoluble difficulties, the truth of the matter is that there is nothing wrong as far as God's administration of affairs is concerned, no, not in any respect (v. 11). It may even be asserted positively that, because of His accurate timing of constructive seasons over against seasons of apparent destruction, everything is actually "beautiful in its time" (*yapheh,* "beautiful," in late usage stands for the *tobh,* "good," of earlier days — *Hertzberg,* or, as *Galling* aptly compares, there is the analogous German use of the word in the phrase *schoen und gut.*) A harmony of purpose and a beneficial supremacy of control pervade all issues of life to such an extent that they rightly challenge our admiration. Nor has He, the divine Disposer of things, left man without the faculty of appreciating the lasting import of things; how, namely, the present builds itself upon the long past that precedes it (*'olam,* "eternity") and how the present is built with an eye to the interminable future that is to come ("eternity").

Man has a deep-seated "sense of eternity" (*Delitzsch*), of purposes and destinies. Yet even then he is not able fully to master the problem, for the reach of eternity involved is too vast for him. Or, to quote Koheleth, "only that man cannot find the work which God doeth from the beginning even unto the end." He may well know of God's blessed power and His purposes and yet not be able to trace them through in detail as God operates. Occasionally man catches glimpses of God's high and holy purposes and must trust God for the rest which he cannot see and understand.

The rendering of *mibbeli* "yet so that" is unsatisfactory. It places the blame on God that man has no success in his investigations. Also note that nowhere in the Bible does *'olam* mean "world."

Verse 12. This piece of definite knowledge and understanding (*yadha'ti*, "I recognized") grows out of the preceding observation that, as far as man's living among men is concerned, there is no better course to follow than to keep a merry heart as a result of trust in God's excellent rule and also to get such good as may be gotten in the course of one's life. Fretting is to no purpose. Trying to rectify what is above our power to set right can serve only to embitter a man's life. — The rendering of *'asoth tobh* as "do good" does not harmonize with the spirit of the passage. It is better to translate "to get good," as also *Luther* renders it, *sich guetlich tun*. A.R.V.m. also has this translation.

Dull resignation apart from all thought of God as our only prospect is far from the writer's thoughts. He is not a pessimist. Even if man takes delight in material gifts that God permits to pass through his hands, such delight is nothing that man creates for himself. It is the gift of God (v. 13), who is the absolute Ruler and Giver of all things. In every case, then,

the attitude to be cultivated is one that is the outgrowth of true godliness.

A well-tested and carefully arrived at conclusion
is offered in vv. 14 and 15. It is submitted in reference
to the preceding observations about God's supreme
rule over all things for the good of the church. It rules
out the thought that man's effort to set things right
could even in a measure contribute to God's efforts, as
little as, on the other hand, man's efforts to frustrate
His purposes can subtract anything from His achievements. When men have observed that all depends on
God's achievements and not on ours they note that
this very arrangement of things is to teach man due
reverence for God. In this scheme of things no variation
occurs. Nothing is now but what has always been;
nothing will ever be that can depart from this fact.
Yet for the special comfort of all poor sufferers whom
the evil times have caught and hold suspended the
thought is inserted that in God's wise care of all they,
the poor "persecuted ones," are also regarded and shall
be delivered in God's good time.

Unfortunately this thought is almost lost by the
peculiar translation given to *nirdaph,* nifal participle
or *radhaph,* which plainly means "the one pursued or
persecuted," not *das, was vergangen ist* (*Luther*), or
"what is passed away"; better is the A.R.V., margin
"driven away," but it is still neuter without reason.
Williams quite appropriately draws attention to the
Hebrew form of the thought voiced in Ecclus. 5:3,
which may well be based on our passage: "Say not who
can prevail against His [or any] strength, for the
Lord seeketh such as are driven away." The objection
should not be raised that such a translation, namely,
"him who is persecuted," is foreign to the context as
Williams thinks, inasmuch as the background of the
book is throughout that of a people suffering persecu-
tion and oppression, and it is just at points such as

this where the background gleams through and helps us to discern more clearly the situation of the children of Israel. — Note the sign of the accusative (*'eth*) before an indeterminate noun. It is used here to avoid ambiguity (*KS* 288g and *GK* 117c).

The whole passage, vv. 1-15, is pitched on a higher level than the commonplace: Be sure you time your actions rightly so that they may harmonize with the times and the seasons that are preordained of God — which, in the end, turns out to be a bit of futile advice. For no man can know the times which God has set in His own plans. Our interpretation ought not to be rejected as being farfetched. It does justice to the peculiar statements found here and offers us a passage that is singularly helpful and comforting in every day and age.

3. Even perversion of justice must serve His sovereign purpose (v. 16-22)

(16) **And besides I saw under the sun that wickedness had come into the place of justice, and that wickedness had come into the place of righteousness. (17) I said to myself, Both the righteous and the wicked God will judge, for there is a time there for every affair and for every work. (18) I said to myself: This happens because of the children of men that God may purify them, and that they may see that they are no better than cattle, they for themselves. (19) For what befalls the children of men also befalls the beast; one and the same thing befalls both; as the one dies, so dies the other, and the same breath is in both; and there is no advantage of the man over the beast. (20) Both go to one place; both are of the dust, and both return to the dust. (21) Who knows the spirit of man that goes upward and the spirit of the beast that goes downward to the earth? (22) So I saw that there is**

nothing better than that a man should rejoice in his works, for that is his portion. For who shall bring him to see what shall be after him?

God's absolute rule over His people has just been considered (v. 1-15). One striking experience of the times certainly seems to be oddly at variance with this principle, and that is the flagrant maladministration of justice of which Israel was the victim. As long as such experiences were more or less common in Israel it could hardly seem as though God's rule was entirely supreme. Yet there are certain higher points of view in regard to this seeming irregularity which serve to harmonize this experience with the sound principle just established. This section adjusts the seeming irregularity.

A new and disturbing observation made in everyday life is introduced (v. 16) as usual by "besides I saw" (*'odh ra'ithi*). Into the place where justice should be administered (*mishpat*, objective judgment that is made in all fairness) wickedness (*resha'*, bending or perversion of the right) had crept. Into the place where fair-minded and upright men should have been found (*tsedek*, subjective righteousness on the part of the incumbent in office) the same wickedness had wormed its way. The solution of the difficulty, which clamors loudly for an adjustment, is given in a twofold way. The first is offered by v. 17.

The author says that God will ultimately take the case in hand. And since the two types of men involved constitute a clear-cut issue of right and wrong, the objects of God's judicial activity are placed first in the sentence — "the righteous and the wicked." This form of statement indicates also that only in such cases where a clear perversion of justice was evident, not in imaginary ones, will God rectify what man has confused. The fact remains: God's judgments straighten unsettled scores of justice maladministered, yet, at the same time, these readjustments come only in God's own time and season. Men cannot hasten, men cannot delay the time that God's sovereign wisdom fixes.

The last word of the verse, the adverb "there," may, at first thought, seem somewhat vague. It is plain, according to the subject matter of the verse, that it points back to God with whom the ultimate readjustments lie. It could also have been spoken with a gesture that points to heaven, where God is, who watches over all such cases and finally proves His sovereign control over even what seemed momentarily to have eluded Him.

The second solution (v. 18) is appended directly and is introduced exactly as was the first (v. 17), namely, by "[then] said I to myself." This solution resolves itself into a double one. In the first place, God lets things happen thus so that He might "purify the sons of men." "Purify" (*lebharam* from *barar*) means to "separate," to "winnow," to "prove." A proving process certainly goes on when men suffer injustice. That which is in their heart is certainly made apparent. Insincerity becomes manifest; true fidelity approves itself; and the whole experience also serves to clarify issues and to bring the actual attitude of men to light.

The second gain that those involved have from such an experience is the realization that they are but cattle. The author does not say *as* cattle but uses the stronger expression *hem behemah*, "they are cattle." Yet the limitation of the thought follows at once, "they for themselves," namely, apart from any higher values God may have granted them. Just how this is to be understood is explained in v. 19.

It is not necessary to sense here something akin to brutality on Koheleth's part. His statement is very strong, but it is not an overstatement. It is an unfair charge to make against our author to say, "This is a brutal way Koheleth has of gloating over his own impotence *in maiorem Dei gloriam"* (to the greater glory of God) — *Hertzberg.*

Verse 19. Life consists, to a very large extent, of chance happenings over which we have no control, and the occurrence of which we are quite powerless even to foretell. So little are we masters of our own life and fortune. The thought seems to be rather emphatically expressed by the pointing of the Hebrew text, which, translated as it stands, reads: "For a chance are the sons of men, and a chance are the cattle." In each case *mikreh* is absolute state not construct, according to the Hebrew vowel points. But that would amount to an unbiblical overstatement of the case. All the versions preferred the reading that has the construct ending as we have done above, which would have read literally, "For the lot of the children of men and the lot of the beast — one lot is theirs." This could be rendered more idiomatically and correctly as we have rendered it above: "For what befalls the children of men also befalls the beast." We thus also avoid the terms "chance" and "fate" which are used by some, for *mikreh* means "happening" or "that which happens to a man."

True as it is that there is a tremendous difference between man and beast, just so true it is that there is, on the other hand, a tremendous similarity. The individual that has not recognized this may be inclined to think too well of himself, better than *he* should who is of the common stock of men as all those are now to be classed who are born after the common course of nature since Adam's fall. God lets certain things befall them such as being the victims of the miscarriage of justice that they might be made to feel how low they really rank in some respects, for a proper appreciation of a man's low estate is salutary for him.

The similarity between man and beast is especially apparent in the manner of their death. For to tell the truth of the matter, one breath is in both, namely, the vitalizing breath of God; and death is the withdrawal of that breath or spirit. We observe the same point of view in Gen. 7:22, where those creatures that perished in the Flood, man and beast, are comprehended under one term: "all in whose nostrils was the breath of life, of all that was on the dry land, died." The *ruach*, the breath of life, animates both (it is called *ruach* or *nishmath chayyim*.) From that point of view truly man has no "advantage" or pre-eminence over the beast. The author has, however, intentionally excluded all consideration of higher values and has kept entirely within the sphere of the things that are "under the sun," as v. 16 carefully noted. Leave out the spiritual assets and possibilities of man, and he is absolutely in the category of the beast.

This truth is of sufficient import to have a still clearer statement of the case sum it all up (v. 20). There is nothing about it that is in any way one-sided.

There is nothing unusual about the verse inasmuch as it merely explains what that "one place" is to which both groups go, namely, the dust from whence they were taken. It is quite proper that, now that sin has entered the world, both should return to the dust. Cf. Gen. 3:19; Ps. 104:29; Ps. 146:4. And any unseemly high thought that man may have concerning himself should dissolve before this inescapable fact. This verse does not, of course, deny any of the deeper truths concerning man's future. The following verses correct any misapprehension one might have had on that score.

Verse 21. Unfortunately, this turn of the thought has been obscured and largely lost through the influence of the rationalistic commentators who have followed the old versions, the LXX, Vulgate, Luther, etc., in their interpretation of this section. Conceiving Koheleth as a man who is struggling in a maze of doubt, they have one of his doubts find expression here.

This doubt they seek to soften down by saying that
Koheleth does not deny the doctrine of eternal life but
merely expresses an uncertainty with regard to it,
which uncertainty had again vanished by the time
Chap. 12:7 is reached (cf. *Delitzsch*).

They can make the claim for this rendering that it
apparently fits more smoothly into the context. We
say "apparently," for it is clear that the author is
using an argument concerning which he is in doubt, for
he says, "Who knows?" Contentions are, however, not
bolstered by doubtful considerations. *Volck* seems to
sense this and says that the meaning of the verse is
this: "No man knows whether there is a difference
between the death of man and the death of the beast,
a difference of such a sort that God takes the vital
breath of the one unto Himself in a different manner
than He takes the other." But that fits into the context
rather poorly, for the author's discussion concerns the
ways in which man is like unto the beast, not the manner
of God's taking the vital breath of the two to Himself.

Practically all these interpretations of the ration-
alists and some men of faith have their root in the
presupposition that the belief in a resurrection was
of late origin in Israel. It was not held before the
Persian era. Starting with this untenable supposition
and adding to it another that is equally untenable,
namely, that Koheleth is wading through a number of
doubts in the course of the book, they interpret the text
from that point of view. Many do not even make an
effort to refute the other view; they assert with dogmatic finality: "It is against sentence structure and
context" (*Zoeckler*) ; or, "It is a dogmatic correction"
(*Hertzberg*). Hardly a commentator of later days interprets otherwise. *Taylor Lewis* and *Hengstenberg*
are exceptions.

First of all, just how does the text read? Just as
we have translated it: "Who knows the spirit of man

that goes upward?" "Spirit" is followed by *ha'olah*, "the one going upward," the participle with the article, *ha*, which, mark well, has a long *a*. The interrogative particle would have been *he* with a short *e*. Likewise before "that goeth downward" there is the article, not *he*, the interrogative particle.

The statement begins with the interrogative "who knows?" *mi yodhea'*. The claim that this must be followed by an interrogative, which some commentators make, is not borne out by Hebrew usage. Upon examining the nine passages where the expression occurs, we find that in *three* instances it is followed by the interrogative (*'im* or *ha*, or *mah*, Esther 4:14; Eccles. 2:19; 6:12). In three instances it is followed by a direct object (Ps. 90:11; Eccles. 3:21; 8:1). Twice it is followed by the imperfect and means practically "perchance" (Joel 2:4; Jonah 3:9). Once it occurs as a kind of afterthought (Prov. 24:24) which is also a kind of "perchance." Since, therefore, three possible usages occur, the context must decide which is to be chosen.

The traditional pointing of the Hebrew text should not be rejected unless it is proven untenable. *Delitzsch* has shown conclusively that the Hebrew scribes did not intend to write the "*he* interrogative." They intended to write the article with the participle. *Barton*, who denies this, cites one instance as an exception. On closer inspection this instance (Numb. 16:22) proves to be *he*, the article, and not *he* interrogative.

Nor are we safe in arguing that the traditional vowel points express merely the belief of the men of a later age, for the painstaking care with which the Jews established a very sound tradition in adding the vowel points is evident on every hand.

Those interpreters who find a doubt expressed here have the author contradict himself, for in 12:7 he distinctly claims: "The spirit returns to God who gave it." If, then, the author finally did penetrate through his doubts and overcame them (as some of these commentators state) why should he here express a doubt on the matter? Is the book only the effort of a man with a doubt-ridden soul to work through his problems and to give a record of his struggles with doubts as they progressed step for step? Certainly not; we have every reason for believing that he was a competent teacher, firm and sound of belief, who, because his own faith was so firm, could venture to impart stability and settled convictions to his contemporaries. The whole book testifies to this fact.

We shall not demonstrate how greatly the opinion that Koheleth here expresses his doubts militates against the doctrine of inspiration. Inspiration, as the church holds that doctrine, would simply be impossible in that event.

We have, then, this thought in this verse: (paraphrasing the first part) "There are not many who take to heart as they ought to the fact that the spirit of man goeth upward, and that the spirit of the beast goeth downward to the earth." The most natural procedure is to take the verse as it stands and to see how it fits into the context. This verse is not a continuation of the thought of the preceding verses. They have shown in how far man and beast are alike. Now there comes a statement in how far they differ. Apparently, then, this is a corrective that is inserted against a misapprehension of the preceding verses. True, man is in some ways like the beast; but, on the other hand (the Preacher says it with a certain sadness) there are none too many who consider the opposite truth, namely, that the spirit of man goeth upward whereas that of the beast goeth downward to the earth. This thought is inserted parenthetically, and thereafter the author promptly concludes the preceding argument (v. 16-20) by a practical application (v. 22).

This verse looks back to the beginning of the chapter. If God is the sovereign Ruler of His people, and men cannot contribute anything to shape their destiny; and if, furthermore, perversion of justice must serve good purposes, under God's direction, in properly humbling man, what attitude should man then assume? One of dull resignation? Since *exultant* faith was not the order of the day, there is a better course, and that is, that man "rejoice in his works." What it is his business to do, let him do and take pleasure in the doing. For our daily tasks afford us all manner of enjoyment if we will but take it. That, in fact, "is man's portion." God wants him to do so. The things that will develop after the present situation (for that is the meaning of "after him," *'acharaw*) that lie beyond his ken and his jurisdiction "who shall bring him to see them?" Therefore he should surely not trouble about them and in a distressed way wonder how they may shape themselves. Since the future course of events lies hidden from his eyes, that is all the more reason for being content with that which is his portion, namely, "to rejoice in his works."

In regard to the expression *sheyyihyeh 'acharaw*, "that shall be after him" (as used here and in 6:12; 7:14; 9:3), it is enough to note that it does not refer to the future life or to the future destiny of men but to future events as they shall develop (*Zoeckler*), especially in reference to the church and her welfare.

CHAPTER IV

C. Another Group of Things by Which Vanity Is Demonstrated (Chapter 4).

The theme of the vanity of earthly things is still being proved and exemplified in this chapter. The author's reason for developing this theme becomes clear in reference to his contemporaries when we consider how very prone to overvalue earthly possessions they were. Malachi indicates how they sought satisfaction in the acquisition of wealth by unjust means (Mal. 3:5). Ezra and Nehemiah portray them as men who were, due to the disordered circumstances of the times, ready to take unjust advantage of their own countrymen by withholding wages, loaning money at usurious rates of interest, and even enslaving their fellow Israelites if possible (Neh. 5:1). This shows that in those poverty-stricken days men were prizing too highly the earthly possessions that they, for the most part, could not acquire, and for the acquisition of which they were oftentimes ready to ignore the commandments of the Lord. For such times and conditions it is essential that the vanity of all things under the sun be most emphatically demonstrated, especially by means of such experiences as were common in those days. Therefore Koheleth demonstrates the vanity of all things by the sad lot of the oppressed.

This chapter might be given the heading, "Social Problems" (*Williams*), for the four illustrations used are taken from the area of social issues. But not social issues as such are being discussed but primarily the fact that the social problems make the issue under discussion plainer, and that issue is the vanity of all purely earthly values.

1. By the sad lot of the oppressed (v. 1-3)

(1) And again I saw—all the oppressed that are mistreated under the sun; and, lo, there were the tears of the oppressed, but there was no comforter for them; and in the possession of their oppressors was power; but still there was no comforter for them. (2) So I sang the praises of the dead who died long ago rather than of the living whose life is still going on. (3) And as more fortunate than both of them did I esteem him who has not come into existence; because he has not seen the wicked things that are done under the sun.

"I returned and saw," as the Hebrew has it, equals, "and again I saw" (see *GK* 120d). This time it was the oppressed whom he considered. The verb "saw" (*ra'ah*) has been used repeatedly to introduce a new phase of the author's subject which he turns to contemplate (2:9, 16). Even if "I returned" (*shubh*) were always to be taken in that sense, the meaning would ultimately resolve itself into, "I saw again." Koheleth looked at the "oppressed" (*ha'ashukim*), not the "oppressions," for the participle that is used is simply the masculine passive of the kal. The examples cited by *Barton* to the effect that the word means "oppressions" — Amos 3:9 and Job 35:9 — do not establish the point. It would be passing strange if the same word were used twice in the same sentence and should have the meaning "oppressions" and then "the oppressed." Our translation agrees with the verb used in the relative clause — *na'asim*, nifal participle plural, for *'asah* means "make," and the oppressed "are made" what they are.

The unfortunates to whom Israel as a people belonged in those days are regarded in their lot only as a people "under the sun," and the estimate put upon their lot expressly leaves out of consideration all hope and comfort that they might derive from a higher source. The feature, however, that in this instance demonstrates so forcibly the vanity of earthly things is the "tears of the oppressed," one of the common signs of those days. What made their lot all the more pitiful is the fact, twice repeated, that "there was no comforter for them." What made the lot of these poor sufferers more intolerable was the fact that the oppressors were actually in possession of power, *koach* ("power"). This word is here not used in an evil sense (which the word never has) but the situation implies that they who have this power will not make good use of it. The mournful repetition, "there was no comforter for them," pictures a hopeless lot.

For anyone who wishes to put an estimate upon life as it is with all its oppression and its injustice, apart from the things that another life and world have to offer, there is but one possibility, and that is, that such life is a possession of rather doubtful value: the dead are to be praised rather than the living, because life is so miserable (*shabbeach,* infinitive absolute, continuing the construction of the finite verb, a construction that is not so uncommon in Hebrew, *GK* 113gg and *KS* 218b). This is not a cynical attitude but the expression of a sober truth. Life has absolutely no worth for the man who seeks his good things "under the sun." Another statement of the case is this: "more fortunate (*tobh*) than either the living or the dead is he who has not yet been," for till his existence begins, he does not have to share in that ghastly mockery of happiness called life.

There is nothing skeptical or cynical about such an attitude. It is the only permissible estimate that can be put upon earthly values apart from the heavenly. Classical writers occasionally utter kindred thoughts, but they never knew how to rise superior to them. To charge Koheleth with being "completely wanting in hope of a future life" overlooks the force of "under the sun" (v. 1). Nor is Koheleth involved in a self-contradiction as might at first appear when one reads 9:4 and 11:7ff., for he is here pointedly thinking of the situation which he has sharply outlined: men living without recourse to higher values.

2. By the futility of earthly endeavor (v. 4-6)

This also proves the vanity of earthly things, for the possibilities to which men might resort in an effort to make this bare earthly life worth while have not yet been exhausted. There is work as such, faithful and excellent performance of it in everyday tasks or special achievements. Such work cannot in the nature of the case afford satisfaction.

(4) I further took note of all the toil and all the competence that is achieved, that it is the result of rivalry of man over against his fellow man. This, too, is vanity and a striving for wind. (5) The fool folds his hands and devours his own flesh. (6) Better to have a handful of rest than two fists full of toil and striving for wind.

What Koheleth observes in regard to such endeavor is this: first, "toil" is required to achieve anything worth while. It may then deserve the word "competence" (*kishron*) or "a skillful and successful piece of work," for this is what the Hebrew word implies. That which proves such an achievement for all that to be a hollow one is not only that men to a very large extent have only envy for him who made the achievement, as the current versions indicate, "for this a man is envied of his neighbor." Our author penetrates deeper into values. For a man might be content with his achievement in spite of what envious detractors might say. But the worm that destroys the true satisfaction to be derived from any such endeavor is the fact that the very motive from which such endeavor springs in men who deal only in natural earthly values is tainted with the spirit of "emulation" (*kin'ah*) a word which *KW* renders very well as *Rivalitaet*, "rivalry." Such achievements are the outgrowth of plain "rivalry," the desire to be distinguished above others by such a piece of work. If, then, the motive out of which it grows is tainted, how can the fruit actually satisfy? Achievements that men praise and admire resolve themselves into a procession of displays of human selfishness or, to revert to the keywords of our book, "vanity and striving after wind."

Another attitude is possible in regard to labor and successful work (v. 5). It is the attitude of the "fool," *kesil*, "stupid fellow," "dullard," "sluggard." That type of fool is rightly introduced who has no ambition whatsoever to achieve a successful piece of work. Over against the zealous endeavors of the man pictured in the preceding verse he is content to fold his hands and to eat his own flesh, that is, do nothing and subsist on what he has like a hibernating bear, with the result, of course, that "he destroys himself." If the two are to be contrasted, the fool, though he is a fool, and by that very name stands condemned, yet has an advantage over the diligent man just described in that he has peace or better "quietness" in the enjoyment of his one "handful" whereas the other man's "two fists full" are accompanied by labor and striving after wind. This fact by no means commends the fool as though he had chosen the better part. He remains a fool for all that. A second disadvantage with which the enterprising man finds himself is indicated: this namely, he must do without "quietness." Therefore the author adds v. 6.

The sixth verse is more emphatic than the use we made of it (under v. 5) indicates. Nor is the A.V. exact in rendering, "Better is a handful *with* quietness than to have both the hands full *with* travail and vexation of spirit." For this rendering conceives the hands as being filled with food: on the one hand with a meagre portion, on the other with a generous amount; the attendant circumstances, however, are in the one instance "quietness," in the other "toil and vexation of spirit." The Hebrew construction is complete without supplied prepositions. The infinitive "to be full" takes as its object, in the one case "hand," in the second, "two fists." We, therefore, translate literally: "Better the filling of a hand with rest than," etc. The emphasis thus lies strongly upon what these two men have, not on the manner of their taking their meals. The enterprising man has a rather generous amount of toil and striving after wind. The fool has a relatively small amount of quietness.

Perhaps we gain a still better meaning and also a better sequence of thought if we regard v. 6 as being the utterance of the fool referred to in v. 5. Verse 6 expresses very correctly the fool's sentiments: "Rather would I have my ease, though I possess but little, than acquire more and have all the vexation that goes with it."

The whole section, vv. 4-6, presents two extreme attitudes that are disappointing. One is that man may achieve something in life by toil and dint of hard work, but, unfortunately, the motivating force behind such toil is too often nothing better than rivalry or envy. Seeing this, the fool (v. 5f.) prefers not to strive and toil but to enjoy what he can, an attitude that surely produces no substantial achievements. To the persons that assume these attitudes all is surely vanity. And so the author has again proved his point.

3. By the futility of the acquisition of riches.
(v. 7-12)

This subject, too, is considered only as further demonstrating the vanity of earthly things. It is but natural that the author also make a specific investigation of riches, which certainly have very frequently been considered as a possible source of true satisfaction. In Koheleth's day, too, many had their heart set on the acquisition of wealth.

(7) **Again I saw—another instance of vanity under the sun. (8) There may be a man who stands alone without a partner, having neither son nor brother, yet there is no end to all his toil; nor do his eyes ever see their fill of riches. "And [he says] for whom am I toiling and denying myself enjoyment?" This, too, is vanity and bad business. (9) Two are better than one, for they get a good reward for their toil. (10) For if they fall they can help one another to their feet; but woe to the one that falls and has nobody to lift him up. (11) Furthermore, if two sleep together they keep warm; but as for the lone man, how can he keep warm? (12). Also if someone should overpower a single man, two could stand up against him; especially a threefold cord is not quickly broken.**

The customary formula introduces also this section, indicating on the one hand that a new subject is being taken in hand; on the other, that values of a purely earthly kind alone are under consideration.

The emphasis of this section does not lie only on the fact that the individual under consideration stands alone (although *'echadh* here means "a lone one") but also and primarily on his being set on acquiring "riches" (*'osher*). Since he wants these riches for himself he withdraws himself from others so that he may not in any way be obliged to share with others what he acquires — a typical miser. He may have a son or a brother, but they are excluded from associating with him. His loneliness is, therefore, considered only in so far as it is brought upon himself by his inordinate desire of wealth. Wealth, so the conclusion runs, must, therefore, be a pretty sorry thing to acquire if it isolates a man and robs him of some of the finest of helps and joys that he might have had in life.

Having, then, isolated himself, this man gives himself unremittingly to that which has become the obsession of his life — the acquisition of wealth: "there is no end to all his toil." As was before indicated, it lies in the very nature of the case that satisfaction cannot follow from this pursuit because the eyes cannot be sated with riches (1:8). There must be a continual hungering that attends the poor miser. *Tisba'* means "be satisfied" and is used in reference to the satisfying of hunger or the quenching of thirst. The subject is plural, "his eyes," a reading that is to be retained as being the more difficult though it is a bit harsh.

The typical miser is then introduced as communing with himself after some time has been spent in the pursuit of riches. He speaks in the unrest of his heart. He asks himself: "For what am I toiling?" We must insert "he says" or something similar before his words. The author has thought himself into this man's position so deeply that he involuntarily voices the other man's thoughts. The miser admits that no one derives profit from what he labors for so painfully. He must continually deny his soul the things it craves. Such self-denial causes some discomfort, but the question keeps recurring: "For whom do I thus deny myself enjoyment?" Since no one profits, and he himself does not (for his eyes cannot be satisfied) the whole undertaking proves itself "vanity and bad business," *'inyan ra', schlimme Beschaeftigung* (*KW*).

One aspect of this poor fellow's situation is developed a bit more at length, namely, his unprofitable isolation into which he has secluded himself in order to have undivided enjoyment of his riches (v. 9f.).

Such "reward" (*sakhar*) as men have "for their toil" (*beth equivalentis, KS* 332o) is in a large measure denied the man that stands alone. The tenth verse exemplifies this. It is surely a reward, when one man falls, to have a faithful friend stand at one's side who is ready to raise one up. Only the one man is thought of as falling (*KS* 265e). This is true of actual falls which occur physically as well as in reference to any reverses that a man may encounter. He that has kept aloof from others finds none to raise him up just at the time when he experiences as he never did before how much men are dependent upon one another. The fidelity of friends is not experienced by those who have selfishly ignored others. All they have of their business is toil. — *Yakim* is a potential imperfect, "he may raise him."

A second instance (v. 11) establishes the point as to how foolish the rich man is. We refer, of course, to the miser mentioned in v. 8. A literal comparison would not do full justice to the case, for the rich man can provide himself with sufficient covering to become warm. In his need of being warmed by the love of associates the rich man becomes like unto the poor man who has but his own garment with which to cover himself. And so, being alone, the rich man suffers grievously. Association with others would have provided for his want. The case is stated rather concisely. Stated at length, it might have run as follows: Suppose this man happens to be traveling. At nightfall he must lodge wherever he can. It may be cold. *Two* men traveling together could warm one another by snuggling closely together. The lone individual has no such prospect. He always operates alone. On occasion that may prove very uncomfortable, to say the least.

Again, any form of opposition is covered by the incident referred to in v. 12 — not only physical attack and defeat. As the one man goes down under an onslaught, those whom he has befriended, and who feel themselves near to him, will out of love for him spring to his defense; and so he shall be rescued. The sweetest feature of the experience will be the fact that true friends intervened. Such friendship is an imponderable asset that is valued most at such a time. — The verb *yithkepho* has an indefinite subject, "if *someone* should overpower."

To sum it all up: such faithful holding to one another is what gives men the victory: "especially a threefold cord is not soon broken." A third man is brought into the picture, for where the spirit of true association prevails, it will always be more than a single friend who is won. The whole group will uphold a man. But within the group, as experience demonstrates, there are frequently a certain three who are most closely attached to one another, cf. II Sam. 23:18, 19, 23. Such combinations are the invincible triumvirates, groups that have dominant influence in an outstanding way. (There is no reference here to the Trinity as some of the ancients surmised). The argument is still concerned with the folly or futility of riches because the very attitude of the rich miser precludes all worth-while and profitable associations with others. There is nothing autobiographical about the case described. There is nothing in the text that suggests that Koheleth once strove to attain riches so eagerly.

4. By the vanity of high station (v. 13-16).

There follows a demonstration that *high position or station in this world* can afford no true satisfaction to those who make it the chief object of their endeavors. The point to be considered is the instability of the holding of any high office.

The situation that is described is in the nature of an illustration. Koheleth is practically saying: "I saw an event of this sort take place." He is not claiming that men in high station are regularly and unfailingly supplanted by poor upstarts or successors who come forth out of anonymity. Still he seems to imply that the sort of thing he describes happens commonly enough.

(13) **Better is a youth, poor and wise, than a king, old and foolish, who no longer knows enough**

to accept advice. (14) For from the prison the former went forth to become king even though he was born poor in the kingdom of the other man. (15) I saw all the living that walked under the sun, that they were with the second youth that arose in the old king's stead. (16) There was no end to all the people, those that constituted his followers. Yet the next generation will not rejoice in him. This, too, is vanity and striving for wind.

Much ingenuity has been employed by commentators to find some historical incident to parallel the situation here described. No instance has yet been found that would fit conveniently. Most precarious are all endeavors that attempt to find here material for fixing the date of our book. Of the long list of suppositions that have been given we may cite: Joseph, David, Rehoboam, Onias, Herod the Great, etc. *Williams* remarks very appropriately: "All the critics seem to forget that there were many kings and kinglets in those days, and that Koheleth may have referred to some persons well known to his first readers, who yet are quite unrecorded in history."

Some of the translations of this passage leave the reader in doubt as to the number of persons involved. There seem to be several poor youths. *Williams* reflects this approach in his remark: "Koheleth says no more about that youth [he means the one of v. 13] but speaks of another, who is at first welcomed with enthusiasm, and is afterward disregarded." Yet it is hardly likely that the author would have written so confusedly. All one needs to do is to point up some of the pronominal objects a little more sharply, and the whole narrative stands out very clearly, saying, in effect: "A poor youth takes over the kingdom of an old king, who once did well but has now grown too old; but even this poor youth will in like manner see the day come when his own popularity wanes."

The king is merely the representative of those who have attained to high position. What is recorded is a common observation with reference to those who have held a prominent position for some length of time. Theirs will usually be a downfall that is all the harder and the more disappointing because, the longer they held such a position, the more do they cherish it and make it the goal of all their aspirations and tenaciously cling to it even after the period of their usefulness has come to an end. What usually happens is what is recorded: the king, having become old, grows self-sufficient and refuses counsel — "He no longer (*lo' 'odh*) knows enough to accept advice." At one time this poor, erring mortal was ready to accept counsel. Self-sufficiency is a grievous fault that will most likely be found in those who are growing old. He that cannot accept correction is one who has outlived his usefulness, and a wise youth, even though he is poor, is certainly to be preferred.

Experience, too, has shown that the latter often supplants the former. This supplanting is not maneuvered by the craft of the youth as if *chakham* were here to be taken in the sense of "crafty" or "cunning," a sense it sometimes has. For the section demonstrates the instability of popular favor and the fact that it brought even this wise youth low. When the youth supplants the old king, that very event is a demonstration of the vanity of high station; for, certainly, the man who had stood high and then fell in his old age will be best qualified to say whether high station satisfies and least ready to claim that it does because his downfall will rankle in his heart. Incidentally this king proved himself a "stupid fool" (*kesil*) by the attitude he took throughout the situation.

The emphasis in v. 14 rests primarily on the uncertainty of such a high position. There are a rise and a fall; one man is on the ascendant, the other is descending. Such is the common phenomenon in regard to high station. What seems to be implied in addition to the fact that is here stated that the ascent of the youth, Joseph-like, takes its beginning from the prison, is that the youth was, perhaps, imprisoned by the old king who considered him a dangerous aspirant for the throne. Some reversion of popular feeling accompanied by a popular uprising leads to the rise of the one and the fall of the other. What makes the contrast the more startling is the fact that, while the old king was in office, his successor was born of a poor family. So the mighty are put down from their seats, and those of low degree are exalted. However, we cannot help but notice the insecurity of all those who come to the throne thus or in any other way. The day of their downfall may soon follow.

That thought must be developed. First, however, a picture is to be presented of the youthful king in the heyday of his glory (v. 15).

For a time our new young king enjoys all the glory that he could desire. He has a following. All acclaim him as the man of the hour. They support him. In reality, only those will entirely pin their hopes on him who are persons "under the sun," that is, such who do not recognize the true and abiding values.

This picture incidentally transcends the narrow limits of Israel, e.g., in Solomon's time. For at that time there were as yet no empires that embraced "all the living under the sun" — another indication of the Persian period when world empires are known. To call this hyperbole, as many interpreters do, overlooks the fact that hyperboles dare not be too extravagant else they fail of their effect.

The first part of v. 16 pictures the new king still in the day of his success. He is visualized as standing up, and before him are those that do him reverence. They cannot be counted, so numerous are they.

The second part of the verse pictures him as meeting the common fate of rulers. The next generation comes up, i.e., "they that come after him." They treated him "too" (*gam*, "also") as the preceding generation had treated his predecessor: they take no delight in him. He also ultimately succumbs to the fickleness of their favor, and the cycle is again complete.

The third part of the verse echoes the now stereotyped conclusion which is proved to be applicable also to high position: "All is vanity."

Grammatical Notes

v. 14. The second clause is concessive in character, "even though" (*KS* 394f).

The form *hasurim* is contracted from *ha'asurim* and therefore means not "rebels" but "prisoners' (cf. *KW* under *hasurim*).

v. 15. The expression "arise under or after" has a parallel in II Sam. 10:1.

CHAPTER V

The connection of thought with what precedes seems to be this: having demonstrated quite fully that all things are vain, the Preacher feels the desirability of warning his readers lest, being set in the midst of so much vanity, *they themselves* become vain. He warns them to watch that area of life where such vanity is most likely to gain entrance, namely, the area of worship.

D. **An Inserted Exhortation** (5:1-9, according to the English)

1. **Warning against formalism.** (5:1-7)

(1) **Watch your step when you go to the house of God; and to draw near to hear is better than that fools should bring sacrifice; for they are ignorant, and so they do wrong. (2) Be not rash with your mouth, and let not your heart be hasty to utter a word before God; for God is in the heavens, and you are upon the earth; therefore let your words be few. (3) For dreams come as a result of a great amount of business, and the voice of a fool as a result of a great amount of words. (4) When you make a vow unto God, do not defer to keep it, for He has no pleasure in fools. What you vow, keep! (5) It is better not to make a vow than, having made it, not to keep it. (6) Do not allow your mouth to make your flesh guilty; and do not say before the messenger that it was an error. Why should God be angry at your voice and destroy the work of your hands? (7) For where there is a great amount of dreams, there are also many vanities and many words; but do you fear God!**

For the first time the Preacher resorts to admonition, and it is direct and extended. There was need of comforting the poor and oppressed people of those days. There was just as much need of warning those who had substituted the sin of formalism for the sin of disobedience. The first flush of enthusiastic faith that was born out of the experience of the Return from the Exile soon died down, and the people began, at least in one respect, to mend their ways. They no longer openly despised the Word of God. That despising had brought upon them all their grievous calamities. Their outward attitude in obeying the laws and the ordinances of the Lord was, for the most part, irreproachable. Yet the inward obedience was not running parallel to the outward observance. Neh. 13:10-20 shows that tithes in support of the sanctuary as well as observance of the Sabbath were grievously neglected. Mal. 1:8 indicates that sacrifices were offered, but that blemished victims were deemed sufficient. Outward obedience, coupled with inner disobedience and reluctance, were the order of the day. To persons who were thus minded the Preacher addresses this very apt warning.

The *Keri* (marginal reading) of v. 1 unnecessarily substitutes the singular "foot" for "feet." The plural is used in Ps. 119:101. This may not be the English idiom. The difference may be eliminated in the translation.

The custom of going regularly to God's house was apparently being strictly observed, so regularly, in fact, that in the case of this generation it had become a mechanical performance of religious duties. What would normally be regarded as a commendable practice is here described as being a course of conduct that is fraught with dangers as long as men drew near in their present harmful attitude of formalism. For such persons the road to God's house is like unto a rocky road that might bring men to fall. Therefore the caution, "Watch your step." The "house of God" here referred to is unquestionably the Temple at Jerusalem, to which men were going regularly; cf. the use of this term in Ezra 1:4; Dan. 1:2; I Chron. 9:11. The synagogues had not as yet been developed, nor were they designated "houses of God."

The construction of the second half of the verse is not difficult: "And to draw near to hear is better than that fools should bring sacrifices; for they are ignorant, and so they do wrong." Where God's Word is to be heard as was, no doubt, the case in the Temple in the days after the Exile, there man is to hear it. Such hearing is the primary duty. That it involves obeying goes without saying, so that we need not make "hear" mean "obey" as it does in I Sam. 15:22, etc. Drawing near to hear implies to be "ready to hear" (A.V.) and would, therefore, be devoid of formalism.

Such drawing near to hear is in every way far better than what deserves to be described as fools bringing sacrifice. The individual who has dropped to the level of formalism in religious practices has sunk to the level of "stupid fellows" (*kesilim*) of whom it is further said that they "are ignorant" (*'enam yod-he'im*, here used absolutely). The result of such conduct is *la 'asoth ra'*, "and so they do wrong." This clause does not express purpose. The infinitive *karobh* is simply the subject of the clause (*KS* 223a). The *min comparative* is used, and so it becomes unnecessary to use the adjective *tobh* ("is good") which is implied in the context, see *K.S.* 308c. The most general word for sacrifices (*zebhach*) is used as if to indicate that, as long as a sacrifice was brought, it was at that time of little moment to him that brought it, whether it was the most appropriate or not.

It must finally be remarked that the concluding clause of cause depicts the unfortunate state of the poor formalists in worship. They have dropped to a level of stupidity that prevents their seeing or understanding that what they deem to be the doing of good is in reality the doing of evil. Surely, there could hardly be a sadder delusion: the works done are the very opposite of what they are thought to be. To find here the thought that "the old opinion that it is essentially dangerous to have any dealings with God, shows its influence here" (*Hertzberg*) is not a statement that is worthy of its author.

The warning against formalism now turns to the subject of *prayer*. A degenerate age is content with offering words by way of prayer and will usually make many of them because prayer has become an empty ceremony. Feeling the emptiness of what they offer, men will attempt to make up the deficiency in quality by increased quantity. Therefore the warning, as before to guard the foot, now to take heed lest the sin be that of the mouth. We have the unusual construction, "Be not rash *upon* thy mouth," *'al*, "upon," indicates the base upon which the rashness is reared, namely, the mouth. Delitzsch compared the German idiom, *"auf der Floete blasen."*

Futhermore, as if to check the rapid chatter of worthless prayer, the warning continues: "Be not in haste to take a word before Jehovah." To make the form of the warning as strong as possible, the Preacher bids men to be careful about the bringing of even a single word (*dabhar*) before Jehovah. The situation as such, if viewed rightly, is sufficient to dictate caution, for it is this: "God is in the heavens, and thou art upon the earth." This very fact points to God's divine and supreme station in contrast with which we are mere earthworms. Our lowly condition over against the divine majesty should inspire us with due caution, for what miserable and lowly creatures we are!

And, surely, our humble position should check any presumptuous approach to the Almighty that we might make. The least that we could do in view of our position would be to let "our words be few." Garrulous chatter is a mark of disrespect to him to whom it is addressed. The thought expressed by this verse appears also in Christ's warning against using "vain repetitions" (Matt. 6:7) as well as in the Lord's Prayer, "Our Father, *who art in heaven.*" Unusual is the word, "few," here plural — apparently a late usage which occurs only a few times.

The "dreams" are referred to only by way of comparison. By this we mean that there is no thought that the dreams are one of the things that mark the fool. The first half of the verse implies an unexpressed comparison with the second: "as dreams result from a multitude of travail, so a multitude of words, etc." This type of comparison is common enough in the Book of Proverbs. No matter who it is that speaks, if he speaks much, he shall presently make a fool of himself just as surely as persons who fret over a multitude of things fall into dreams at night. Linked with the preceding verse, this means: A man can make a fool of himself even over his prayers if they are unwisely offered. — The article before "dream" is the generic article (*G.K.* 1261), and we therefore translated "dreams."

Another form of externalism receives a rebuke — the vain making of *vows.* Deut. 23:21-23 is the basis for the passage, being cited almost word for word. The connection is not difficult to establish. Vows are no vital part of the Old Testament religion. The laws respecting them do not *command* that vows be made; they are merely a regulation of such vows as a man may feel inclined to make. Such relatively unnecessary elements of religion have apparently been moved to the forefront in a decadent age. However, they are being dealt with in an almost frivolous spirit by Koheleth's contemporaries; they are rashly made and just as rashly broken. The old prescription of Deuteronomy has to be renewed in this respect; not to make a vow is far preferable to a making that is followed by rash breaking. — The first word of v. 4 (*ka'asher*) is really a bit stronger than "when"; it equals "just as," thus at the very outset stressing the thought that this is a department of life where fulfillment must be exactly as it is stipulated. Parallel in thought are Acts 5:4 and Ps. 50:14.

Carrying the thought of the abuse of vows farther, Koheleth condemns that rash mode of trying to dispose of a rash vow by the mechanical presentation of a *sacrifice* to cover the seeming deficiency. The warning first again touches upon the rash uttering of a vow: Do not give thy mouth (cf., the German *hergeben*, (*G.B.* 1g, *titten*) to render thy flesh (here "body") guilty. This meaning of *lachati*, viz., "to cause to be guilty," must be maintained here rather than A.R.V., "to cause thy flesh to sin," because the Old Testament point of view never conceives the "flesh" as the agent of sin. The only alternative is "to bring thy flesh into punishment" (BDB), which stresses the necessary outcome rather than the state into which a person places himself by such rashness.

The "messenger" (*mal'akh*) spoken of is the priest, to whom the guilty person appeals for atonement. That this interpretation is correct appears from Mal. 2:7, 8, where the priest is distinctly so called. The term also applies to prophets, cf., Hag. 1:13 and Mal. 3:1; but the case before us requires a priest. To translate the term "angel" and let it stand for "God" is rather far-fetched. What the man who has made the rash vow wants of the priest is to procure him to offer for him a "trespass" or "error offering." Cheerfully he approaches the priest: "It was a *sheghaghah*, 'an error,' that I made this vow; offer the requisite offering for me." So simply does he expect to dispose of sin. Those who trifle thus with vows are reminded that such levity rouses God's just anger and induces Him to destroy "the work of the hands" of such a person. This last statement implies rendering unsuccessful whatever a man attempts. God's blessing cannot attend such a one who so flippantly seeks to dispose of religious obligations. — On questions that use *why?* for a wish, see KS 354e. Luther catches the spirit of the last statement by rendering: *Gott moechte erzuernen ueber deine Stimme,* etc. "God might be angry at your voice," etc.

By a comparison, like unto the one used above in v. 3 (2), Koheleth suggests that, where dreams are, there will vanities be found (v. 7). In other words, the thought is not that the worshiper has engaged in vanities and has, therefore, been dreaming overmuch. Rather only this: *As* where men are busied in vanities they cannot avoid idle dreams, *so much the more* where there are many words there must also be vanities aplenty, also in all matters of worship. For, surely, dreams are vain and empty things, so there will be vanities where many words are used. By this general precept of weighing well one's words Koheleth suggests that restraint might also be practiced in the matter of making rash vows. The best corrective of all is that fundamental principle of setting oneself into the right relation to God, this deep spiritual principle which is the basic note of the book and its chief counsel: "fear thou God (*'elôhîm*). This implies that man, the earth-born creature, learn to observe due reverence over against God. — The final *kî* before "fear thou God" means "but rather," *aber vielmehr,* (*Zoeckler*).

The warning against formalism includes all forms of religious observances, especially those that are performed at the sanctuary. After the general observation that all formalistic worship is a "fool's sacrifice" Koheleth dwells on two areas of worship where formalism is most liable to show itself, prayer and vows, and supplements the discussion by an indication of the

cheap spirit of bargaining in religious duties into
which formalists are apt to fall.

3.   Comfort in the face of oppression   (5:8, 9)

**(8) If you notice instances of the oppression of
the poor and exploitation of justice and righteousness
in the province do not be unduly amazed over the
matter. For one official watches over the other, and
still higher ones watch over these.   (9) It is an advantage for a country on the whole that there is a
king over the cultivated field.**

The admonition just addressed to his externalistic
coreligionists being disposed of and properly concluded,
Koheleth proceeds to comfort, for there is much need
of kindly words when men find themselves in a difficult
situation. Oppression seems to be the almost universal
lot of his people. In so far as such oppression is unjust
and undeserved, the comfort of v. 8f. applies.

"Oppression of the poor" was a common enough
sight; for the poor man, being without means, is the
most helpless of all. The "exploitation (*gezel* really
means 'robbery') of justice and righteousness" is a
necessary sequel to the oppression of the poor or is a
parallel evil that will be found wherever there are
men who prey upon the poor. "Justice" covers "just
decisions" by judges. "Righteousness" is a personal
quality of fairness. Both are lost in evil days, and such
irregularities were a common sight "in the province,"
far from the center of authority as Palestine was in
those days. *Medhinah* is a late word that first appears
in reference to the provinces of Ahab that had princes
over them and is then used in reference to Babylonian
provinces; it is used repeatedly in Ecclesiastes.

One attitude to assume in the case of such irregularities is not "to marvel at the matter" (*chephets* is
used in the general sense of the Latin *res*). For in
reality it was a common evil that honeycombed the

entire fabric of government throughout the various grades of officialdom. Over him that was high there was another that was higher, who was also on the watch as to how he might gain advantage over his inferiors (*shomer,* "watching" in an evil sense as in I Sam. 19:11 and elsewhere, see BDB p. 1036 1c). Surely, at such a time men are not to think it strange concerning the fiery trial that does beset them (I Pet. 4: 12). *Gebhohim* cannot here be a plural of majesty, akin to 12:1; for though, as to form, this is admissible, yet if God is thought of here, the reason advanced why a man should not marvel does not fit the matter it is supposed to explain. But surely there is a congruence if men are bidden not to marvel because the spectacle is so common, yea, well-nigh universal, contaminating all ranks of officials in a satrapial form of government.

Still there is a true "advantage" or "profit" in every way in the land. Such profit, however, does not lie in corrupt and oppressive measures that are resorted to by officials high and low but is to be found only in the King, that is, the Lord God Almighty who has all such matters entirely under His control. Wherever the "cultivated land" is, that is, where men are engaged in gainful occupation working the field, the best "advantage" of all is that there is one supreme King over it all. This statement, considered in the light of the closing verse of the last section (7), suggests that those who suffer from oppression should consider all their advantage and profit to be this, that there is a true and supreme Ruler over all puny and corrupt officials in a realm that is marked by much corruption on the part of men in authority.

We cannot view with favor those translations that find here the praises of a king who devotes himself to agriculture, being "a king who is served by the field." Such purely utilitarian suggestions are not of the nature of this book. Furthermore, *ne'ebhadh* (nifal) is always referred to tilled soil and therefore modifies "field" and not "king." Besides, such an interpretation would have offered no comfort to those who were suffering from oppression. They would be treated merely to a sound economic reflection: better than to have a land build its fortunes on oppressive practices is the building of the fortunes of a land on a sound agricultural basis of patriarchal simplicity. True enough, but the book of Ecclesiastes is not a textbook on political economy nor a treatise on statecraft. This same criticism applies to *Barton's* translation: "But an advantage to a country on the whole is a king (i.e.) an agricultural land." *Galling* removes the difficulty by a radical revision of the text, a procedure which always allows for a broad scope of clever notions. He translates: "A king is at hand for the prince and for the serf."

To give *ne'ebhadh* the meaning "appointed" is untenable because there are no Hebrew parallels but only some Aramaic parallels. *KS* 286d has apparently invented his grammatical explanation without consulting the usage of language when he translates: *dem Felde dienstbar.*

E. The Third Group of Things by Which Vanity Is Demonstrated   (5:10-6:12)

1. The vanity of riches (5:10-20)

a. As being unable to satisfy   (5:10-12)

The vanity of riches is one of the subjects that requires manifold and complete treatment, first, because there are so many sides to riches, and, second, because the number of those who are entangled by the allurements of riches is very great. The danger of loving them was especially great in Malachi's time, when men had so little of them as was indicated above.

(10) He that loves money will never be satisfied with money, and whosoever loves wealth will have

no gain from it. This, too, is vanity. (11) When goods increase, they that eat them increase in numbers. What profit have the owners thereof except the gazing upon them with their eyes? (12) Sweet is the sleep of the laborer whether he eats much or little; but the satiety of the rich man will not permit him to sleep.

We have first the general proposition that satisfaction cannot come from riches. He that turns to the gathering of them is, however, rightly described as a "lover" (*'ohebh,* participle) of them, for they do beguile the heart into caring for them. Besides, not the general term "riches" is used but the word "money" (Heb., "silver") inasmuch as in those poverty-stricken days gold was very likely in evidence very little — another feature that fails to agree with the era of Solomon.

The parallel expressions that are used describe the case quite realistically. "Abundance" really means "murmur," "roar," "crowd," for there is plenty of noisy tumult in crowded marts where men seek to acquire silver. For "silver" the parallel expression "increase" is substituted (*tebhu'ah*), the regular word for the increase of the fields, apparently derived from the root "to come," therefore, that which comes from the field. For in seeking to acquire wealth in an agrarian population men must deal largely with the products of the field. If acquired riches in any form cannot satisfy, then the usual conclusion fits here most aptly: "This, too, is vanity." — *Mi* practically equals the indefinite pronoun "whoever."

A few shrewd observations (v. 11) now establish the point that is being made. The first is, "as goods increase" the establishment of the owner (*be'aleha,* singular, though plural in form, *KS* 263k) assumes larger proportions unless a man is of the type described in 4:7ff. And so the number of those that consume things grows, and just as little usually remains as remained previously before the establishment grew. What, however, does remain, according to the next shrewd observation, affords a peculiar kind of "success" to its owner. *Kishron* meant "skillful or successful work" in 4:4; "profit" is a very apt rendering here. By a quiet irony the Preacher boils down the efficiency or success of such acquisition to this: A man has the privilege of gazing upon a little more than some are privileged to gaze upon — a rare achievement. Such sterile success is, however, accompanied by certain more or less painful losses. One of these is suggested in v. 12.

Inability to enjoy normal sleep is always a painful loss to a man. Because of the satiety acquired without the laboring man's bodily exercise to balance his heavy diet, the rich man finds his rich and undigested meal keeping him awake. Incidentally, even if the poor man's meal may not have been quite sufficient, physical weariness has made his body ready to sleep. As for the rich man, his very abundance of means imposes a disadvantage upon him. — *'Obhedh* is "laboring man," not *'ebhedh,* "slave," as the *Septuagint* has rendered it.

b. **As being a harm to man**   (v. 13-17)

(13) **There is a grievous evil which I have seen under the sun—riches kept by their owner to his own hurt. (14) Those riches may perish in some unfortunate enterprise, and if he becomes the father of a son, there is nothing in his hand. (15) Just as he came forth from his mother's womb, naked shall he go again just as he came, and he shall take nothing for his toil that he may carry in his hand. (16) Besides, this is a grievous evil that in every respect just as he comes, so he also goes, and what profit is there for him in that he toils for the wind? (17) Also all his days he eats his food in darkness and is sore vexed and has sickness and anger.**

A climax is reached in this verse: first riches are shown to be unable to satisfy (10f.) ; then they rob a man of his sleep (12) ; finally the keeping of them is said to be an *evil* in itself. Surely a climax or, from another point of view, an anticlimax. The man who strives for riches considers them "good"; they are now seen to be "evil." This applies, of course, to those who stay "under the sun" in their endeavors and their aspirations. The following verses exemplify what the author meant about riches' turning out to a man's hurt.

Some "unfortunate enterprise" (v. 14) A.R.V. or "bad business" (*BDB*) brings about the collapse and utter loss of his fortune. The author does not imply that this happens regularly. It is merely one of those things that may come to pass. The loss is so complete that his son, who follows him, never gets a cent of the paternal fortune. It is better for such a man not to have had a fortune, for the loss of it brings with it much distress and disappointment that would never have been experienced had he not grown rich. The text does not make it plain whether it is the father or the son who has "nothing in his hand." In fact it is true of both.

Just the sober but very true reflection is offered in v. 15 that riches can never be a permanent possession. This may well come under the "evil" of v. 13. A man acquires riches merely in order to give them to others. For we come naked and go naked. Paul uses this thought in I Tim. 6:7. So there follows the conclusion expressed in v. 16, concerning which it is to be noted only that, in view of the case as it stands, riches are called "wind."

The conclusion of the story of the man who suffered grievous financial reverses is given in v. 17. The gloom of his sad experience spreads over him because he has hung his heart on riches. When he sits down to eat, his painful loss is felt most by contrast when he considers to what excellent repasts he was once privileged to sit down. So the case is stated thus: "He eateth in darkness." The thought of the many things involved in his reverses — how others perhaps cheated him, how still others profited by his downfall, the dissatisfaction with his fate — produces vexation, sickness, wrath as his usual mental state. To make "in darkness" an allusion to the dark workroom of the person in question and so to conclude that he is a fanatic about work puts too much into the words "in darkness." — The suffix on *cholyo*, which would give it the meaning *"his* sickness," seems best explained by the assumption that the *waw* was written twice by a mistake of the copyist — dittography — and so it should be dropped and the unmodified word *choli*, "sickness," read in its stead (*KS* 23).

This is one of the nine verses in the Hebrew Bible that does not have the accent *athnach* to mark the middle of it.

c. Brief exhortation to enjoy the gifts God permits (18-20)

(18) **Lo, what I have seen to be good is that it is a very fine thing for one to eat and to drink and to enjoy life in all his labor wherein he labors under the sun during the course of his life which God gives him, for that is his portion. (19) Every man also to whom God gives riches and possessions and enables him to eat of it and take his portion and be happy in his toil—this is the gift of God. (20) For he does not much remember the days of his life, for God allows him to keep occupied with the joy of his heart.**

Though this seems to be the oft-repeated counsel of the wise Preacher, it drives home a vital point and adds to it such excellent supplements to round out this sage advice that we do well to observe these new elements. First, he dwells on the fact that the course that he suggests is not only "good," i.e., morally unobjectionable in itself, but also "a very fine thing," to follow, of course. *Koenig* (*KS*) has the best rendering of these words: *"Was ich als probat erfahren habe war, dass es trefflich sei zu essen, etc.";* our translation seeks to imitate this. A part of the counsel suggests that a man eat and drink. The spirit of such eating and drinking is indicated by the next phrase, "to enjoy life in all his labor"; for one side of that labor is that it is toilsome, cf., "wherein he laboreth under the sun." The other side of it is that it has pleasant features here and there.

He is bidden not only to enjoy these but to "look" upon these, which suggests a definite turning of the eyes to that which can be enjoyed. That, of course, means "to enjoy life." So the eating is to be carried on in the spirit of determined rejoicing over the good which is certainly at hand. The under-the-sun aspect of it all is one that continues only a limited number of days, for "all the number of the days of his life" is again a reference to the short space of life — a common use of the word "number" (*mispar*). The words, "for this is his portion," have a very useful directive: that is the "portion" God has allotted to him, nothing else. If he receives it, let him be glad.

Verse 19.   The thought of this verse is not that wealth is the gift of God, but rather that the gift of God is that He giveth to a man "to eat of it and take his portion and rejoice in his toil." Man is by nature not free to enjoy in such a harmless fashion whatever of earthly goods he may happen to have. The squandering spendthrift, of course, does not come under consideration at all. But the usual experience of men who have accumulated wealth is that *they* stand under the power of their *wealth,* not *wealth* under *their* power. Therefore freedom from such domination and the judicious enjoyment of such things as are their own are possible only as a gift of God. This commendable, carefree state of such a one whom God has indeed set free from the love of money is described more at length in the last verse of the chapter (v. 20).

True, these verses (18-20) that we are here regarding as an exhortation are as to form merely an observation. Yet it is an observation upon which Koheleth apparently expects men to act. For this oft-repeated observation (2:24; 3:12, 13, 22; 8:15) in 9:7 finally has the imperative form. Nor would an observation that could be translated into deeds be repeated so frequently if it were not anticipated that it would be acted upon.

Such a man's days are pictured (v. 20) as passing away so quietly and undisturbedly that he does not especially remember them. True, there are no remarkable experiences of good. How can there be in the depressed days of the Persian domination? But it is just as true that there are no days that are marked by particular evils. Days that run along in a quiet, even tenor are the days that are least remembered as the years go on though in some particulars they are the best of life. The reason for their running along smoothly is that God hears or answers his prayers which voice the desire of his heart, as the more familiar translation has it; and such desire or "joy of his heart" is that he may have a quiet and peaceable life in all godliness and honesty.

Another approach is to regard the verb (*ma'aneh*) as being derived from a different root, which *KW* lists as *'anah II*, and to which he assigns the meaning *sich abmuehen lassen mit*, which may be translated: "God keeps him occupied with the joy of his heart." *Gesenius-Buhl* similarly lists an *'anah III*. All of which is, in the last analysis, a return to Luther's translation, which simplified a bit by rendering: "For he does not give much thought to the days of his life because God makes his heart glad." Our rendering means that if, according to v. 19, a man would cultivate a cheerful use of the gifts God gives, God would let the resultant joy drive out the anxious thoughts that might otherwise fill the heart, and so life would pass swiftly, and the passing days would scarcely be remembered. The net result of the two interpretations is about the same.

The days of evil are, by God's grace, rendered so quiet as to be forgotten. To have as one's goal that amid the various evils of this life one's days pass thus, is entirely wise and good.

So ends the counsel of this chapter.

CHAPTER VI

2. The vanity of possessing goods that cannot be enjoyed (6:1-6)

Still more needs to be said to Israel to help the covenant people to get their bearings on the question: "What is wealth worth?" and so to curb envious thoughts that might spring up in their hearts in their present impoverished state.

(1) There is an evil which I have seen under the sun, and it is common among men: (2) A person to whom God gives riches and wealth and honor, and there is not wanting to his soul anything that he desires, yet God does not make it possible for him to enjoy it; for a strange person enjoys it. This is vanity and a grievous misery. (3) If a man has a hundred children and lives many years, so that the days of his life are really many, but his soul is not satisfied with good, and he does not get buried, my verdict is that a premature birth is better off than he. (4) For it comes to no purpose and goes on again in darkness, and its name is shrouded in darkness; (5) besides it does not see the sun nor get to know anything, yet it has rest rather than such a one. (6) And if he lives a thousand years twice over but doth not get to enjoy things—do not all go to one place?

To introduce a discussion on the value of riches with the statement, "There is an evil," ought to help men to get their bearings. The case here described manifestly constituted an "evil" even as do many other cases. In fact, this is an evil which is "common among men," not one of the incidental ills of mankind. *Rabbah* really means "great," i.e., practically "common" (A.R.V.) or *gemein bei den Menschen* (*Luther*). That which is "common among men" may be described as "heavy" as is done in 2:21; 8:6. — The qualifying phrase "under the sun" has again been inserted, for only a man who puts his confidence in earthly possessions can have the experience here described.

There follows the statement of the case for which v. 1 has prepared. This statement is very paradoxical, well calculated to remove any misapprehension men may have in regard to riches, "a man to whom God gives." Even that statement of the case indicates that in no instance is the acquisition of wealth merely an outright achievement of man. Man can acquire nothing unless God permits him to have it. The man under consideration has a great variety of things that are esteemed good. "Riches and wealth" cover this in the broadest sense. Besides, he enjoys a good name, having "honor" before men as one of his notable acquisitions (cf. the same order of words in II Chron. 1:11ff.). An ideal case is selected to make the contrast all the more striking. "There is not wanting to his soul anything that he desires." The present participle *chaser* pictures him as living along in this state and condition, which he, because of the enormity of his resources, naturally deems unalterable, a state of lacking nothing that he has sought to acquire.

We ask: "Is any particular instance under consideration?" *Delitzsch* points to the case of Artaxerxes III, Ochus, whose fate was like that of the man described. *Hengstenberg* refers to "the Persian," meaning, no doubt, the rich man among the Persians generally speaking. It seems best to consider the reference as applying to any rich man of the time who might have had such an experience, although the spirit of inspiration apparently cast the statement into such a form as to make it particularly apropos with reference to the Persians, many of whom will have met the fate here described. If the allusion seems somewhat veiled, 10:20

describes why it was necessary that all such statements made with reference to persons of influence or to authorities had to be guarded. Chapter 11:2, 3 gives a few more statements of a kindred kind. This apparent reference to the Persians is all the more timely inasmuch as at the time of writing the only rich with whom Israel came into contact were the Persians.

Wherein does the particular evil consist which this man's lot exemplifies? Answer: "God does not make it possible for him to enjoy it." A rich man is being thought of who never gets beyond the painful process of acquisition. He stays in the thraldom of his avaricious bent. Actual enjoyment, which is the gift of God, is never his in connection with his wealth. Of course, the expression found in the original, "eat thereof," means, "to enjoy it," as Isa. 3:10 and Jer. 15:16 show. A calamity intervenes. Even if it had not intervened, this man could not have risen to the point of enjoyment. The calamity itself and all the grievous misfortunes that befall him are enumerated to make the case all the more drastic as an illustration. That calamity consists, in the first place, in this, "a strange person eats it." *Nokhri* applies regularly to those of another nation, "aliens." This was most decidedly true in reference to the Persians. When their downfall came, those of another nation, foreigners, were the ones who enjoyed the Persian wealth. There is a singular irony in having not even those of your own relationship, no, not even those of your own race, receive that for which you toiled. There is actual pain in such an experience. Mark well that the author does not imply that this happens regularly to rich people. But it certainly is one of the things that *may* happen. There is more to this calamity as v. 3 now indicates.

Situations like those spoken of in Ps. 79:3 are thought of, when the nations devastate God's people — a common experience in the Preacher's time. Though

the man in question may have had the good fortune
to beget numerous offspring, a thing which was always
esteemed a very great blessing in days of old (Judg.
8:30; II Chron. 11:21; II Kings 10:1ff) yea, though
his days may have been very many — and long life
has always been counted a rare good fortune — yet if
his soul derives no satisfaction from the good that he
has acquired, his wealth, his offspring, and the length
of his days; and if, besides, he faces the double calamity
of having another, "an alien," devour his wealth, and
he himself after his overthrow has not even a "grave,"
or "does not get buried" — what a sad lot! For the
thought is that after the fortunes of war the enemies
have overthrown his people and cared so little for their
honorable dead as not even to provide burial for them.
Who now, in viewing the dead bodies of those who were
once wealthy and are now rotting under the skies and
in thinking of the joyless life and the miserable death
accompanied by much suffering, would not join in the
conclusion here given: "An untimely birth is better
than he"? This appears to be a reference to Job 3:16
(cf., Ps. 58:8) even as in 5:15 there was a reference to
Job 1:21. Also Isa. 14:19f, and Job 21:32f. may be
compared to show that to remain unburied was regarded
as very unfortunate.

It matters little whether one at this point thinks of
a typical Persian man of wealth or of one of the rich
Israelites of that time or of any time.

It would be a misunderstanding of the situation
if the statement made in this verse were unduly
generalized as is done by some commentators. It should
be especially remembered that these verses have in mind
a case "under the sun," in which a man disregards all
higher values and seeks his treasure exclusively in
earthly things, cannot even enjoy these, and finally
has not even a grave for burial. *Delitzsch* cannot reconcile himself to such conclusions and, as the case is more

fully unfolded in vv. 4 and 5, says: "It is true that this contains a thought to which it is not easy to reconcile oneself." Again, "The saying of the author cannot bear the test of exact thinking from any point of view." Again, "The author misunderstands the fact that the earthly life has its chief end beyond itself; and his false eudaemonism, failing to penetrate to the inner fountain of true happiness, which is independent of the outward lot, makes exaggerated and ungrateful demands on the earthly life." It is not Koheleth who has misunderstood the facts; it is Delitzsch who has misunderstood Koheleth, for Koheleth distinctly indicated, on the one hand, that he was giving the story of a man who disregarded the higher values (cf., v. 1, "under the sun") and has shown on the other hand, where true values lie. See 5:7, "Fear thou God." Where human life remains persistently separated from God, too low an estimate of its value can hardly be given. Since the events recorded in Gen. 3 human life as such is a miserable thing.

Galling makes the issue revolve about the very incidental point that *nephesh,* "soul," is used several times (see vv. 2, 3, 7, 9). This word, which we have translated "soul" in vv. 2 and 3, "appetite" in v. 7, and "desire" in v. 9, refers, as lexicons rightly say, "to all functions through which life is maintained or strengthened, or to experiences through which it is affected" (*Buhl*). It may, then, mean "appetite" and the like. By using a highly specialized meaning of the Assyrian equivalent for *nephesh,* i.e., *napishtu,* which means "throat," *Galling* arrives at the unique interpretation that this is the meaning of *nephesh* in this section — a point that might be well taken if he were dealing with an Assyrian text — and then concludes that the subject matter of the chapter is the case of a man who is suffering from a severe throat malady and therefore cannot eat. This leads *Galling* to reject

v. 6 as being a corrupt reading because it does not refer
to this throat ailment (!). His interpretation is a case
of determining the meaning of Hebrew words by non-
Hebrew standards and not by Hebrew usage as such.
It often also involves textual alterations, which show
an interpreter's ingenuity but are not always exegesis.

The last statement of the author concerning the
untimely birth requires some elucidation. Therefore
he adds vv. 4 and 5. The neuter pronoun "it" is to be
preferred to the masculine "he" (A.V.). *Luther* also
has "sie," referring to *unzeitige Geburt*. For undesir-
able as such a lot may be, coming "to no purpose"
("vanity") ; going on again "in darkness"; never acquiring a name; never seeing the sun; never knowing
anything — yet all the disquiet and the vexation of a
life of pursuit after unsatisfactory riches are spared
such a being. It has what the unfortunate rich man did
not have — "rest." By a proper estimate, with the
restrictions that Koheleth imposes, upon each of the two,
it will be seen that the conclusion drawn is not an
exaggeration. Why *Barton* should suggest that this
estimate of "rest approaches the Buddhistic appreciation of Nirvana" is hard to discern. Any reasonable
man might put the same evaluation on rest.

If, however, the unhappy rich man had had one
other advantage, one that is very highly esteemed,
namely, long life, might there not then be some reason
for altering the verdict: "an untimely birth better
than he"? The preacher reckons with that fact in an
effort to make the statement of the case as exhaustive
as possible.

Verse 6. Long life is considered a blessing (see
Exod. 20:12; Ps. 49:11). Granting to the man in question that it had been his good fortune to enjoy double
the span of patriarchal length of life, yet continue the
one outstanding disadvantage above named, namely,
that "he does not get to enjoy good things," the situation

is still the same as our author contended above. This time the stronger phrase "see no good" is used to indicate how very far removed from good he really is. It does not even come within his reach, let alone afford him any enjoyment. But the conclusion is this time not stated as, perhaps; "An untimely birth is better than he," but: "Do not all go to one place?" This must be interpreted so as to fit the context. The sameness of the lot of all people cannot be the outstanding thought. Apparently, the nature of that place in reference to his not having seen any good is primarily under consideration. Only in so far is the thought of the sameness of the place for all under consideration as, namely, that all have the same experience there, that whatever they may have failed to achieve during the span of their earthly existence cannot be retrieved in that one place. That one feature of that place is commonly conceded: it is not a place for making up lost opportunities.

One feature of the preceding instance (v. 1-6) must be borne in mind. It takes as an example, not what is the general rule, but a hypothetical case for illustration's sake. *Hertzberg* does not do well to call this type of reasoning "casuistry."

3. Why a man cannot be satisfied with riches (6:7-9)

The author feels that this matter of man's being unable to be satisfied with riches requires looking into. As he throws a stronger light upon it by means of his explanation he at the same time establishes his point a bit more firmly.

Everything to the end of the chapter is still dealing with the matter of riches and their vanity.

The beginning of the deeper search into the matter is the seventh verse, which finds a peculiar trait in man, a native flaw, which makes such a thing as true satisfaction by such means simply impossible.

(7) **All of a man's toil is for his mouth, and yet
his appetite is not appeased.** (8) **For what advantage has the wise man over the fool, or what
advantage has the poor man that knows how to walk
over against the living?** (9) **Better is the sight of
the eyes than the straying about of the desire. This
also is vanity and striving for wind.**

We learn what a peculiar kind of soul man has.
Nephesh ("soul") may be translated "appetite," but
there is no getting away from the fact that it is the
soul which has the appetite. It would seem that the
translation "soul" might after all, in spite of *Delitzsch's*
strictures upon *Zoeckler's* interpretation, be used to
very good advantage. That does not, however, imply
that "mouth" represents lower desires, and "soul" is
"the organ of the higher, spiritual aspirations." The
"soul" is the center of corporeal activities such as
desire for food, see KW *sub voce*. So, in the last analysis,
"appetite" covers the case.

A strange situation is depicted. Natural man's toil
is primarily for his mouth so that, though secondary
objects may come to the forefront and seem to crowd
out this primary effort, in mankind at large this effort
is so very preponderant that the statement must go
unchallenged. The article before *'adham* is, therefore,
generic, and the word refers to "mankind." In spite of
man's pouring the sum of his acquirements into this
one narrow orifice, the mouth, the soul that sits behind
it all with its insatiable appetite stubbornly refuses to
cry, "Enough!" A morbid insatiability has possessed
it. Something is radically wrong where such a state
of affairs prevails. Clearly, the soul has departed from
its true functioning and is pitiably damaged. It now
becomes clear why no amount of wealth acquired by
man can satisfy him. The way is paved for trying better
sources of satisfaction, sources that will first heal the
soul's sad derangement.

It is now shown (v. 8) that even some of the covenant people show marked traces of the same disorder, for they are charged with the same insatiable desires and failure to find satisfaction. In the Scriptures the wise man (*chakham*) is uniformly one of the people of God whereas the "fool" (*kesil*) must here be sought among the surrounding heathen nations. The "poor man" is, likewise, one of the people of Israel, who suffers in manifold ways, also in having a smaller measure of earthly goods. That such a one is meant becomes clear beyond controversy if we consider the words: "Who knoweth how to walk over against the living." The only people who really knew how to walk over against all those living upon the face of the earth were the Israelites to whom God had given statutes and ordinances. These showed them how to walk according to a rule that was well-pleasing unto God and, therefore, entirely acceptable to man as certain passages also state. Cf. Deut. 4:5, 6: "I have taught you statutes and ordinances. . . . Do them; for this is your wisdom and your understanding in the sight of the peoples that shall hear all these statutes and say, Surely, this great nation is a wise and understanding people." Cf. also Ps. 147:19, 20, especially v. 20: "He hath not dealt so with any nation, and as for His ordinances, they have not known them." If any of the "wise" inclined their heart toward deceitful riches in spite of this superior knowledge, which extended also to the problem under consideration, they could have no profit from such living. For the fact that some were wavering by letting their soul go out in pursuit of untried wealth is apparent from v. 9.

There would be no need of rebuking men for the "straying about (literally, 'the going about,' *halokh*) of the desire," if they had not been guilty of this. The wandering is the lustful straying about from one thing to another in quest of true satisfaction. This is possible to the children of Israel only when they fail to regard what they have. That is here designated as "the sight of the eyes" (*mar'eh 'enayim*). In all cases except this one and another in Eccles. (cf. *BDB*) *mar'eh* refers objectively to that which the eyes see. Since that meaning is quite appropriate here, it may be regarded as established. That which their eyes see is the good that God has given them as a nation. This they should have regarded rather than to let their eyes rove about, as they were now doing, in quest of something that is satisfactory. The present course of some, eagerly desiring wealth as they were, was certainly "vanity and striving for wind."

So the deep-seated ailment of mankind has been uncovered: the ravenous appetite of a sick soul, which infects all men and also infected many in Israel at this time.

4. Why it is useless for a man to strive for riches (v. 10-12)

Bringing this phase of the discussion to a close, the Preacher points out that in the very nature of the case man should desist from the vain quest after riches inasmuch as he cannot acquire any unless God wills that he should do so.

(10) **Whatever one may be, his name was given him long ago, and it is known that he is man, neither is he able to contend with Him that is stronger than he. (11) If things are increased, vanity is increased by them. What profit has a man? (12) For who knows what is good for a man in life for the number of the days of his vain life which he spends as a shadow? For who can tell a man what will be after him under the sun?**

It is very difficult to translate the first part of v. 10. Our translation has the merit of being understandable and, we believe, correct. The root of the matter is laid bare as the Preacher goes back to the

beginnings of the human race. What type of being man
actually is, Koheleth claims, is fully revealed for present purposes by the name that was given him long ago,
that is, the name "man" (*ha'adham*) which, as Gen.
2:7 indicates, is his because of his being taken from
the earth (*ha'adhamah*), a fact which the English
might approximate by saying: "His name is earthling
because he was taken from the earth." The point the
author wishes to make is this: can any such frail being,
having such an humble origin, ever dare to attempt to
strive with God or contend with Him? For God is the
one that is meant when "the One that is stronger than
he" is referred to. Does God not have the supreme control of all things in hand? (3:1ff); or does He not
ordain times and seasons? Also, who shall be brought
high or low? Man's attempting to achieve riches, if
God has not willed to give them to him, is a striving
of the "earthling" with the Almighty (cf. Isa. 45:9).
That is not only futile, it is the sin of "revolt." Man's
name (*shemo*) which has been given him long ago
shows him his proper place.

If the verse is translated as we have rendered it
above, the whole verse presents a consistent and a
unified thought. *Hayah* would naturally first suggest a
masculine; then, if that is impossible, a neuter (A.V.).
The one doubtful word can be read *shehithqiph* (hifil)
or *shettaqiph* (a noun). The net result is the same.

Verse 11. In the case of such a being as we have
just described (v. 10) there can be but one outcome
if "things" increase (the only meaning for *debharim*
permissible here is "things"). That is, "they will be
increasing (*marbim*) vanity." They have no intrinsic
worth in themselves. Being "vanity" in themselves as
belonging to the things under the sun, the acquisition
of them is an accumulation of "vanity." The logic is
inescapable; and man's inability to be satisfied by them
is definitely illustrated: "What profit has a man?"

One telling argument is yet to be added in v. 12.

By beginning with the close of this verse we shall most readily see how it fits into its connection. No man is able to discern what is coming after the situation in which he now finds himself. What the next turn of the road will bring is completely hidden from him. Why, then, make extensive preparations along one line — like amassing riches — if a man has absolutely no knowledge as to whether that will happen to be the thing that he should really have acquired? Here are cases that may develop: he may later require patience, but he laid up a stock of gold; he may require strength of character, but all he has is a strong fortune; his particular situation may call for Christian hope, but his hope is built on uncertain riches. Such a situation is a downright calamity. To nothing more proper than to calamity may the acquisition of wealth be likened. These days of man are insubstantial enough as it is: he spends their slight number as a shadow. ("number" = fewness, cf., 2:3). There is no retrieving lost days. To follow such unsubstantial pursuits as acquiring wealth makes them still more unsubstantial, "as a shadow" — a figure that is employed also in I Chron. 29:15; Job 8:9; Ps. 102:11; 144:4.

It should be noted that *'acharaw* must mean "after him," not in the sense of "after the termination of this life" but in the unusual sense of "after the present situation in which he finds himself." It refers to future events that may occur *before* his death. Otherwise the causal clause of this verse, "for who will tell, etc.," fails to agree with the first half of the verse.—*'asah* has the unusual meaning of "to spend" or "to pass," which will not seem so strange if it is remembered that a parallel use of the verb "make" can be found in German, viz., *abmachen* (*Hertz.*) Note also that *'asher* explains the *ki* palindromically (*Ks.* 389a).

CHAPTER VII

III. **Counsel for Days of Suffering** (7:1-12:7)

  A. **The Value of Suffering** (7:1-10)

1. **Its value by way of comparison** (v. 1-4)

In their depressed situation after the Return from the Captivity the children of Israel were not yet prepared to meet their lot and to be victorious after every shock to which they were exposed. The futility of riches has just been dealt with. Suffering in various forms was still upon them. The suffering itself constituted a serious problem. Instruction as to how to meet it without suffering a damage to faith was a necessity. That instruction begins at this point. What if they are in a gloom of mourning and sorrow! It is here demonstrated that such a situation has greater advantages than have days of laughter and joy.

As to the spirit of the passage *Hertzberg* makes a very good remark when he says: "This very *carpe diem* ('enjoy each day') in the sense in which Koheleth means it grows out of a right apprehension of the *memento mori* ('remember that you must die')."

Some interpreters have been influenced at this point by a purely formal matter, namely, the fact that a certain outward similarity of initial statements appears in the first eleven verses of the chapter. For in vv. 1, 2, 3, 5, 8, 11 there are found clauses that begin with the word "good" (*tobh*), which is usually translated "better" because of the obvious Hebrew comparative that is involved. However, this repetition is largely accidental, and when it is closely examined it bears little weight. To give to the section (v. 1-12) the heading "Better Things" is to be overimpressed by an almost accidental external circumstance.

(1) A good name is better than precious ointment, and the day of death is better than the day of one's birth. (2) It is better to go to the house of mourning than to go to the house of feasting inasmuch as that is the end of every man, and the living take it to heart. (3) Sorrow is better than laughter, for by sadness of countenance the heart is improved. (4) The heart of the wise is in the house of mourning, but the heart of the fools is in the house of mirth.

Though "good" (*tobh*), as noted above, stands first in the Hebrew, it is not intended to have any special emphasis, for it is the predicate, and the predicate normally stands first in a Hebrew sentence. Besides, though the word for "name" is without the adjective "good," yet since "name" commonly means "reputation," and only a *good* reputation is obviously thought of, the translation "a good name" is quite in order, cf., Zeph. 3:19 and Prov. 22:1 for a similar usage.

A kind of paronomasia is to be found here: *shem* vs. *shemen*. This has been rendered aptly in German: *Besser ein gut Geruecht als Gerueche*. *Williams* renders it rather cleverly: "Better is a name than nard and the deathday than the birthday." However, this half of the verse has no particular emphasis. It is employed only as a type of comparison such as is found in 5:3. Two groups of things, one of which is better than the other, are simply set side by side. So this becomes the meaning: *"As* a reputation is better than precious ointment, *so* the day of death is better than the day of birth." Ointment refers to the liquid perfumed oil that is used in the East on joyful occasion, see 9:8; Amos 6:6; Ps. 45:7; Cant. 1:3 (*Williams*).

The author's statement seems to be quite extreme. It would seem to imply that life as such is so doubtful a value as to be classed as being inferior to death, and, therefore, "the day of death" is preferable "to the day of being born." However, the Preacher's attitude seems to be this: In particular situations death is preferable to life for some persons if their life has been crowded full of an unusual measure of evil. As far as earthly values are concerned, death confers a benefit on such persons by releasing them from misery. However, that is but one side of the matter, and if men of Koheleth's day would have been inclined to advance this one-sided claim, the author would grant it without further argument. This makes those with whom he deals more susceptible to further instruction. He, however, proceeds at once to limit the statement to its proper scope in the following verses and goes on to show men a more desirable viewpoint to hold. That he cannot grant the truth of this statement absolutely appears from 9:4, "For to him that is joined with all the living there is hope, for a living dog is better than a dead lion." Verses 2 and 3 must, therefore, be closely joined with the preceding (v. 1). Perhaps a more satisfactory approach would be to say simply: "The first verse must be kept in close connection with what follows. The day of death is better than the day of birth insofar as good lessons are to be learned by those who go to the house of mourning with their hearts open for instruction."

We, therefore, do not agree with *Delitzsch* who remarks in reference to this statement: "A saying such as 1b is not in the spirit of the Old Testament revelation of religion." Behind such a pronouncement there lies a misapprehension of the purpose of the whole book and a conception of this passage which argues that this section offers a number of disconnected words of practical counsel. So *Volck* judges that these are *Lebensweisheitsregeln*. *Delitzsch*, too, sees no more than the word "good" as the bond that these scattered sentiments have in common and so affixes the heading: "Proverbs of better things, things supposed to be better, good things, good and bad days." Commentators who judge thus have failed to fit the words here written into the situation of the children of Israel and still put them into the mouth of a half-philosophic skeptic, who, Faust-like, broods over issues that, by the way, never arose in Israel's life. Neither can we say that Koheleth "here gives way to the feeling of despondency that sometimes overtakes him" (*Williams*).

The proper limitation of the general statement whose validity the Preacher granted in v. 1, viz., that "the day of death is better than the day of one's birth" must now be made (v. 2).

In this one particular respect there is an advantage in death: it brings about sober and salutary reflections on the part of "the living." Death, the common "end of all men," produces a readiness to consider sober realities as nothing else can. To go into the house of mourning after death has removed one of its inmates, therefore, has advantages in teaching a man certain necessary lessons as nothing else can do, even if one has gone only to comfort the bereaved. For the visitor in such an instance is the man who is referred to as going into the house of mourning.

The profit of such an experience can never be gained by "going into the house of feasting," for revelry never actually betters a man. In the Hebrew "feasting" is "drinking." But that is not an unseemly thought, for the drinking that marked the feast usually stayed well within the bounds of sobriety. Add to all this the thought that Israel was in these days "in the house of mourning," in fact, had been compelled to go there, and one sees why this comparison is employed. So it appears from this illustration that "the day of death is better than the day of birth" whereas, perhaps, only feasts mark the occasion.

Koheleth delves deeper into the matter. The verse that follows (3) is again intimately bound up with the preceding.

The thought of what men do after having gone to the house of mourning is not abandoned, it carries over into v. 4. The "anger" or "vexation" is the result of the sobering experience referred to in v. 2. The force of *ka'as*, as *Hengstenberg* contends, cannot be restricted to "vexation," though that is, of course, its primary meaning. It is but a short step from "vexation" over sin to "sorrow" over sin, and "sorrow" fits very well into the context. The vexation caused by such an occasion is the personal displeasure at one's own sins, the thought of which involuntarily arises on such an occasion. This thought occurs also in II Cor. 6:10, "as sorrowful, yet always rejoicing," and in II Cor. 7:10, "For godly sorrow worketh repentance unto salvation, a repentance which no man regretteth."

It cannot be denied that such sorrow is far more profitable than is "laughter." This sorrow is the murmuring over our own sins, which the Scriptures recommend so highly (Lam. 3:39, Luther's translation). "The sadness of countenance" (*roa'* is infinitive) that accompanies such an experience is by no means evil. It yields, in fact, a definite profit, which reaches down into the heart, and that profit is that "the heart is improved." If the day of death can produce such salutary effects it is certainly to be preferred to the day of birth.

We do not understand why *Barton* should remark on this verse that "the thought, however, is foreign to Koheleth, who never seems to grasp a moral purpose in suffering." Must every thought expressed by an author be supported by some other statement of his in a given book before it attains to any validity?

Ginsburg interprets as he translates when he renders
the first part of the verse: "Better is thoughtful sadness than wanton mirth." This interpretation is much
to the point.

The expression "the heart is improved" has definite
moral implications. It must be admitted, however, that
it is used elsewhere with a nonmoral connotation (cf.,
Judg. 18:20; 19:6, 9; I Kings 21:7; Ruth 3:7; Eccles.
11:9). Though this difference of usage may well indicate that the language of Koheleth is late, it by no
means follows that the verse or expression must be a
gloss as *Barton* claims. Such a conclusion is an obvious
non sequitur.

Verse 4. The resorting to the one or the other of
the two houses mentioned is a characteristic trait, on
the one hand of the wise men if it is the "house of
mourning," on the other hand of "the fools" if it is
the "house of mirth." A bit more lies in the thought:
since the *heart* is said to be in the one or the other, the
idea implied is that, prompted by their inmost character and nature, men resort to the one or the other.
They do what is entirely in harmony with their nature
when they resort to the place they prefer. In other
words, the wisdom of the wise expresses itself in their
vexation and grief over sin as occasioned by a sober
consideration of death; on the other hand, folly stamps
itself as folly and runs true to form when fools resort
exclusively to houses where there is mirth.

What excellent light this passage throws on the
problem as to how Koheleth means his exhortations to
enjoy the good of this life appears in a statement made
by *Vaihinger*: "It appears from this passage how,
when the Preacher exhorts to enjoy life, he never takes
this as implying boisterous amusements and blind in-
dulgence, but rather a worthy and grateful enjoyment
of such good and beautiful things as God provides.
Such type of enjoyment, however, is not only possible

if there be a sober cast of mind, but only to be attained where such an attitude prevails." *Galling* gives a good summary explanation: "It is better to look death squarely in the eye than to dull the thought of death in drinking bouts."

So the claim that the day of death is better than the day of birth has been upheld from the point of view set forth above, and from this point of view no man would dare question the propriety of the statement. Vv. 1-4 must be treated as an unbroken unit. To take v. 1 alone leads to a misconception. — V. 4 has the accent *zakeph katon* rather than the customary *athnach*.

2. The value of the rebuke of the wise in times of suffering (v. 5-7)

Having by way of contrast or comparison demonstrated the value of suffering, which for the present appears as grief, the author goes on to show how we are to meet suffering if it is really to prove valuable to us. It is to be met by hearkening to the rebuke of the wise. In this instance the Preacher again employs a contrast, dwelling primarily on the wrong way of meeting it inasmuch as this way was by far the most common.

(5) It is better for a man to hear the rebuke of a wise man than to hear the song of fools. (6) For like the sound of the nettle under the kettle, so is the laughter of the fool. This, too, is vanity. (7) For oppression makes the wise man foolish, and a bribe destroys the understanding.

When times of suffering come, God aims to correct men by the use of them. What His correction is, what it implies, is best shown by men who are at home in divine truth. Such men are the "wise." Among those of this class God's prophets were outstanding. Such a one was Malachi, who specifically entitled his book "The Burden." Reproof such as he administered through it was the thing that the Israelites were to give heed to when, for example, they were "in the house of mourning" — for this thought has not yet been abandoned. When the heart is sobered by death, and the grief over sin has set in, you have a ready soil for the proper sowing of the seed of the Word.

Another possible course at such times would be to try to have the heart avoid such earnest thoughts by "listening to a song of fools" that scatters a man's thoughts and fills the mind with silly and trifling ideas. "Drinking songs are not elevating" — *Williams*. Such sources of comfort are, to say the least, quite shallow and unsatisfactory. Such a manner of meeting days of suffering is certainly wrong and a grievous mistake.

Barton very properly remarks that *'ish* is introduced before *shomea'* because the two hearings are supposed to be acts of different individuals.

The shallow nature of what the fool's mind produces is now set forth in order to establish the claim just made. By means of a striking pun (v. 6) the author makes his point quite emphatic. Several remarkable points of similarity are prominent in the comparison. Strictly speaking, the term used does not signify "nettles" but "thorns." The Hebrew has: *sirim* under *sir.* Charcoal is the regular fuel in the Orient (cf., Ps. 18:8; 120:4; Isa. 47:14; John 18:18). Thorns are sometimes used for fuel under kettles, especially since fuel is often scarce.

The first feature that attracts attention in regard to such a fire is the sharp, crackling sound heard as the thorns blaze. So irregular and noisy is the fool's laughter. Besides, the thorns are soon consumed and furnish but little heat. So this shallow laughter is soon spent and fails to produce the substantial warmth of true humor. To go to men who produce such shallow matter in an effort to obtain comfort from their jollity

in days of suffering is really a very foolish course
of procedure.

An explanation, by way of one example, is now
offered to show how the fool came to be so inconse-
quential a fellow. "The reason is here assigned why the
happiness of the fool is so short," says *Hengstenberg.*
That does not agree with the statements made in v. 7,
which treat, not of the brevity of his joy, but of how
he became foolish. *Delitzsch* makes a difficulty of what
certainly lies pretty near the surface. He states that
no one has yet succeeded in showing how v. 7, beginning
with *ki,* "for," shows the cause of what v. 6 claims.
However, if v. 6 speaks of fools and v. 7 of their becoming foolish, the connection must be an attempt to
show how they became the shallow fools they are. One
instance only is given, nor is it claimed that the reason
assigned covers all cases. In the case of loud-mouthed
Persians, who were blatant fools, this explanation is
most apropos. We cannot agree with *Delitzsch* who
assumes that a verse has dropped out between v. 6
and v. 7. Such conjecture allows a great deal of license
in interpretation. *Barton* shows to what extremes such
positions lead when he makes v. 5, 6, 7, 8 glosses, and
then 11 and 12 likewise.

Equally untenable is *Hertzberg's* solution. Acting
on the assumption that there is no connection between
v. 6 and v. 7, he rearranges the verses as follows: 6,
11, 12, 7. That produces a new thought sequence. But,
we ask, how did vv. 11 and 12 slip so far from their
anchorage? Such treatment of a text makes room for
hundreds of possible changes, all perhaps equally
clever, but all also equally uncertain. Such a procedure
cancels the authority of the Word and substitutes for
it the subjective fancies of clever commentators.

Nothing is gained by regarding the words, "this,
too, is vanity," as being introductory to the thoughts
that follow, as also the *Kittel* text does. For it seems

rather unnatural to let the very next statement begin with a "for" (*ki*).

Verse 7. These men then — the Persian magnates of that day may be thought of — may have been in the class of the "wise," but they resorted to "oppression" and, becoming corrupt, allowed themselves to be influenced by "bribes." Wicked conduct always has a definite result in the form of deterioration of a man's moral fibre (cf., Exod. 23:8; Deut. 16:19). To cover the whole situation — they become "fools" (*yeholel* means "to make foolish"). How could anything substantial be expected from such a one? He that has properly weighed all this, though he is one of the afflicted and oppressed Israelites, will hardly look with envious eyes at the gay and apparently successful Persian officials. Such men deserve only pity.

Note: In v. 7b we have a feminine noun with a masculine verb because verbs that stand first in a sentence often begin with the masculine till the subject rectifies the assumption (*GK* 145a). Also, in 7b *'eth* is used before an indeterminate noun to remove ambiguity as to the object.

3. The value of patient endurance of suffering
(v. 8-10)

He that knows what has thus far been set forth is not yet sufficiently armed against suffering. He still needs to cultivate the spirit of patient endurance. What a valuable asset such endurance is we now see unfolded in a telling way.

(8) **The end of a thing is better than its beginning, a patient spirit is better than a proud spirit. (9) Do not soon be vexed in spirit, for vexation abides in the bosom of fools. (10) Do not say, How is it that the former days were better than these? For you have not asked such a question out of wisdom.**

If empty-headed fools seem to be successful men, the issues are not yet at the point where the final outcome is visible. Much may change before that time. To conclude that something or even our course of conduct is a failure, would be quite premature. The latter end of all things is all-important as is the case in all contests, for example. Momentary setbacks are trivial. *Ende gut, alles gut.* "All's well that ends well." If the end of our policy proves successful, that is the thing that counts. Consequently the man that can wait until issues have resolved themselves and come to their logical and only possible conclusion is the man who weathers storms. In other words, "patience of spirit" gives him a share in the final and inevitable victory of the cause with which he, as a member of God's people, is truly identified. "Pride of spirit," though apparently bold and victorious, fails to carry a man through difficulties such as these. Here true steadfastness is the cardinal virtue (cf., Ps. 37:37f.; Lam. 3:24ff).

The course of conduct that such true patience will induce a man to follow is now more explicitly outlined (v. 9). To be "hasty in spirit" is akin to having "vexation." The "spirit" (*ruach*) is in the Hebrew regularly regarded "as that which breathes quickly in animation or agitation — temper or disposition" (*BDB* p. 925, 3). To grow vexed in time of distress is only harmful and foolish in every way. It involves a man in difficulties with others and induces rash thoughts in reference to God's dealings (Jas. 1:19). In short, the bosom where anger dwells is the bosom of the fool.

A further tendency of those who will not have recourse to true patience is to look backward with many a sigh to the bygone times and to wish them back. But such a course of conduct does not savor of wisdom (v. 10). It will be observed that this is a reference, first of all, to a specific situation, namely, when men are grievously disappointed in the present. It is only at such times when men particularly allude to the so-called "good old times." The statement here given covers all times and all circumstances. According to the connection in which this statement occurs, the author clearly upholds the thought that the ultimate conclusion to which God will bring things (v. 8) is far better than any stage of development that may be arrived at previously. To the glorious outcome which God will bring about a man should turn his hopes and expect far better things, otherwise he "asks not out of wisdom in regard to this matter" (*'al zeh*). The spirit of the times is, however, admirably displayed in sayings that are attributed to his contemporaries by Malachi, who says, 2:17: "Ye have wearied Jehovah with your words. Yet ye say, Wherein have we wearied Him? In that ye say, Every one that doeth evil is good in the sight of Jehovah, and He delighteth in them; or where is the God of justice?" (cf., also Mal. 3:14, 15). These words give evidence of a lack of "patient spirit" (v. 8), of being "hasty to be angry" (v. 9), and "of not enquiring wisely" (v. 10).

B. The Value of Wisdom at Such Times (7:11-29)

1. Wisdom, a fine regulative in days of suffering (11-14)

From this point to the end of the chapter wisdom is under consideration in relation to the times and the needs of Israel. Israel must not conceive its lot as being only one of patient suffering. It would be a pity, indeed, if nothing more were found among God's people. There are among the Israelites certain resources that should not be forgotten, rich treasures, in fact, that the people still have, because of which they dare rightfully claim that they are rich. One of these treasures is wisdom. It is in itself a great advantage by showing men how to regulate their thinking and their conduct. To think of it from this point of view was suggested in v. 10, "thou dost not ask in regard to this matter in accordance with wisdom."

Some interpreters may question the propriety of our caption in that it introduces the term "suffering." They claim: the word "suffering" appears nowhere in this section. But, pray, are men not living in days of suffering when situations are met with such as are here referred to? In v. 2 of this chapter there was "mourning." In v. 10 men are comparing the present with the past and deeming the latter better. The emphasis in v. 14 suggests that "the days of adversity" are actually present. Verse 9 points to a situation that causes men to grow angry. According to v. 13 certain things are so definitely askew as to warrant the statement that God "hath made them crooked." Surely, the thought lies near that these are not purely academic discussions but a treatment of living issues that reflected the times. Besides, since so many things in the book of Koheleth point to the days of Nehemiah and Malachi, we must remember that these were days of suffering for Israel.

But what was the use to which wisdom was to be put? The section vv. 11-14 gives the answer.

(11) **Wisdom is as good as an inheritance, yea, an advantage over it for them who see the sun. (12) For as money protects a man, so does wisdom; and the advantage of knowledge is that wisdom gives life to him that has it. (13) Consider the work of God, for who is able to make straight what He has made crooked? (14) On a good day be of good cheer, and on an evil day consider: God has made the one side by side with the other in order that man may not find out anything that shall be after him.**

The thought is not as A.V. states it, "Wisdom is good with an inheritance." For, though the original could, indeed, be translated thus, yet in this book Israel appears as a nation that has been despoiled of its possessions; therefore, it cannot lie within the purpose of the author to show how the possession of wisdom enhances the possession of an inheritance. Besides, the rest of the discussion deals with "wisdom" as the only possession that is left to Israel. And again, wisdom is good without an inheritance. Therefore the *'im*, "with," before the word "inheritance" must be taken as the *'im* which coordinates; cf., 2:16 (*BDB*, If, p. 768). *A.R.V.* is correct.

In likening wisdom to an "inheritance" the Preacher establishes the fact that an inheritance is a permanent possession of a man, which, especially in Israel, was received from parents and passed on to children. The permanence of such a possession is emphasized. This treasure abides with a man through all manner of vicissitudes.

But a stronger statement of the case must be made. As a wise teacher, Koheleth begins by making a milder claim, to which he has reason to believe all who hear him will give assent. Having secured approval of one statement, he proceeds a step farther by making the next statement the one that finally conveys the claim that he is most intent upon advancing, viz., "Wisdom is more excellent than an inheritance for those who dwell under the sun," that is to say, for all who live upon the earth. On this claim the Preacher builds up further claims one by one until he has presented a rather complete development of his topic. He has thus for the time considered the work of consolation by pointing to rich treasures that certainly should be tapped in days such as these, for they ease the load of evil tremendously. The next aspect of the thought follows (v. 12).

As in the preceding verse a comparison was drawn between wisdom and possessions, so in v. 12 we have another comparison although the verse reads literally: "For in the shadow of wisdom, in the shadow of silver."

Perhaps, as the majority of the versions suggest, we should read correlatively *ketsēl . . . ketsēl* as in Gen. 18:5 and Hos. 4:9, rather than *betsēl . . . betsēl*. Still the Masoretic text is not difficult, and it makes good sense as it reads. However, the rendering above seems to be most natural because of the similar comparison found in 5:11. The translation, "wisdom is a defence even as money is a defence," is very much along the same line (A.R.V.), save that "shadow" (*tsēl*) does not imply so much "defence" as "protection" generally (cf., Ps. 91:1). The thought is derived from the fact that shade is at times a necessity for actual defence against the danger of the hot rays of the Oriental sun. So "shade" becomes a strong synonymn for "protection." The reason for our preference of "protection" is that "defence" may include an active part taken by such means whereas the part played by wisdom is here according to the comparison entirely passive. This is, however, only because of the thought developed: wisdom is a shield against the hot rays of adversity.

Wisdom can do more than that: it also "gives life to him that has it." For though the statement itself is a bit longer, "knowledge" in the first part of it is only a synonymn for "wisdom," emphasizing that one side of wisdom. For wisdom has many sides; the knowledge (*da'ath*), however, that is stressed here is a very vital element in it. Its benefit is said to be that it "gives life." Such potent knowledge actually dwells in wisdom: it gives a higher life which cannot be smothered or submerged by the floods of suffering that may surge over a man. What a valuable possession that must be which also supplies "life" in the highest sense of the term, life that adversity cannot extinguish! Surely, wisdom is a precious possession!

We justify the translation, "it giveth life," rather than "it preserveth the life," because, though the Piel of *chayah* has both meanings, we feel that the parallels

that supply the first thought lie nearer. *Chayah* in the
Piel applies to divine activity in passages such as I
Sam. 2:6; Hos. 6:2; Ps. 119:25, where it has the
meaning "to make alive." However, it is also true that
the achievements of wisdom are parallel to divine
activity in passages such as Prov. 8. Therefore these
parallels are the more appropriate here. Besides, in
the progressive series which the author builds up,
"giving life" is a better climax than "preserving life."
This rendering has the support of the LXX, ζωοποιήσει,
the Vulgate, and Luther, *"Weisheit gibt das Leben."*

After speaking about the value of wisdom the
author makes an appeal to use it in the situation immediately under consideration without, however, specifically saying that this is what he is doing. His
summons to "consider the work of God" is the
equivalent of saying, "Now put the knowledge which
wisdom grants you to use and consider the work
of God."

There is something about the manner of God's
working that only wisdom can discern, and that is
that what He seems to have thrown out of alignment,
or what He has allowed to be "crooked," tangled, or
sadly disorganized certainly cannot be made straight
by man. The outreach of the passage is limited too
much if the bent back of the old man is thought of
exclusively as the "crooked" thing under consideration
(*Galling*). Many a thing, indeed, appears to man as
though He, the Supreme Governor of all things, "has
made it crooked." A similar thought is voiced in Ps.
146:9: "The way of the wicked He maketh crooked"
(A.V.: "He turneth upside down").

The thought implies no actual criticism; it merely
presents the appearance that situations have in the
nearsighted estimate that man puts upon them. To
attempt to right such things is from one point of view
nothing other than an assumption of divine preroga-

tives, a tampering with God's government. Surely, from one point of view there are many things that we can and must do by way of extricating ourselves and others from the morasses into which our clumsiness plunges us. But the idea that we could actually straighten out what He has made crooked is unpardonable and presumptuous arrogance. Wisdom shows the right point of view.

Wisdom, in fact, teaches not only the correct negative attitude but also the correct positive standpoint (v. 14). Since it does not lie within our power to change existing conditions, that fact should not lead to a dull resignation or apathy; for men should also remember that a most competent Ruler administers the affairs of the world. *His* work should be considered (v. 13). That will lead to an attitude of good cheer in good as well as in evil days. This trust in God's providence alone is sufficient to outweigh all the evil of the evil day. Our rendering of the verse disregards the accents and thus makes far easier reading. We regard *re'eh* ("see") as equivalent to *hinneh* ("behold') and as introducing the new clause. The same use of *re'eh* is found also in 1: 10; 7:27, 29.

Both good and evil days serve the higher purposes of God which lie beyond the immediate enjoyment and vexation of men. Therefore God is said to be the One that makes one kind of day as well as the other. Since, however, man will never be able to discern the good that comes from evil days, the situation will be one that continually reminds him of his inability to see what will come next upon the earth. Here, as in 6:12, *'acharaw* does not refer to things that come to pass after a man's death. *Zoeckler* shows how our idiom takes an opposite viewpoint, for *'acharaw* = that which lies *before* a man, or, as *Barton* puts it, this "refers to what will be in this world."

This effect on man is designed by God for the very purpose that man may recognize how little he can do, and how cheerfully he ought to trust God. Such an attitude is the attitude of true wisdom as it helps a man to get his bearings in days of suffering, especially when everything seems to have been thrown into a hopeless tangle. *'Al-dibhrath shelo'* is an obvious Aramaism and a late usage.

2. Wisdom, the golden mean (v. 15-18)

This section, to which *Delitzsch* gives the title: "Injuriousness of Excesses," and *Barton* less aptly: "Another Arraignment of Life," stands between subdivisions that show how wisdom proves itself a valued possession in days of suffering. Since it does rightly inculcate the principle of the golden mean, it must, therefore, present this attitude as the outgrowth of wisdom. Therefore our title above.

(15) **All manner of things have I seen in the course of my vain days: there is a righteous man perishing in spite of his righteousness, and there is a wicked man prolonging his days in spite of his wickedness. (16) Be not overly righteous and be not excessively wise. Why should you destroy yourself? (17) Be not overly wicked, and don't be a stupid fool. Why should you die before your time? (18) It is a good thing for you to take hold of the one and not to withdraw your hand from the other. For he who fears God will come forth from every such case.**

The opening *'eth-hakkol* should not be translated "all this," for such a rendering fails to fit into what follows. The common meaning "all kinds of" (cf. *KW sub voce* 2, a) should be used here. In fact, it seems quite proper to consider the use of *kol* as being very loose and meaning nothing more than "both" as the following words suggest (*Galling*). This is then in the following at once limited to two concrete cases, which must be regarded as matters of common observation ("I have seen").

The days the Preacher has lived hitherto he terms "the days of my vanity" because since the fall of man all existence is subject to the law of vanity. This suggests that "short life" could be substituted for "vain days." In entire conformity with verses 13 and 14 cases are cited which show that God works in a manner that often proves very puzzling to men. Nothing can so disturb a man's sense of right and wrong as does the injustice of seeing a man perish "in spite of his righteousness" and in seeming contradiction to Exod. 20:12; Deut. 4:40; Ps. 91:16. We have translated *be* "in spite of" because we regard it as the "*be* of concomitant conditions," *BDB* III, c.

Equally disturbing is the opposite experience of seeing "a wicked man live long in spite of his wickedness" in seeming contradiction to Ps. 55:23; 58:3-9; 73:18. This was one of the forms of suffering to which Israel was exposed. For as a general thing the "righteous man" would be the Israelite whereas the apparently successful "wicked man" would be sought among those that ruled Israel.

A peculiar type of righteousness was beginning to manifest itself in Israel, an overstrained righteousness which lost sight of the ever-present sinful imperfections of men and felt strongly inclined to argue with God and to find fault with Him because He was apparently not rewarding those righteous men as they deemed they deserved to be rewarded. A generous dose of work-righteousness was, therefore, mingled with this attitude. Of these persons Malachi complains in 2:17; 3:13-15 of his book. This righteousness was, therefore, imperfect and unsatisfactory though the term "righteous" is still used in connection with it even as in the New Testament, Luke 5:32, we read:

"I am not come to call the *righteous* to repentance."
Only as we bear this thought in mind do we see the
close connection between vv. 15 and 16.

The tendency of recent writers (e.g., *Galling*) to
find in this verse a strong reaction against the traditional "catechism faith" of the orthodox is quite
one-sided. Yet Koheleth does imply that to try to cover
all situations by convenient formulations of divine
truth fails to account for all the issues that may arise.

Verse 16. An overstrained righteousness which
grows out of conceit and stands ready to challenge God
for His failure to reward is plainly under consideration. For both the righteousness and the wisdom that
are here spoken of are of a kind that can "destroy"
a man. The author refers to a righteousness that is
beginning to go to seed, a righteousness that will
flourish in its most distorted form in the days of Jesus,
in regard to which Jesus will be moved to say: "Except your righteousness shall exceed the righteousness
of the scribes and Pharisees, etc." (Matt. 5:20). In
the light of the New Testament facts it may, then, be
regarded as a straining out of many little externals,
which make of it a stricter type of righteousness than
God had commanded.

Coupled with it was that overstrained quest after
wisdom which led the Pharisees to love to be called
"Rabbi, Rabbi" (Matt. 23:7). The golden mean then
suggests a striving after true righteousness and true
wisdom as God has defined them and not encumbering
these two virtues with human accretions which completely destroy their true nature (*tishshomem* is hith-
polēl with assimilated *t*). This is surely more than
the purely utilitarian advice to "mix freely with both
righteous and wicked." We furthermore believe that
those interpreters have misunderstood this passage
who take it to mean: "A morbid scrupulosity often
leads to mania" (*Williams*), as well as those com-

mentators who have it mean that "Koheleth undoubtedly implies . . . that man may sin to a moderate degree" (*Barton*). *Ginsburg's* suggestion may well be noted; he believes that *tishshomem* could be taken in the milder sense of "thou wilt only make thyself to be forsaken," but no parallel for this meaning can be found in Biblical usage.

The other side of the matter is at once presented lest men veer into the opposite extreme.

Verse 17. Some of the interpretations of this verse have it advocate a rank opportunism and result in doubtful ethics. *Barton* says: "Some commentators, as *Delitzsch,* hesitate to admit that Koheleth really implies that one may sin to a moderate degree. That, however, is what he undoubtedly implies." If the connection with the preceding verse is borne in mind, and it is remembered that the course of conduct here outlined is the outgrowth of true wisdom that is motivated by the fear of God (v. 18), only one explanation will prove satisfactory, namely: all who possess wisdom will recognize that a residue of the old Adam lurks in every regenerate life. This seems to be suggested as a corrective to the overstrained righteousness. Recognizing this sad but inevitable truth, a wise man should, nevertheless, see to it that the ebullitions of the remnant of the old Adam are restrained as much as possible, for simply to swerve into the attitude: since I am not to be overstrict I shall let human nature express itself as freely as it will — this is an attitude that is fully as dangerous as is the other. He who assumes it deserves the title "stupid fool" (*kasal*). He as well as the overrighteous man is the cause of his own destruction. But in the case of such advocates of license the end will come before the "appointed time." God cannot tolerate such impudence. Cf., Prov. 10:27; Ps. 55:24.—"Time (*'eth*) with suffix means the proper or fitting time for a thing, cf. Ps. 1:3; 104:27."

Verse 18. Both situations described in v. 16 and in v. 17 should be carefully heeded, and the counsel given there should be followed. That is the attitude of the God-fearing man, and as a result he shall escape both these dangers. *Yatsa'*, as *Delitzsch* reminds us, is used here in the sense found in the Mishna, "be quit from." So the admonition has come to a conclusion in the spirit of wisdom. Cf., Matt. 23:23, where the Lord apparently cites this verse: "These ought ye to have done, and not have left the other undone."

3.   The self-restraint of wisdom in the face of humiliation   (v. 19-22)

Just as, on the one hand, wisdom teaches a man the proper course of conduct in reference to what might be called "the golden mean," so it also aids him in shaping his course in days of the nation's humiliation. What man needs above all in such days is a generous measure of self-restraint. Wisdom teaches him just that. — When writers call v. 19 an interpolation because "it is impossible to find an intelligent connection for this verse with the preceding context," their chief difficulty is that they have not grasped the thought involved.

(19) Wisdom provides strength for the wise man more than ten rulers that are in a city.   (20) For there is not a man upon earth so righteous as to do good and not to sin.   (21) Furthermore, do not pay attention to all the things that men say lest you hear your servant cursing you.   (22) For your heart knows right well that many times you yourself have cursed others.

Without indicating the specific need that he has in mind, the Preacher shows what a strong ally a man has in wisdom, an ally that stands boldly at his side to help him. The verb "is strong" (*ta'oz*) is not to be translated "strengthened" (A.V.), for that is not its meaning (cf., *Barton*). Wisdom may strengthen a man; but the thought developed here is rather that wisdom is a mighty hero who places himself at a man's side to help him in combat. *KW* translates the verb well *kraeftig eintreten,* i.e., "intervene mightily," therefore the dative very properly follows and is not, as in Aramaic, the use of *le* to express the direct object.

The aid that wisdom furnishes is superior to that which ten "rulers" may give. Rulers who are competent and actually exercise rule are under consideration, for the word *shallet* is translated "having mastery." To make the comparison more forceful, they are thought of as being "in a city." In a larger city, therefore, where the rulers will ordinarily be of the better type because they are selected from a much larger population. This has the force of a kind of superlative. It may be true enough that in those days there was a committee of ten prominent men "who often managed Hellenistic towns." It is also true that the author lived close to the Greek period. But it is highly improbable that he lived in any other than a Palestinian city. To find here a reference to the ten-men-committee is, therefore, not plausible. Even with such allies at his side, a man would not have the aid that wisdom affords for the support of a wise man. — *Lechakham* is a dative of advantage.

Verse 20. This statement is not a general dictum that shows the universal depravity of mankind but is specifically connected with the preceding and demonstrates why we all stand in need of that close alliance with wisdom, whose advantages have just been described. We all fail of attaining to the ideal of truly right conduct, that is to say, of being righteous (*tsaddiq*). Though it is not expressly said, it is assumed as a matter of common experience that such failure on our part to meet the necessary standard is the factor that weakens us most and makes it needful that we form a close alliance with wisdom. The phrase "as to do good and not to sin" is merely an exposition of what the term righteous involves. — Cf. on the verse I Kings 8:46; Job 15:14-16.

The Preacher goes on to show (vv. 21, 22) in regard to the strength that wisdom supplies that it is of particular use in the evil times in which his contemporaries lived. In other words, he cites an instance where wisdom gives a man proper self-control.

It would surely be quite out of proportion to let so weighty an introduction on the subject as to how wisdom proves herself a strong ally to the man who needs her be followed by nothing more than the rather commonplace counsel to employ this tremendous power merely to restrain oneself when one's servant curses. That would be a case where the mountain travails and brings forth a mouse.

The author is not dealing only with a petty domestic issue but is concerned about one of those matters which in the evil days after the Captivity grievously disturbed the whole nation. Israel is regarded as the "master"; the "servant" are the Gentiles. A parallel passage is 10:17. This is a common point of view in the Old Testament. Israel's exalted position over against the Gentiles first finds its expression in Exod. 19:6: "Ye shall be unto Me a kingdom of priests." This word implies that this nation has a regal as well as a priestly character. This regal character expresses itself in relation to the other nations as v. 5 indicates. Again, there is Deut. 15:6, "Thou shalt rule over many nations, but they shall not rule over thee." This is the ideal state which shall obtain if Israel remains true to the Lord. Such rule, however, is conceived of as having its essence primarily in spiritual dominion. There is also Deut. 28:1: "Thy God will set thee on high above all the nations of the earth." Deut. 28:13 conveys the same thought. Isa. 45:14 gives the same idea from another point of view, namely, in the fulfillment, where the voluntary submission clearly points to dominion in spiritual things. "The labor of Egypt and the merchandise of Ethiopia, and the Sabeans, men of stature, shall come over unto thee, and they shall be thine: they shall go after thee: in chains they shall come over; and they shall fall down unto thee, and shall make supplication unto thee, saying: Surely, God is in thee; and there is none else." This is another way of saying, "Salvation is of the Jews." We all acknowledge their rule over us when we, too, cheerfully receive the riches that God had prepared in their midst for all nations. This was Israel's destiny: "to rule over the nations." For Israelites to refuse to believe this would have been a criminal rejection of God's gracious offer.

In saying this it should be self-evident that we associate with all this nothing of carnal pride or self-exaltation on Israel's part, no despising of Gentiles or a haughty feeling of racial superiority. If Israel believed God's Word she had to consider the nations as her servants, potentially and according to God's purpose — a conviction on Israel's part that was not only compatible with humility but was possible only to those who were spiritually-minded enough to be humble.

How were the Israelites to employ the valuable strength that their ally, wisdom, furnished for their use? Answer: By bearing with equanimity all that their oppressors might say in scorn or with the express intent of galling Israel, now that she had lost the position for which she was destined. That is the meaning of the words, "Do not pay attention to all the things that men say lest you hear your servant cursing you." *Mekallel* = "revile" (*Barton*); cf., the rendering of Symmachus λοιδοροῦντες. "Giving the heart to things" means letting them touch you too deeply. That might lead to unnecessary vexation or even to thoughts or acts of revenge or reprisal, which could not do anything other than to make Israel's unfortunate position doubly unfortunate. Wisdom, the strong ally, would help Israel to bear such "words" and to take refuge in the promises of God that can be depended upon.

There is, however, another side to the matter (v. 22). There are some proper thoughts of a disturbing kind that should arise in the heart — and here the Preacher turns to reproof. In the promises of God Israel's remaining in her exalted condition was made contingent upon her fidelity in abiding by His Word. If at this time the outward circumstances were at variance with her exalted destiny, disobedience on her part was the simple explanation. In this case, however, the explanation given does not touch upon all the instances of sin of which Israel was guilty but only upon that particular instance which made the present suffering of Israel appear as nothing other than perfectly just retribution. Instead of regarding herself as God's missionary to the Gentiles, Israel had often forgotten her duty and in vexation at the unfair conduct of these neighbors had often cursed rather than blessed. Now the same experience was brought upon Israel's own head. Wisdom, therefore, which showed both Israel's noble destiny and her sad mistakes, doubly equipped the people for these days of suffering by inculcating a noble self-restraint by these very means.
—Note: *'asher* is used as late Hebrew for the earlier *pen*.

4. The difficulty of attaining unto true wisdom
(vv. 23-29)

Since wisdom has been recommended from so many different angles, the Preacher finds it necessary to speak a word of caution at this point lest men take their quest after this valuable ally too lightly. This caution may be summed up thus: Wisdom is not so readily attained. This caution should spur men on to strenuous and never-ceasing efforts to attain this priceless virtue.

(23) **All this have I put to the test by wisdom. I said: I will be wise, but it was far from me. (24) Whatever is is far off and exceedingly deep; who can find it out? (25) I turned about, and my mind was set to know and to explore and to seek wisdom and the reason of things, and to know that wickedness is folly, and foolishness is madness. (26) And I found more bitter than death itself that kind of woman whose mind is snares and traps, and whose hands are fetters. The man that pleases God will escape from her, but the sinner will be caught by her. (27) Look, this is what I found, says the Preacher, weighing one thing after another to find the net result, (28) which I am still seeking and have not finally determined: one man out of a thousand did I find, but a woman have I not found among all these. (29) Only, behold, this have I found that God made man upright, but they have sought out many devices.**

The topic of the next phase of the discussion on wisdom is first stated. The "all this" refers to the statement about to follow, especially to "it was far from me." However, with deep truth the author indicates that wisdom is to be employed in the quest after wisdom — as he did in 1:13. The verb *nasah* ("to put to the test") implies making a careful trial. So then, having resolved "I will be wise," the Preacher most studiously attempted to acquire wisdom. While he was making this thoroughgoing attempt he began to discern that the perfect achievement of the goal was "far from him." — *'Ethkamah* is the only instance of the cohortative in the book (*Barton*).

The thought is clearly developed. In the test that he made the Preacher sought to find out "whatever is," that is to say, the actual essence of things or what actually is. 3:11 offers a parallel thought: "Man cannot find out the work that God does." As man attempts to delve into any one thing that God has made he has the feeling that the thing keeps on eluding him. It stays in the distance, "far away." Or if he does seem to get it within his grasp and seeks to fathom it he is amazed at the unfathomable depths of it that he will never be able to plumb. — "Exceedingly deep" is really a simple superlative, "deep, deep" — *GK* 133k; *KS* 309m.

All this was only a general statement of just what he did in this quest, so the author goes on to say just what goal he aimed at, and how he conducted his test (v. 25). The beginning of the taking up of the new problem is indicated by the expression "I turned." (See on 2:20; here the verb implies a turn to another aspect of the same case, not to an entirely new subject). The intensity of the search is indicated by the sentence, "My mind was set to know." There was nothing superficial about the attempt. It was not a mere mental process. The heart was in it. Besides, the three infinitives, "know, explore, seek," indicate careful study from every angle of the case.

The whole task was one of proving "wickedness" to be "folly," which really means "being blinded." This gets pretty deep into the essence of things. In the last analysis "wickedness" is "stupidity," for *kesel* means primarily just that kind of folly. Nothing more stupid than sin! Now, by a kind of chain reasoning, having arrived at "stupidity," just what is that? (*Sikhluth* plainly comes from the same root as *sekhel*, being only a longer form). It is that form of folly which is called *holeloth*, which means "being blinded," and so the resultant "madness." Something has beguiled a man into expecting true values from that which has only outward glamor. By getting so far into his investigation the Preacher has really gotten pretty deep down into the roots of the matter. But was this ultimate wisdom? Hardly. Yet it was one of the things that constitute a very important part of the findings of those who go on the quest after wisdom. On the whole verse compare 1:17.

Another basic finding needs to be recorded (v. 26). To regard this statement as referring to loose women fails to do it justice. Such a warning against bad women is out of keeping with the purpose of this section. Besides, it does not require particular researches, conducted by wisdom, to discover the danger of being ensnared by such a woman. Many a fool has been beguiled thus and, remaining as much a fool as he ever was, could yet have subscribed to the statement that such a woman was "more bitter than death."

Nor is it satisfactory to establish a connection in thought by saying: "Koheleth finds that a very serious hindrance on the way to wisdom is to be found in sensual beguilements; they make the heart impervious to wisdom." For that matter, the same could be said in regard to practically every sin, and it is by no means apparent why sensuality should be singled out.

Since at the beginning of the chapter the discussion is still on the subject of wisdom, it cannot seem strange if we claim that here the discussion centers wholly on the same subject. Otherwise we run into the reprehensible interpretation which has the author, without any apparent warrant, yea, without rhyme or reason, skip from one subject to another that is quite unrelated to the preceding.

We maintain, then — with *Hengstenberg* and *Michaelis* — that the strange woman is *heathen philosophy* or any form of human philosophy, even as she is in the book of Proverbs. Since Ecclesiastes freely cites earlier books, we need not be surprised to find this book taking the same view as Proverbs does on this matter. It seems quite obvious that Proverbs cannot have intended anything other than that the warnings against the "strange woman" be construed as referring to heathen philosophy. Chapter 5 of Proverbs contrast two women: one, the legitimate wife; the other, the strange woman. Chapter 7:4 describes *wisdom* as a true sister, and faithful clinging to her is taught to be an effective antidote against the beguilements of the "strange woman." As in this contrast the one feature is unquestionably figurative, so, we argue, it was to be conceived in chapter 5 and in both parts of chapter 7. The case becomes clear beyond a shadow of doubt in chapter 9 of Proverbs, where the two women again appear, both striving to win the heart of the youth, the one being specifically called "wisdom" (v. 1), the other, by virtue of the contrast and in the light of chapters 5 and 7, must be the "strange woman" that is called "folly"; for her modes of enticement are the same as those employed by the "strange woman." To cling too tenaciously to the sense of the letter only in the face of these arguments and in spite of the fact that the book of Proverbs 1:6 indicates that deeper things are meant than meet the eye ("to understand a *proverb* and a *figure,* the words of the wise and their dark sayings"), to cling to the plainest literal sense in the face of all this is unsatisfactory interpretation, and, as *Hengstenberg* remarks, a substituting of Occidental literalism for the plain symbolism of the Orient. Even Prov. 2:16f. introduces us to false wisdom in showing that heathen wisdom originated when the heathen turned from God.

Galling observes very correctly: "If we try to find parallel passages for this verse, it becomes apparent immediately that Koheleth is not at this point describing the nature of woman, but of the 'strange woman' who seduces the wise man." He then cites the passages from Proverbs that we have just alluded to together with Ecclus. 6:2-4; 9:1-9. But he fails to evaluate the parallels cited.

The New Testament treads on the same ground in Jas. 3:15, when it speaks of the wisdom that is "earthly, sensual, devilish," cf., also Col. 2:8.

Nor should it be forgotten that in v. 27 an ideal female personage is speaking (note the feminine of the verb *'amerah*). The noun "Koheleth" is here construed with the feminine verb. This places us into the very situation found in Proverbs 9.

Now to examine this warning. The construction refers to a result that is the outcome of some common experiences in life, for it begins with the present participle, which seems to have special significance (*contra KS* 239g). False wisdom rears her head continually and keeps on offering her enticements, but, on the other hand, the offers keep proving themselves unsatisfactory. As in everyday life a man who has been beguiled by a loose woman may be ready to admit afterward that death cannot be a more bitter experience than to fall prey to the allurements of such a one, so in the search after true wisdom any man who yields to false wisdom will readily grant that its allurements can lead to a taste of suffering that is more bitter than death. Such a temptation is pictured as being very strong when she is said to be a woman who is "snares and traps" such as the hunters use to catch their prey, and when her hands are said to be "fetters." Worldly wisdom, having beguiled a man, clings to him in a singularly tenacious way and binds him.

The Israel of these days needed the warning here given, for men will be inclined to listen to the wisdom of the nation that has enslaved them, if for no other reason than that it belongs to the *Zeitgeist* and happens to be the order of the day. Or it may be that men have the impression that the victor's philosophy must be the successful one. There is, however, no historical indication of Israel's being threatened particularly by the danger of being beguiled by prostitutes in the days of Koheleth.

Falling prey to false wisdom is explained as being due to the providence of God; on the other hand, he that pleases God escapes the wiles of the temptress. Nor is it a virtue for which man can claim credit when he effects this escape: it is the gift of God. On the other hand, the sinner is the one whom God punishes by letting him fall into further sins. The case is stated thus to induce men to shun sin and amid such dangers to seek safety under the sheltering grace of God.

Since wisdom is so difficult of attainment, the Preacher concerns himself with the problem whether there can be such a thing as actual achievement in the case of some few men, perhaps, lest his hearers regard the quest as entirely too difficult. He, therefore, indicates (v. 27f.) that there are a few cases on record where favored individuals have arrived at the goal.

This word can mean but one thing since it occurs in the connection of seeking after wisdom, and that is: One man of a thousand did I discover who actually finds wisdom, but not a woman among all the seekers. The peculiar form of introduction to these findings indicates that thus far a certain result has been arrived at, but that the author is still on the quest to let his investigations be made more and more thoroughly ("which I am still seeking and have not finally determined"). "To find the net result" (*metso' cheshbon*), which A.R.V. renders "to find out the account," means about as much as "to strike a balance." *Buhl* says rather well that it is *Denkergebniss*. We have here an indication of the thoroughness with which Koheleth went to work on his various problems.

The term "thousand" is apparently used loosely for a "great number." To understand the author's conclusions it must be borne in mind that in v. 23 he has classed himself among those that had not found wisdom.

He can hardly be saying anything harsh or cynical if he predicates the same thing of women. He has, however, found that some few men can be said to have arrived at this goal. It appears that he had in mind worthy men of God like Abraham and Joseph and Moses and Samuel and David. We should hardly care to question his conclusion.

A kind of side light is thrown on the problem when we observe that in the Old Testament as well as in the New not one woman was honored by being chosen to write a Biblical book. That is a task for which truly wise men only happen to be chosen. Yet the unwarranted inferences that might be drawn from this fact as to woman's place in the kingdom are offset by the fact that individual women have produced sacred songs which the church has not been reluctant to use (cf., Miriam, Hannah, Mary, Deborah). Nor, for that matter, has it ever been the province of women to produce by constructive wisdom works or systems of thought that are truly creative in the realm of revealed truth. Koheleth, therefore, speaks no slander but utters what our present-day observation still substantiates. This shows the untenableness of the position of all who remark somewhat after the fashion of *Barton*: "This implies that Koheleth was somewhat of a misogynist," and again, "He has apparently had some bitter experience with a member of the opposite sex." The whole statement involved must continually be related to the passage as a whole, which is concerned with the quest after wisdom.

To round out the subject properly, one last aspect of it must be touched upon (v. 29). It is no fault of God's that man does not succeed in attaining unto wisdom. "Only" introduces that kind of a complementary afterthought that is calculated to convey this idea. Koheleth was apparently engaged with the problem of discovering how this all came about. When he had concluded his investigations he was able to say that he had "found" the explanation in this, that man was originally made to be "upright," but failing to abide in this upright state, he has resorted to all manner of "devices" or "speculations," which are evidence of his ability to reason and calculate cleverly, but are departures from uprightness. For "devices" (*chishebhonoth*) are contrivances which clever thinking is able to make up. So the charge of man's failure is to be laid at his own door. — In *ha'adham* the article is obviously generic.

Commentators such as *Siegfried, Barton, McNeill,* etc., find it difficult to fit the author's thought into their outline. The verses that do not yield the sequence of thought they presuppose are labeled "glosses." In this chapter the following verses are so labeled: 5, 6, 7, 8, 9, 12, 29. They speak of a glossator who broke up the coherence of sections of the work. Yet no one apparently took any exception to such procedure at the time. It is difficult to explain why anyone with a literary sense should follow or tolerate such a procedure. That is a literary license that is unheard of.

CHAPTER VIII

C. Problems on Which Wisdom Throws Light
(8:1-10:20)

1. Submission to the heavenly King (8:1-8)

In evil and depressed days, if they continue long, it is essential that there be manifold instruction. So the thought of "How to Meet Suffering" (chapter 7) is still being developed.

One issue that will very likely arise at such times is the problem of discontent with the divine government of things. The wisdom of the King may be questioned. How utterly subversive of all true faith and godliness such an attitude at once becomes need not be demonstrated. To submit cheerfully to His governance, sure that the reins have not slipped from His hands, is a very advantageous position to occupy as is about to be demonstrated.

However, a major exegetical problem is whether the King referred to in v. 2 is actually the heavenly King. That this position is the only satisfactory one appears from the evidence that is to be submitted as we proceed. To brush it aside lightly without refutation as is done by almost all of the later commentators is not a fair treatment of this position. Let only the following facts be considered before we examine the individual verses. In the first place, the whole passage has a more substantial meaning and touches upon more vital problems if it is interpreted in the light of an admonition to submit to God's guidance. Submission to temporal rulers is wise and good, but extended counsel, such as is here given, is prosy in comparison with the richness of godly instruction that the other interpretation offers. "Reflections on Despotism," as *Barton* labels this section, vv. 1-9, does not pitch the passage on a very enlightened level. Besides, the widely divergent interpretations given to verses 6-8, when this latter interpretation is followed by commentators, shows under what difficulties they labor. In addition, it is strange that a refutation of the claim that the heavenly King is under consideration has hardly been offered. That view has been lightly brushed aside by an offhand assertion or two but has not been disproved. Lastly it should be observed that v. 1 indicates that a figurative saying is about to be offered when it is claimed that wisdom knows the "interpretation of a thing." The very nature of the statement leads us to expect one of the "dark sayings" (Prov. 1:6) or the figurative forms of discourse that abound in Wisdom literature. The mode of approach that we challenge fails to put an "interpretation" upon the passage and clings merely to the plainest literal sense. This explanation of ours is also in harmony with 5:9 with its reference to the King.

It should also be noted that every reference made to the King, vv. 1-8, fits the heavenly Monarch, in fact, applies to Him more aptly than it does to an earthly ruler. This fact leads *Williams* to adopt the unique position that in the middle of the discussion, namely at v. 5, the writer suddenly drops the consideration of the earthly ruler and takes in hand the heavenly, for he says: "In v. 2 the writer enjoined keeping the charge of the king. Here his thought is chiefly of a greater King."

It could also be noted that the interpretation we advocate is suggested already by the *Targum*, which paraphrases the first part of v. 3 as follows: "And in the time of the anger of the Lord do not cease to pray before Him, tremble before Him, go and pray and ask for mercy from Him." With the exception of the

Septuagint, the *Targum* represents the most ancient exegetical tradition that we know.

(1) Who is like the wise man, and who knows the interpretation of a thing? A man's wisdom illumines his face, and the hardness of his face is changed. (2) I counsel you to heed the command of the King, and that because of the oath of God. (3) Do not be hasty to be out from His presence, and do not stand firm in an evil cause. For He does whatsoever He desires. (4) Inasmuch as the King's word is all-powerful, and who would dare say to Him, What are you doing? (5) He who keeps the commandment shall experience nothing bad; and the wise man's heart knows time and judgment. (6) For there is a time and judgment for every matter, for the evil of man is great upon him. (7) For he does not know what is to be, for who can make known to him how it shall be? (8) There is nobody who has authority over the spirit to hold back the spirit; neither has anyone authority over the day of death; nor is there discharge in war; neither shall wickedness deliver him that does it.

To begin with, this first verse with its strong emphasis upon the use of wisdom in furnishing the right understanding of things is almost meaningless unless what follows is one of those passages for the right apprehension of which a wisdom that delves beneath the surface is requisite. A recommendation of wisdom and its use such as we have here must be bound up most closely with what follows. It is, according to our interpretation.

The form of the question, "Who is the wise man?" implies that there is none that excels him (cf. BDB f (c) sub *mi*). There is no syncope of the article (*kechakham*) such as is frequently found in later writers, e.g., Ezek. 47:22; II Chron. 10:7; 25:10; 29:27; Neh. 9:19. From what point of view the usefulness of wisdom is here considered appears in the statement that is appended directly: "And who knows the interpretation of a thing?" From the first half of the verse some addition such as, "like the wise man," must be supplied. It would, indeed, be strange to praise with particular emphasis the virtues of wisdom and then continue with a matter that is foreign to this quality of wisdom. It must be borne in mind that the eulogy of wisdom is not the beginning of a dissertation on wisdom but only the introduction to the subject that is about to follow. To seek to put a deeper interpretation upon what follows would be quite in keeping with this introduction. This is the initial argument that leads us to understand "the king" in the sense of the heavenly King.

The second half of the verse continues the thought: "A man's wisdom illumines his face, and the hardness of his face is changed." The shining of a man's face is indicative of joy: joy illumines it. The parallel expression in Ps. 19:8 suggests this. So the insight which wisdom affords a man makes his face to glow with inner joy and satisfaction. The "hardness of face" referred to appears, from passages like Deut. 28:50 and Dan. 8:23, where the adjective from the same root is used, and where the translation is "of fierce countenance," to be a hardness that is caused by sinful passion. Therefore *BDB* renders "impudence," which is akin to the German *Trotz*. Where wisdom shines into a heart with her clear and cheery light, there the harsh effects of sin disappear, and the evidence of the change is apparent externally as well.

A man who has himself experienced what this means is in v. 2 speaking to persons who are also familiar with what he means. Such men will observe the higher import that lies behind his words. Construed thus, the close connection between v. 1 and v. 2 becomes apparent. These two verses cannot be re-

garded as being unconnected. This would be a violation
of even the simplest laws of coherence in composition.

We dismiss, as lying on too low a level and as being
out of harmony with the introductory verse, all thoughts
of an injunction to inculcate obedience to civil authorities. Historically there is no ground for supposing that
Israel leaned toward rebellion. For diminutive Israel
to attempt anything of this sort against Persian
authority would have been foolhardy madness. Why,
then, counsel men so earnestly to abstain from what
they would not dream of doing?

There is sufficient indication that on previous
occasions, without further explanation, *God* had been
designated as the *King*. See Ps. 20:10; 5:3; 10:16. —
After "I" (*'ani*) some verb must be supplied. It is
simplest to supply "counsel."

The Hebrew reads: "Observe the *mouth* of the
King." By a simple synecdoche this means "command,"
as also Gen. 45:21 indicates. The question then arises:
Does the expression, "and that because of the oath of
God," perhaps, after all refer to the oath of allegiance
made in the name of God, to the ruler of a given time?
It could, no doubt, grammatically do so. Several considerations have, however, suggested a higher point of
view even though we could cite instances from the
Scriptures where Israel rendered an oath of fidelity to
the Babylonians, cf., II Chron. 36:13, where Zedekiah
is bound by such an oath. Grammatically there is nothing to prevent construing the term as referring to an
oath that is rendered to *God*. In Gen. 24:8 "my oath"
is the oath that is rendered *to* me. In Josh. 2:17 "thy
oath" is the oath that is rendered *to thee*. In Deut. 29:
12 "the oath of Jehovah" is the oath that is rendered
to Him, so also "the covenant of Jehovah" is the covenant that is made *with* Him. The history of these times
informs us that, according to Neh. 10:29, Israel "entered
into an oath (*shebhu'ah*) to walk in God's law." That

Israel had in an outstanding way covenanted by an oath is beyond a doubt. Such a solemn oath should induce Israel to obey God's commandments. — Instead of the usual construction (*be* followed by the person attesting the oath) the construct relationship is used; as also in Exod. 22:10; II Sam. 21:7; I Kings 2:43; cf., KS 336t. The *waw* before *'al* is the so-called *waw augmentativum;* see *KS* 375d.

What are the substance and the practical value of this bit of counsel for evil and bitter days? This: When God allows His people to suffer, they should on that account in no wise grow remiss in obeying His holy commandments. They stand solemnly pledged by covenants that were made at various solemn and important junctures in their history and by solemn oaths to abide by His will in every situation of life. Refusal to keep His commandments faithfully would be tantamount to saying: "God has not kept His part of the covenant; we shall neglect ours." Such an attitude is defection from Him. The Preacher counsels that, even if God does not at once do what we should prefer to have done, we still cheerfully do all His will. Our oath of allegiance to Him is not to be lightly set aside. Surely, such counsel was more necessary for Israel than were exhortations to obey civil rulers.

That the counsel thus far given implies faithful adherence to God appears from the next verse (3), which further unfolds this thought. This admonition has been applied to the case of a man who finds himself in the presence of an earthly ruler. But an individual from so insignificant a nation as Israel was would scarcely be offered the opportunity to stand in the presence of the Persian king. The book of Esther shows how difficult it was to come into his presence. Other historical facts also reveal the extreme reverence in which the person of Oriental monarchs was held. Even if a man had been permitted to appear before the king, court etiquette so completely regulated every step of his conduct that no man would ever have thought to vent his displeasure at a royal decision by hastily leaving the august presence. Unless one desired to court certain death, departure would be made only upon a sign from the monarch. Some interpreters recognize this difficulty and give the phrase "to go out from his presence," literally, "his face," the meaning to revolt from allegiance to him—a rather unnatural and forced meaning.

These difficulties of interpretation are avoided by thinking of the *heavenly Ruler*. Departure from God's presence is apostasy, cf., Gen. 4:16 in reference to Cain, who "went out from the presence of Jehovah"; cf. also Hos. 11:2. The advice given is in complete harmony with v. 2. It is this: "Do not be hasty to cast off your allegiance when the Omnipotent does not grant you instantaneous relief." Such a purpose is thought of as "an evil cause," and to carry it through would be "to stand in an evil cause." The figure used here is easily understood. Such a foolish course of action is conceived as the ground occupied; on it you stand as long as you are intent upon persisting in such a purpose.

These first two clauses, therefore, give the same counsel, only from slightly different points of view. The first advises not to forsake God; the second advises him who has forsaken Him not to persist in his evil purpose. The verb is ultimately synonymous with "persist" (A.R.V.), but the original meaning "stand firm" is much simpler.

This point is clinched thus: "For He does whatsoever He desires." This is not a threat, not even a wholesome warning, but a good, solid reason for cheerful submission: God does what pleases Him. Since we can never keep pace mentally with all His plans and His desires, it behooves us to admit that we know little of the why and the wherefore of His doings. So it must be if He is the great King that we believe Him to be. Only such a course of conduct is worthy of Him. That explains our difficulty more fully. It is only this: His divine rule completely transcends our thinking. When we cannot follow His higher and better plans, that certainly is no reason for wanting to cast off His leadership. We should rather regard it as His divine prerogative and as an indication of a government on His part whose deepest ends we can never trace.

That these words, "He does whatsoever He desires," are applicable only to God Himself appears clearly from the mode of speaking that is observed in the Scriptures, cf., Jonah 1:14; Job 23:13. To refer them to an absolute Oriental monarch would ascribe a divine prerogative to an earth-born ruler.

Verse 4. God's unquestioned sovereignty is still being insisted upon inasmuch as those people whom Koheleth addresses are perfectly ready to grant that He is sovereign. If He rules, there is an excellent propriety about having His Word simply prevail and order one thing after another. We may not be able to follow it as to all its purposes, but it is still perfectly clear that God's government brooks no interference. Who dares to challenge Him or take Him to task for a certain course that He has chosen to follow? It seems as though Koheleth is letting the difficulties that arise from God's doings as regarded from one point of view be settled by matching them with another unquestioned attribute of His — sovereignty; and letting the consequences of the latter remove the difficulties of the former. For, surely, none would have questioned that God reigns supreme.

That the challenge, "What are You doing?" should not be addressed to *God* appears from such passages as Job 9:12; 23:13; Isa. 45:9; Dan. 4:32-35. It is in harmony with this Biblical usage when we say that God is under consideration in this passage rather than an earthly king. This mode of speech regularly applies to Him.

The good fruits of the course recommended in v. 2 are now set forth in v. 5. If a man faithfully keeps God's commandment he shall meet with no evil. *Men* cannot guarantee to man such immunity against evil. Furthermore, it is in the nature of the case that such a course of conduct bears good fruit, even as it is also written, "All things work together for good to them that love God." The term "know" means as much as "know by experience" or "to experience." Indeed, there may be seasons of waiting until the set "time" of God comes, or until God's "judgment" for the defence of the righteous and the rebuke of the wicked comes to pass. But the righteous man knows that there is a time when God's judgment comes due, and he can wait till such a time. In fact, such knowing and such waiting are characteristic of the "wise heart."

We still have a unified paragraph under consideration (v. 1-8), a paragraph that is instructing men how the wise face suffering. That *God's* commandments are being considered appears from the context and from the fact that the phrase "keep the commandments" elsewhere refers to God's commandments, cf., I Kings 11:34; Prov. 19:16. The second half of the verse is unsatisfactory if the verse is regarded as teaching obedience to civil rulers.

Verse 6. We need not insist that *chephets* has kept the root meaning of the word in this verse and must, therefore, be rendered "desire." For though other passages demand this meaning, here, as most dictionaries agree, the word has the very general meaning of "thing or matter" (*Sache, Angelegenheit*). The verse then ties up very intimately with the preceding. The truly wise man is aware that God's "time" and "judgment" are decisive factors in determining the outcome.

This rule does not apply here and there; it holds good for *"every matter."*

The second half of the verse shows that there is a reason why God should have times and seasons for interference. That reason is that God's children find that the evil that man lays upon them lies heavily upon them. Their being thus burdened stirs God's pity for them. He prepares His aid; but this aid is conditioned by the "time" that is most suitable for its being brought to men, and, on the other hand, it is conditioned by God's "judgment." What He has judged, that is the outcome. So the verse is a composite whole. In this case "man" refers to the oppressor that may happen to afflict the godly. "Man" is, therefore, a subjective genitive.

In v. 7 the reason is given why evil men will afflict the godly: they are persons who do not know what course things will take, that, namely, God has His time and His seasons for judging. Being ignorant, therefore, of such settling of accounts, they believe they can lay a heavy hand upon the righteous, and do it with impunity. Those who could instruct them in this matter are despised by them. So it naturally remains true: "Who can make known to him how it shall be?"

In v. 8 good counsel is still being imparted to the man who is being oppressed. This verse seems to contain only very general statements on the universal impotence of man in certain directions. In its connection, however, it becomes a prediction concerning self-satisfied oppressors, who seem to succeed particularly well in oppressing the godly. It shows in particular that these oppressors are not men who are especially to be feared. For there are certain necessary events that will ultimately come to them and prove them to be quite frail and helpless. These eventualities that must transpire are, however, under the full and absolute control of the heavenly King. But they do demonstrate how little the oppressors are to be dreaded.

One of these happenings that does, indeed, befall all men and will sooner or later be encountered by the Persian oppressors is the hour of departure when the "spirit" returns to Him who gave it. Let a man try, he will not be able to "hold back" the spirit from going when it must. This is really the meaning of the verb *kelo'*. We have translated it "hold back" and not "restrain" — another legitimate meaning — because the latter suggests thoughts about self-mastery, which are not at all under consideration here.

Those commentators who translate *ruach* "wind" instead of "spirit" — though both meanings of the word are common enough — have several serious objections to their rendering to face. One grows out of the parallel statement which follows concerning the having power over the day of death. To speak in one breath of so quixotic a thing as seeking to master the winds and in the next of trying to postpone the day of death would lead any reader to wonder how things that are so widely different get into parallel statements in a series. But to have retaining of the *spirit* under consideration quite naturally suggests another side of the same experience — the inevitable coming of the day of death.

In the second place, there is difficulty in determining why the somewhat preposterous thought of controlling the wind should serve as a charge against any man in any situation. Nor are our contentions invalidated by those interpreters who claim that man can "restrain his spirit" and refer by way of proof to Prov. 25:28, "ruleth his spirit"; for this verse has nothing to say about self-control as does the passage in Proverbs; it refers to keeping back a spirit that is about to depart from the earthly tabernacle of this body. Any oppressor who appears as the frail being that he is when the summons comes to yield up the spirit certainly amounts to nothing by comparison with Him who is the "God of the spirits of all flesh."

Viewing the situation from an equally legitimate angle, the author places the oppressor face to face with the day of death. Israel's Ruler has control of such events. But how about the poor wretch who oppresses God's people? Has he any control over the issues? Absolutely none. He must cringe and grovel before the mighty terror and appear as small as he in reality is.

Since Israel's true Ruler has all such matters fully under control, this is true also in regard to the next situation. He is engaged in a conflict with all such enemies of His church. They may regard Him as a feeble opponent. But when He begins to assert Himself, they may prefer to escape, not being desirous to face the ultimate issues of the war in which they have engaged. But they shall find that there is no discharge from the warfare they have undertaken, cf., the case of the Pharaoh who sought "discharge" from the conflict when it grew too vehement.

To refer to the rigors of military service in the Persian army and to the impossibility of discharge from such service is unsatisfactory from at least two points of view. 1) The fine harmony of the whole argument is interrupted. Instead of having a demonstration of the fraility of those who oppose God, one is obliged to construct a sequence of thought out of unrelated materials. 2) Besides, the word used, "discharge" (*mishlachath*), is from the same root as the verb the angel employed when, desirous of becoming free of his opponent, Jacob, at Penuel he said, "Let me go" (*shalleach*, Gen. 32:27). For Him there was no discharge from the battle until He had blessed Jacob. To seek discharge in war would, according to this parallel, mean to seek to desist from a conflict in which one has become involved. Oppressors of Israel have become involved in a conflict with God as their opponent. The struggle will have to be waged to a bitter finish, much as these opponents may by that time desire to withdraw.

Parallel with these situations is the last one mentioned: "Wickedness shall not deliver him that does it." The course followed by the heathen oppressors of Israel was unjustifiable on every score. It was "wickedness." Those that engage in it shall surely gain nothing thereby. By a mild litotes it is said only that they will gain no deliverance as a result of the course they follow. The situation is really far more terrible. The evil of their doing shall come upon their own heads. That is what is implied when reference is made to "not deliver." There must be some danger from which they need to be delivered.

He that thoughtfully considers the four items that are charged against Israel's oppressors ought to be moved to say, "Surely, I should not care to be one of that group." For after careful analysis it becomes apparent that the lot of the oppressors is far more grievous than is that of the oppressed.

2. The oppression of the righteous (v. 9-13)

When evil days have come upon a nation, the problems that cause godly men concern are most varied. Though much counsel has already been given as to how to meet and to stand up under these difficulties, there are still a few such difficulties that can cause grievous concern to the people of God. What if the wicked have the rule and use it oppressively against the righteous and thus expose them to suffering or drive them to sin? The author presents that problem (9b) and suggests two considerations by way of an answer: the first (v. 10) considers the nature of the end to which such wicked rulers come; the second is: Remember the fixed and ever-valid principle that it cannot go well with evildoers (v. 11-13). He that holds fast to these sound considerations should not become disconcerted, no matter how acute the situation may become.

(9) **All this did I see when I gave my mind to all the work that is done under the sun at a time when one man rules over another to his hurt. (10) Such being the case, I have seen that wicked men were buried, and they came to the grave, and they departed from the place of the holy man and were forgotten in the city, they who had done thus. This, too, is vanity. (11) Because the sentence upon an evil deed is not speedily executed, therefore the mind of the sons of men is fully resolved within them to do evil. (12) Even though a sinner does evil a hundred times and lives long, yet I know that it shall be well with those that fear God, that really fear His presence. (13) But it shall not be well with the wicked, and being like a shadow, he shall not prolong his days because he is not a man who is in awe of the presence of God.**

The Preacher introduces his new subject with the words, "All this did I see when I gave my mind to all the work that is done under the sun." "All this" points forward to the problem that is about to be stated and about to be solved. *Williams* remarks that the expression used "seems always to introduce a subject, not to gather up that which has been already described." Koheleth's statement that "he gave his mind to every work that is done" suggests that, in spite of having disposed of certain problems, he recognized that others remained, and he, therefore, "gave his mind," that is, his most wholehearted attention, to another problem that was common enough in those days and worked out the solution that is now to be presented. — *Nathon,* absolute infinitive, is used adverbially and is subordinate to the main verb, somewhat like 4:2, and is, therefore, best translated, "when I gave," cf. *KS* 218b.

The statement that Koheleth gave his mind "to every work that is done under the sun" suggests two thoughts. The one is that the Preacher is intent on scanning the whole complex of situations as they then obtained. The second is that the problems are problems only in so far as they leave out of consideration the higher truths and values that cannot be discerned as long as one keeps on the level that is designated as being "under the sun." In the second half of the verse *'eth* ("time") is an adverbial accusative and should not be translated, "there is a time," but, "at a time when," as shown by *KS* 331b.

The second half of the verse states the general situation that one discovers when he lets all things pass in review before his searching gaze: "Man rules over man to his hurt." The man who is primarily hurt is, of course, the man over whom the other rules. That the ruler is to be regarded as a wicked man appears from v. 10, which speaks of "the wicked." Verse 9 without v. 10 would leave us entirely at a loss or at the best oblige us to resort to vague guesses. Verse 10, on the other hand, cannot be considered as speaking of the death of wicked men in general but must rather speak of the death of wicked *rulers* in particular.

To tell the truth, there are few things that can so completely upset a man as to see injustice done without any apparent sign of just retribution. More grievous by far, of course, is it to be the victim of such unjust dealings. Men have suffered shipwreck of the faith because of such experiences. The Preacher recognizes the need of helping such persons to get their bearings. Nor is this the only Scripture passage that deals with this problem, which was peculiarly postexilic. The 128th Psalm, rightly assigned to this same period, also stresses the thought that they who truly fear Jehovah cannot fail to find God's blessing. Likewise chapter 8 of Zechariah. If so many Scripture passages are concerned with this matter, it must be one of major importance. However, Koheleth gives a very thorough and satisfactory solution in the following verses.

The first solution of the problem is the same as that which is offered in Ps. 73:17: "It was too painful for me [the supremacy, namely, of the wicked] until I went into the sanctuary of God and considered their latter end." There follows in Ps. 73 a sketch of the latter end of the wicked.

Unfortunately, the issue has been confused by inserting into v. 10 the idea that those who were removed from the place of the holy and were forgotten were the *righteous* men. Then hardly any satisfactory sense can be extracted from the verse, nor does the problem under consideration have any light thrown upon it. The whole verse is really quite simple when it is conceived, as it aims to be, as a portrayal of the end of the *oppressor*.

The adverb translated "so" (*bekhen*) is an Aramaism and literally means "in thus," which we prefer to render, "such being the case"; *KW, in sogestalteten Verhaeltnissen.* The meaning is simply this: The situation being as just depicted, the wicked, namely, holding the rule over the godly, I saw this situation now developing in the following manner: Such wicked rulers were buried. — The participle "buried" is used here as it was in 7:21. — The same men still being under consideration, the verb follows, *ubha'u,* "and they came," implying, of course, *to the grave.* There follow the verb and its phrase: "and they departed from the place of the holy man." Now we see what the author is aiming to set forth. These wicked men are removed from the theatre of activity, where, according to v. 9, there were but two actors on the stage — the wicked man and the godly man — or, as the latter is here called, the "holy man." So the holy man stays, being left behind. That is a prominent truth that experience substantiates again and again. The wicked vanish, and their works perish with them. The godly prevail and are preserved by God.

It will not do to translate, "they go from the holy place," for "place" is in the construct state (*mekom* not *makom*) and must be translated: "the place of the holy," *KS.* 305d, "holy" here being the ideal holy person, Israel, an adjective which the Scriptures commonly use with reference to Israel. To this thought the next must be added: "and they are forgotten in the city" — the late use of the hithpael for the passive, *KS* 101. Having been removed from their position and so from the possibility of practicing further unjust oppression, not only do their works perish, but their very memory perishes with them. That is God's judgment; they are wiped out. Is not this a solution of the problem? Has not God interfered when, as so often happens, this result is brought about? The very city that witnessed all the unrighteousness of such men has no memory of their existence. Men are ready and glad to forget such administrators of justice.

The clause, "they who had done thus," closes the account, to remind men that this was the reason for their ignominious end. *Doing thus* demands such a fate. Certainly, their history deserves to be epitomized: "This, too, is vanity."

The attempt to make most of this verse an allusion to the death and the burial of good men finds its chief support in the clause just rendered, "they who had done thus," which is then given this form, "they who had done *right*," and is placed in a different position from that which the Hebrew has. But such a rendering takes a secondary meaning of *ken,* which is less appropriate at this point, and produces confusion in place of an easy and natural sequence of thought.

The removal of the wicked from the company of the godly is one way of curbing their oppression in evil

days. God has other ways. This one is stressed as being
a striking example. The Scriptures frequently speak
of this lot of the ungodly, cf., Isa. 52:1; 49:17; Prov.
10:7; Ps. 73:19, 20. But there is more to be said to set
troubled minds at rest.

Before the comfort is applied, the problem is re-
stated from another point of view (v. 11). For the
situation is still the same as it was in 9b: one man is
ruling over another to his hurt. True, the end to which
the wicked ruler will come straightens out a part of
the tangled thought for the oppressed; but until that
end comes, the temptation that this verse states is
continually assailing them. The well-merited sentence
upon the evildoers is delayed, and as a result many a
temptation to wrongdoing arises in the heart of the
oppressed, sometimes, no doubt, in the spirit of revenge, sometimes in the spirit that says: "If evildoers
prosper in their course, why should I so assiduously
guard myself from doing evil?"

The disturbing factor is the experience that the
divine sentence (*pithgam* — a Persian word) against
the evildoer is delayed. This word, too, points to the
Persian period. It refers to royal decrees (cf., Esther
1:20; Ezra 4:17). Here it naturally refers to a divine
decree or sentence, in regard to which faith well knows
that it has been pronounced but "is not being put into
execution" (*'en na'aseh*). The construction is unusual.
'En, "is not," is here used with the niphal participle,
which places one vividly into the very situation of
waiting: "it is not being executed." The many like
situations of the time, all of which clamored for adjustment, are referred to by a singular, "the evil work,"
for all the situations were in principle the same, and
all called for the execution of the one and the same
divine sentence. It will not do to take the accent
(zakeph) over the word "sentence" as being so
strongly disjunctive as not to allow for a construct

state of that word (as *Hengstenberg* does) and so to make the adverb "speedily" a verb; for the disjunctive accent is at times used with the construct state, cf., Esther 1:4. — *Bahem,* "in them," is pleonastic.

The temptation growing out of the situation just described is worded thus: "Therefore the mind of the sons of men is fully resolved within them to do evil." The figure is both vivid and simple, for the verb is literally "filled up." The mind is regarded as a vessel in which the agitated thoughts collect and seethe. Each new piece of injustice unavenged adds to the contents and the agitation of the vessel until it refuses to hold the total contents, and so the hot mass spills over the brim. This spilling is the "doing of evil." One might translate the verb "fully set" (A.V.) or "emboldened" (A.R.V.), but in either case the picturesqueness of the figure, which *Luther* retains, is lost. The same expression is found in Esther 7:5, where it is rendered "presume," but that again is best understood by a literal rendering.

The opening word of the verse (*'asher*) is in this case to be rendered as a conjunction as it is in 6:12b; Deut. 3:24, viz., "because." As to its use in introducing v. 12, it is there best rendered "if" or "even though" (cf., *Buhl* B4) a meaning that is readily deduced from the relative idea if it is translated: "as to the fact that." The phrase *'al-ken* serves to introduce the apodosis, *KS* 415Q.

Verse 12f. This is not the entire solution of the problem but a contributory factor that weighs heavily in the balance in reaching a satisfactory conclusion. The author, who, it must be remembered, (v. 10) has busied himself intensively with the problem and worked it through in his heart as a personal problem, found it of value to place over against the vexatious thoughts that arise at such a time one of the immutable

principles of Scriptural wisdom that have been inculcated by the Word of God as basic for all moral issues,
the principle: "It must be well with those that fear
God," or its antithesis: "It shall not be well with the
wicked." They out of whose life and experience such
principles have grown find in them an anchor of hope
in the face of vexatious irregularities; and they know
that these problems are a momentary clouding of the
issue and a delay which continues only until this ir-
resistible principle gets underway and clears away all
obstacles which seem for a time to intervene. This
attitude is one of faith and of ripe experience and is
possible only to those who have some spiritual ground
under their feet; but to such it is entirely satisfactory
because they know the nature of these solid principles
which divine Wisdom offers.

We find that v. 12 is intimately linked with v. 11
and in the protasis merely restates the problem, giving a
third statement of it. In this case the emphasis lies on
the many individual instances of wrongdoing of which
the wicked are guilty "a hundred times" (*me'ath*, like
6:3) without being checked in their course in which
they "continue long." It is better to translate thus than
to supply the word "days," namely, "and he prolongs
his days"; for the verb makes perfectly good sense
without a supplied object. When an object is desired,
as is the case in v. 13, it is added. We have this gain
from our translation: it emphasizes what is the
peculiar problem of these verses — the long-continued
and uninterrupted practice of evil rather than the long
life of the sinner.

The principle, the abiding, unquestionable, and un-
failing principle which is laid in the balances to offset
the weight of the above difficulty is simply this: "It
shall be well with those that fear God." That is the
emphasis which the order of the words in the Hebrew
suggests. The verb stands first: "there *will be*." In a

statement of this sort that is the same as saying: God must come to the aid of such as fear God.

However, the Preacher does not trifle with valid principles, nor offer illusory comfort, nor permit any man to deceive himself. He emphasizes that they alone dare draw comfort from this good principle who truly measure up to the demand that it makes upon men. That is the motive for the appositional statement, "that really fear His presence." "They that fear God" was a common term in reference to God's people. It was like the German *die Gottesfuerchtigen.* Common terms are often used idly without weighing their moral demands. Against such formalism the author's remark is a protest. Or the approach of *Williams* may be used who gives a very feasible translation, *"because* they fear God."

The author might have been content with this statement of the case, but having enunciated a solid principle, he applies it more fully also to the wicked in order that the final result of it might comfort the disturbed hearts of the God-fearing.

The emphasis of the statement is now altered. The Hebrew order runs thus: "Good will not be for the wicked." This implies that good fortune is something that, in the nature of the case, cannot fall to the lot of wicked men. There is a contrast between the expression "prolong his days" and the one used in v. 12, "live long," the same verb being used in each case. It might have been rendered into English thus: "though he go on long (in sin) he shall not make his days long." The explanation for this unusual fact is appended, and it is all the more emphatic because of its brevity, "being like a shadow." What a futile life if such a verdict must be pronounced upon it! But the deepest cause of this futility is the fact that they "are not in awe of the presence of God." Rather than marvel at or envy the success of the ungodly, one feels: *They* are the ones who are truly deserving of pity; not God's afflicted saints. The truth taught is the same as that found in Job 5:26; 15:32 ff; 20:5-9; 22:16; Prov. 10:27; Isa. 65:20.

3. The inability to fathom God's doings (v. 14-17)

Though in vv. 14, 15 a particular difficulty is under consideration, a practical conclusion is given not only in v. 15 but also in vv. 16, 17. It is, therefore, best to make these verses one paragraph, 14-17.

The situation is still one that grows out of days of suffering.

The particular problem which is now examined is the observation that what befalls the righteous seems to be what is due to the wicked, and what befalls the wicked would have been more appropriate for a righteous man. This is, no doubt, a very specific and a very disconcerting problem to face.

(14) **There is a vanity which is done upon the earth, namely, that there are righteous men to whom it happens as if they had done the deeds of the wicked, and there are wicked men to whom it happens as if they had done the deeds of the righteous. I said that this, too, is vanity. (15) So I commended mirth; for there is no better thing for a man than to eat and to drink and be merry; for this will stay with him in his toil all the days of his life which God gives him under the sun. (16) When I set my mind to know wisdom and to see the work which is done upon the earth—for both day and night a man does not see sleep for his eyes—(17) then I saw with reference to all the works of God that man cannot find out the work that is done under the sun; because man toils to discover and still does not find; and even if a wise man thinks he knows yet he will not be able to find it out.**

We again meet the familiar phrase, "under the sun," which is used in v. 15, and which in v. 14 has

the wording, "upon the earth." From the purely
earthly point of view, leaving out of consideration the
divine factors, which certainly bear most directly upon
the case, the Preacher finds the problem very difficult.
Why should the destiny of one class fall to the lot of
another? Such a situation is certainly, "vanity," i.e.,
one of those futile situations that prevail so commonly
since sin has come into the world. If men disregard the
heavenly issues, the problem may become so grave as
utterly to confuse a man. As soon as he begins to let
higher considerations influence his thinking, it must
strike him that in all truth there is never a man who
can lay claim to perfect righteousness, and that, therefore, the treatment which an entirely righteous person
ought to receive should be his. The author prefers not
to let the higher issues settle the case in this instance.
He simply lets the case remain at the point first made:
"This also is vanity."

But he suggests two practical considerations: the
one, v. 15; the other, v. 16 f., considerations that also
offer a perfectly satisfactory attitude, and perhaps, in
the light of conditions as he met them, the most necessary approach. The first is v. 15.

Koheleth indicates that he does not propose to draw
upon the higher sources of comfort and counsel (cf.,
"under the sun"). But to let a seeming confusion of
the fate of the just and the unjust induce a man to
forego all legitimate delights and enjoyments which
still remain, and so to make an unpleasant lot still more
unpleasant, surely has no advantages. Therefore let a
man cultivate such harmless good cheer as God lets
him find. The same counsel was previously given in
other connections: 2:24; 3:12, 22. It is just as apropos
here, for men have let such seeming discrepancies of
divine judgment sour their whole life.

Nor is Koheleth's teaching out of harmony with
the sentiments expressed in 7:1 ff., which sought to in-

culcate a spirit of true earnestness and sobriety. Such an attitude does not rule out the joys that are here commended.

Nor can we find good reason for translating as the A.R.V.m does: "this should accompany him." The jussive is as little necessary here as it was in corresponding previous cases such as are told in 3:22, 5:18, where the indicative was entirely satisfactory. There we translated: "this will stay with him" or "accompany him." Such proper enjoyment of good material gifts, if it is rightly entered into, is a thing that accompanies a man all the days of his life and so keeps furnishing some ground for satisfaction.

A second consideration in view of this problem is v. 16 f. This says in substance to a man who is puzzled by this problem: "God's doings cannot be fathomed, not even by the wise." The introductory remark—"when I set my mind to know wisdom"—is not a resolution to engage in the pursuit of wisdom but nothing more than the thought, I let wisdom make her contribution toward the solution of the present difficulty, and this is what she said. The matter that was thus wisely considered was the "work" (*'inyan*) that is engaged in upon the earth, when men, namely, try to find a solution of the particular problem that is in the forefront since v. 14 —the contradictory fate of the righteous and the wicked. This work is described in 16b as being of such a kind that he that attempts to solve the problem is engaged in it with such eager effort that he can find sleep neither day nor night. Such an experience constitutes "work" or "travail." It is sufficiently arduous to ruin a man completely.

The Preacher does not pass over the surface lightly. He gives his "heart" to understand what wisdom can contribute. His final discovery is that, as far as God's works are concerned, it is simply impossible to penetrate into the ultimate depths of them. The best counsel to a man who is wrestling with a problem is sometimes: "You are attempting more than you can achieve." At the same time a judicious bit of explanation is inserted: Just because a man labors to find out a matter he does not of necessity achieve an answer. To believe otherwise is to begin with the rash assumption that all problems can be solved by the intellect of man. For that matter, the last observation is very much in place: Even if a wise man should resolve to know he would not be able to find out. It is this thought which aptly touches upon a grave difficulty. Those who determine most strongly to solve grave difficulties are often the ones who lack the necessary equipment to do so. They are not even truly wise, yet they attempt what transcends the capabilities of the wise.

We believe that this section, v. 16, 17, is a consecutive unit, which has a good logical sequence, as our translation indicates. Strangely involved renderings of these verses are offered in some commentaries. Most of them seem to grow out of a misapprehension of the purpose of the passage. Verse 16 begins with a conditional clause; v. 17 furnishes the conclusion. The *we* before *ra'ithi* should, therefore, be translated "then." The *ki* in v. 17 means, "that namely" (*Zöckler*) cf., Gen. 40:15; Exod. 3:11. "All the works of God" is not the direct object but the accusative of specification—*"in reference to* all the works of God."

A good parallel thought of v. 17 is Rom. 11:33.

The verb "to find" (*matsa'*) has an unusual meaning here, *entirely to understand*, cf., *BDB sub verb*. 2a.

So the conclusion of the matter is: Do not attempt to solve what man cannot solve. This is good counsel to an age that thinks all problems can and must be solved by man.

CHAPTER IX

4. The similar fate of the godly and the ungodly — no cause for pessimism and inaction (9:1-10)

This section is very closely akin to the preceding (cf. especially 8:14). For this reason, too, it begins with a "for," so that some interpreters establish too close a connection (e.g., A.R.V.) and let 9:1 be the closing verse of the preceding chapter. A distinct difficulty appears in 9:1, and it should be considered separately. This difficulty is the similarity of the lot of the righteous and the wicked insofar as it blots out the indications of God's favor or disfavor. This may not be so vitally different a problem from that considered in 8:14, yet a comparison with the contemporary Malachi (see 1:2 ff.) shows that a somewhat cynical spirit had taken possession of the Israelites, a spirit that led them to question whether the love of God which the fathers had claimed for Israel were purely chimerical or a reality. What the Preacher offers shows them how to evaluate the difficulty and how to overcome the dangers that grow out of it.

When passages such as the one before us are misunderstood they lead some interpreters to make strange charges against this book. Nor has the situation been cleared by such commentators as *Delitzsch,* who claim to be voicing very faithfully the problems which the book itself contains. This commentator, for example, has as a heading for these verses—more exactly for verses 1-12—"The Power of Fate and the Best Possible Thing for Man in His Want of Freedom." This ascribes an unscriptural determinism to the author. Again *Delitzsch* finds "an Epicurean thought" in vv. 7-10. This

type of exposition is not willing to give the Preacher
the benefit of the doubt. Though what we have thus far
pointed out might be regarded as a mild criticism, some
interpreters have gone so far as to find, for example,
in v. 9 the thought: "Add to your harem any woman
who charms your eye" (*Cox*). Since this is the attitude
of some commentators, it is hardly to be wondered at
that some persons have had misgivings about this book.

The background of the chapter is the troubled age
after the Exile. This must be borne in mind as it needed
to be borne in mind in a consideration of all preceding
chapters.

In its first part, vv. 1-6, this section sketches the
difficulty that the author seeks to meet. The second part,
vv. 7-10, suggests the spirit in which the difficulty is to
be met.

**(1) For all this did I take to heart, and I ex-
plored all this, namely, that the righteous and the
wise and their works are in the hand of God; and
also no man knows whether it will be love or hatred.
Everything is still before them. (2) All things come
alike to all; there is one outcome for the righteous
and for the wicked; for the good and the clean and
for the unclean; for him that offers sacrifice and for
him that does not offer sacrifice; as is the good so
is the sinner; he that swears rashly is as he that fears
an oath. (3) This is an evil in all that is done under
the sun, that there is one outcome for all; and also
the heart of the sons of men is full of evil, and madness is in their hearts as long as they live; and after
that—to the dead! (4) For whosoever is joined to
all the living he has hope. For a living dog is better
than a dead lion. (5) For the living know that they
will die; but the dead know nothing at all; neither
have they any reward, for the memory of them is
forgotten. (6) They are neither loved nor hated nor
envied any more — all this has long perished; neither**

have they any portion any more in anything that is done under the sun. (7) Come now, eat your food with joy and drink your wine with a merry heart; for God hath already approved of what you are doing. (8) At all times let your garments be white, and let not oil be lacking on your head. (9) Enjoy life with the wife whom you love all the days of your vain life, which He has given you under the sun all your vain life; for this is your portion in life and in your toil wherein you toil under the sun. (10) Whatever your hand finds to do by the use of your strength, do it; for there is no work, or devising, or knowledge, or wisdom in Sheol where you are going.

This problem suggests itself as a result of trying to arrive at a satisfactory solution for the preceding one. There it became apparent that man cannot explain what God does. Still one other of the things that cannot be explained stood out more prominently, even after the author suggested that man can never solve all, and that was the problem: How can we tell whether God is for or against us?

The author was delving deeply into the issues involved: "I did take it to heart," and, "I explored." The construction begins with a perfect and continues with a construct infinitive with "and" and "to." This is done only for the purpose of continuing the thought which has in it something of an element of probing the future. "To give one's heart to a matter" means to look into the future; the infinitive with "to" has the same force. To regard this as a future periphrastic, viz., *eram scrutaturus*, does not yield a satisfactory thought though it is advocated by *Delitzsch* and accepted by *Volck. Bur* is the infinitive from *barar*.

The matter explored is stated only partially in the words: "The righteous and the wise and their works [*'abhadh*, used only here] are in the hand [i.e., power] of God." The rest of the verse shows how this is meant.

So, taking all the remaining elements together, we gain this thought: Men are not directing the course of their lives so that, being wise and good, they can do such works as invariably lead to God's showing favor to them. These persons and the works they do are in God's hands, and He does as He pleases.

This is not determinism although God's sovereignty is strongly stressed, perhaps as strongly as anywhere in the Scriptures; but, as the next words indicate, it is to be understood primarily in this sense: *From the manner in which things happen in his life* a man cannot tell whether God's attitude toward him is one of love or of hatred. "Everything is still before them." This means: practically anything may happen to a man. The "love" and the "hatred" referred to must be thought of as attitudes of *God*, for God was just mentioned as having all issues in hand, and the words that follow suggest that He may send anything. No man has a certainty as to the next thing that shall befall him. Though it is stated as generally as possible—"also no man knows"—we yet see that the one referred to is the *righteous* man, who is concerned about how he stands with God, and about how God does things in governing this world.

The balance of the thought is disturbed, and incongruous matter is introduced if, as *Hitzig* and *Ewald* do, the second half of the verse is construed to mean: "Since man has not his actions in his own power he knows not whether he will love or hate." The translation of *Luther* is grammatically impossible: *Doch kennet kein Mensch weder die Liebe noch den Hass irgend eines, den er vor sich hat.* The same is true with regard to the translation of A. V.

The somewhat enigmatic, "everything is still before him," with which the verse closes, is in need of further explanation. This explanation is given in v. 2.

Throughout this verse the emphasis is on the fact that the fates and fortunes of all men seem to all appearance to be entirely *alike*. The term "event (*mikreh*) must, however, be rightly understood. It comes from *karah,* which means "to meet." That which a man meets with in life is *mikreh*. "Happening," "event," "outcome"—all strike fairly close to the original meaning. Since it means simply *that which befalls one* it is surely not used as a term which is in opposition to divine ordainment, as though according to the point of view of the Old Testament, there were some "power of fate" that, like the fate of classical paganism, could prevail in the face of God. The term is used in opposition to independent action on the part of the righteous, or better, to man's control of the things that shall befall him. As the examples cited clearly show, "the righteous" may do good works, "the wicked" may be guilty of evil. A shallow view of what ought to happen as a sequel, a view that borders on a mercenary spirit, would want to see as the inevitable outcome a prompt reward of the one and swift justice for the other. Koheleth rightly claims (and experience amply substantiates his claim) : What befalls (*mikreh*) may be identical in the case of these two. Of course, an obvious difference in God's treatment of the just and the unjust is oftentimes also discernible.

The citation of the example he now refers to may have been motivated either by the personal observance of special instances of such an outcome or of certain classes that were particularly prominent in his day, namely, such who in a sincere spirit observed all ceremonial demands (therefore "good" and "clean") ; also such who were most exacting in observing what the laws concerning sacrifices prescribed; also such who lived really good lives ; and lastly also such who realized the true import of an oath and would dare to use it only in the true fear of God. The Preacher had not

observed that such conduct, which was governed by
the fear of God, rendered men immune to adverse
"events."

What an effect such an experience had on him and
his contemporaries the Preacher explains in v. 3.

Even *Hengstenberg* seems to charge the author with
unseemly conduct when he says of him that he
"sins with his tongue." For it seems to him that the
Preacher has brought a charge against God when he
says that what God lets happen to good and evil men
alike is an "evil" (*ra'*). It seems that interpreters have
not fully grasped the meaning of the phrase which is
here so carefully inserted — "under the sun." That
always implies leaving out of consideration all higher
values and divine factors and limiting oneself exclusively to values and facts that the natural man can
apprehend. But, if all revealed truth is left behind, and
the difficulty before us is to be judged only by what
man's reason can devise — and that the author purposes to do when he says "under the sun" — then it most
assuredly is "an evil" that "there is one outcome for
all." It certainly looks bad or "evil" to us. The author
rules out the only true explanation there is, viz., the
fact that there is a just Judge of all mankind who
ultimately sets all things right. But why rule that out?
Just because, in judging a problem such as this, men
very frequently do leave it out. For a time Koheleth
drops down to a level on which men's thinking quite
generally moved in his day so that he might the more
clearly state their problem as they felt it.

When thinking on such a lower level is being
followed, another difficulty arises. Seeing that all
efforts at righteousness seem to fail to produce results,
"the heart of the sons of men is full of evil." The same
difficulty arises again that was mentioned in 8:11, but
it is in a slightly different setting. In the latter passage
failure to see God's judgment stirred men to turn to

evil. In this passage the apparent failure of righteousness to deliver a man from evil produces the same
result. The figure is about the same: bitterness is seen
filling the vessel of the heart until it is on the verge
of overflowing. Men practically resolve: "I, too, shall
give myself over to evil deeds; I shall get just as far
as the other man."

However, just how the author stands on the matter
is indicated with sufficient clearness in his next statement which describes these embittered persons: "Madness is in their hearts while they live." Of course, it is
madness for any man to adopt such an attitude. The
term for madness used here (*holeloth* from *halal*) implies "a being blinded as to the true issues" — *Ver-
blendung*. The glare of a certain fact which was beheld
to the exclusion of all things else robbed a man of the
ability to see things rightly (see *KW* on these words).
That is really the state of such poor deluded souls.

Having lived a life that is blinded by delusion, man
has only one tragic outcome to report, and that is:
"After that — to the dead!" The word sounds like a
brief military command which brings the career of a
rebel to a close and must, of course, be carried out on
the spot. A sorry end, indeed! A similar phrase occurs
in Isa. 8:20. — "After that" (*'acharaw*) uses the
suffix in a neuter sense, which gives the word a purely
adverbial force: *Zoeckler-darnach*. Akin is the "after"
found in 6:12 and 7:14.

It is as though at this point the author retraced his
steps for a moment and said: "Though such deluded
souls as were pictured in v. 3 must finally fall away into
death, let's go back for a moment to look at their
situation before the end came." As long as they are
alive they have hope. Or to give the wording of the
case that he employs, "For whosoever is joined to all
the living, he has hope." That attitude of hope is characteristic of men. Our present-day proverb expresses it

less elegantly, "Where there is life there is hope." Or
if one desires another proverbial saying for it, one
might say, "A living dog is better than a dead lion."
In connection with this proverb it must be remembered
that the typical dog of the Oriental city was the con-
temptible cur who ranged the streets as a scavenger
(I Sam. 24:14; II Sam. 3:8; 16:4; Rev. 22:15; Matt.
15:26). Even such a one, while he is still alive, has the
advantage over the regal lion whose carcass lies in
the thicket.

Note that we have accepted the approach of most
of the versions by reading *yechubbar* rather than the
actual text *yebuchar* or *yibbacher*. This necessitates
taking *mi 'asher* as "whosoever" — a meaning that is
common in later Hebrew; which is also found in Exod.
32:33 and II Sam. 20:11.

Verse 5. To dwell a moment longer on this one
advantage that the living enjoy — "they know that they
will die." This seems to be so scant an advantage that
one is for a moment tempted to think that the author
is speaking in a half-sarcastic vein. But it need not be
that. The thought is merely that a living person has
the distinct advantage of knowing that he will die and
be able to arrange many a thing in his life and prepare
to meet the issue. But for the dead every opportunity
for action or achievement of any sort is a thing of the
past: "The dead know not anything at all; neither have
they any reward, for the memory of them is forgotten."
This certainly seems to be a flat denial of all hope of
a hereafter. But *Williams* says quite rightly: "We have
no right to consider the verse as the definite opinion of
Koheleth about the state of the dead in the other world;
he is only expressing the relation of the dead to this
world, as in v. 6." One arrives at the same result when
one keeps applying the limitation expressed in v. 3,
which is still in force here, namely, the phrase "under
the sun." How else can death appear if higher values

and possibilities are disregarded? The dead "have no reward." "They are neither loved, nor hated, nor envied any more" (v. 6) as far as this life is concerned. They are out of it all: "all this has long perished; neither have they any portion any more in anything that is done under the sun."

Taking isolated utterances like this one and insisting that they must be pushed to the limit of possible negative interpretation is not satisfactory exegesis, especially when there are other weighty statements, like 12:7, to the contrary. Against such misconstruction the author has apparently erected a double barrier, for he repeats that he had in mind the possibility of dead persons' having a share in what goes on in this world after they are dead by again adding the phrase as a conclusion — "in anything that is done under the sun."

Quite striking is the parallel between verses 1-6 and Mal. 2:17, where we read: "Ye have wearied Jehovah with your words. Yet ye say, Wherein have we wearied Him? In that ye say, Everyone that doeth evil is good in the sight of Jehovah, and He delighteth in them; or, Where is the God of justice?" In Malachi, however, the situation has, on the part of some, resulted in a direct charge against God, a charge of outright injustice. The Preacher shows how hopeless the situation gets to be for those who confine themselves to the things "under the sun" — they face an empty, hopeless, dreary end.

Vv. 7-10 suggest *the spirit in which this difficulty is to be met.*

We shall presently find (v. 9) that the author is pleased to remain on the lower level of resources and values, viz., of those things that are found under the sun. That it is which gives his present counsel somewhat the savor of earthiness but does not justify the stricture, "an Epicurean thought." For by limiting himself to the earthly the Preacher indicates that he is perfectly aware of higher values. It is, therefore, a procedure that is somewhat like that which we follow when we say, "humanly speaking."

"Come now" implies more than is at first apparent. It is a summons to be up and doing and is directed against the tendency to brood and to ponder over the vexatious problems that marked the age of the author and his readers. The summons "to eat bread" and "drink wine" is directed against the idea of yielding to grief, and for that reason the two qualifying phrases are added: "with joy" and "with a merry heart." The possessives "your bread" and "your wine" imply that these are gifts of God to which one can rightly claim title. The whole of the commandment approves itself as eminently sane, for from every point of view it is better policy to enjoy what may be enjoyed than to brood over insoluble difficulties. Though this counsel has been offered already in 2:24; 3:12, 13, 22; 5:18; 6:12; 8:15, the very simplicity of it is apparently apt to lead men to despise it because it is not a particularly brilliant solution. Since it is really a treasure of wisdom, that recommends itself ever more forcefully each time it is considered, the author keeps on hammering away at it so as to make an impression.

His motivation is in this case entirely different from any thought that has previously been voiced. It runs thus: "God has already taken delight in thy works." This apparently means, in the light of the entire problem under discussion: You, O righteous man, may be sure that God has taken sincere delight in your works that are done in righteousness; uprightness and iniquity are by no means matters of indifference to Him; though He has given few evident tokens of His approbation of the course you are following, rest assured, His attitude is one of sincere delight. By this suggestion the Preacher urges men to persevere in their course of conduct and knows that this certainty of being accepted with God in their works will give the surest grounds for using joyfully what God has given.

Far less in harmony with the context is the interpretation which has this clause mean: such cheerful use of God's gifts meets with God's approval. After this counsel to eat and to drink cheerfully has been given about a half dozen times, it appears as a rather tardy afterthought now to suggest that such a course really does not displease God. Besides, the plural "thy works" would have been used if the author had such a thought in mind. Lastly, the very issue that is at stake would have been ignored, for the major question for troubled hearts was: Do we really stand in God's favor, seeing there are no outward tokens of such favor?

Particular emphasis is lent to the thought by the use of the "already" or "a long time ago" (*laengst*) — *kebhar*. It is not only of late that God has been gradually brought around to this point of view of regarding righteous conduct with favor. The Immutable One has eternally been minded thus.

Malachi presents a kindred solution of the same question in 3:18: "Then shall ye return and discern between the righteous and the wicked, between him that serveth God and him that serveth Him not." Malachi, however, stresses the thought that what is now to be accepted in faith will ultimately be made evident before the eyes of all. Ps. 73:1 has the same thought in still another setting. — *Lebh ṭobh* = literally "a good heart" and means "a merry heart," cf., I Sam. 25:36.

A few additional suggestions are added on the question of how to cultivate good cheer (v. 8), suggestions that have not appeared hitherto. In the light of what precedes we are inclined to accept without hesitation the suggestion of *BDB* that white is here a "sign of cheerfulness and joy," as also commentaries generally agree though the thought offered by others is not foreign to the context when they claim that "white garments become the emblems of purity and festivity" (*Ginsburg*). The use of oil is a symbol of joy as it is in Ps. 45:8 and Isa. 61:3 ("oil of joy"). Grief induced men to go about with hair unkempt and face unwashed. Joy expressed itself in a shining countenance, the effect of which was heightened by the anointing of the head and the face with oil and then properly smoothing and arranging the hair.

Verse 9. Another new feature is added to round out the measure of possibilities of enjoyment in a life that remains quite vain as long as one confines himself to the things under the sun. Our Preacher is apparently not the misogynist that some sought to make him on the basis of 7:28. He knows what a good gift a true wife is, and though in still more evil days Jeremiah was forbidden to take a wife (Jer. 16:1-4), men are now bidden cheerfully to enter upon the estate of matrimony. The suggestion, strictly speaking, is not directed to the married but to the unmarried. We do not find "thy wife" (*ha'ishshah*) but "a wife" (*'ishshah*), which implies choosing a woman to become a wife. The one to be chosen is the one that is loved, and so the injunction practically bids a man to bask in the sunshine of her love. This is, without doubt, one of God's choicest gifts, one that is well calculated to make this vain and toilsome life far more bearable. The fact that God cannot disapprove such an attitude, and that He actually gives His sanction to it, is made clear by the expression: "This is thy portion in life."

It was these features of the book that Luther appreciated and emphasized in his commentary over against a pseudo-asceticism. The emphatic repetition of "all the days of thy vain life" is not "heavy and unnecessary" (*Delitzsch*). It is simply one additional

weighty testimony to the fact that Koheleth appreciates
as few have done how vain life really is if one leaves
the higher values behind as he here does in thought.

Having an interpretation which is in every sense
according to the analogy of the Scriptures and of faith
and unforced, we cannot accept an interpretation that
derives the whole section from a passage in the Babylonian Gilgamesh epic, though that passage does present points of striking similarity. Our chief objection
to such a course is that the spirit and the purpose of the
latter passage are diametrically opposite to those of
the Biblical book. The Babylonian writer actually
counsels pure sensual enjoyments. In proof of this it
will be sufficient to append this fragment. It runs thus:

> Since the gods created man
> Death they ordained for man,
> Life in their hands they hold,
> Thou, O Gilgamesh, fill indeed thy belly,
> Day and night be thou joyful,
> Daily ordain gladness,
> Day and night rage and be merry,
> Let thy garments be bright,
> Thy head purify, wash with water.
> Desire thy children which thy hand possesses.
> A wife enjoy in thy bosom,
> Peaceably thy work (?). . . .

On the strength of this similarity *Barton* concludes:
"The argument is so closely parallel to that of Koheleth
that one can scarcely doubt but that he was influenced
by the passage. . . . This passage shows that the
combination of pessimism and brightness, which we
find in Koheleth, is thoroughly Semitic, and to the
Semetic minds, congruous." The chaste joy that Koheleth counsels a man to take in the fear of God does not
emanate from the muddy fountain of passages such as
these. Those who have the Biblical writers go abor-

rowing from all manner of sources sometimes reduce
the content of the Biblical passages to an extremely
low level in order to secure their parallel. Barton says
on v. 8: "Ginsburg saw in it [viz., in the absence of
the article] a command to embrace whatever woman
pleased one. . . . The analogy of the Babylonian,
which seems to be freely reproduced here, tends to
confirm Ginsburg's view." Conservative Bible interpreters cannot accept such statements.

Verse 10. One thing the Preacher by no means
advocates, and that is a supine attitude, a drifting
along, a doing of nothing on the claim that it avails
nothing, a purely defeatist attitude. There is work to
be done. The strength that we have is to be used, and
where opportunity of putting it to use presents itself,
such an opportunity is to be utilized. This is the
thought presented, not that which the current versions
have: "Whatsoever thy hand findeth to do, do it with
thy might," for the emphasis cannot lie upon putting
one's whole self into the task but upon *putting to use
the strength God has given*. This thought is then driven
home more securely by the reminder that a time is
coming when opportunities for achievement will be
cut off. For all those happy faculties that man possesses for doing work (*ma'aseh*), for devising new
things (*cheshbon*), for employing the knowledge that
he has accumulated (*da'ath*), for employing constructive knowledge that is ethically motivated (*chokhmah*)
— all these rare privileges are at an end.

The Preacher is, therefore, emphasizing only what
no one questions, that in this life certain resources that
are at our disposal may achieve certain results. When
this life is terminated, there is absolutely no opportunity of making up for the tasks left undone, no
matter how many and varied our gifts may have been.
This thought influenced even Jesus when He remarked:
"We must work the works of Him that sent Me, while

it is day: the night cometh when no man can work,"
John 9:4. Since, therefore, this statement says plainly
that earthly activities cannot be continued after this
life, and since this thought is an excellent stimulus to
action in times when enterprise may lag, there is no
call to press out of the statement thoughts it was not
meant to express. There is no attempt here to describe
from every angle the nature of man's existence in
Sheol. Consequently to have the verse express doctrines
that deny a hereafter is a misreading of Scripture.

The section has come to a termination on an opti-
mistic note and a call to action. The Preacher is surely
giving sound counsel for evil days.

5. The higher destiny controlling the final outcome
(vv. 11, 12.)

**(11) Again I saw under the sun that the race is
not to the swift nor the battle to the strong; neither
is there bread to the wise, nor riches to the man of
understanding, nor favor for men of skill; for time
and chance happen to them all. (12) For man does
not know his time: as the fish which are caught in
an evil net and as the birds which are caught in a
snare, so are the sons of men snared in an evil time,
when it falls upon them suddenly.**

A new point of view is prominently stressed in
reference to Israel's downtrodden and unpromising
situation though, of course, the statement of the case
is cast in general terms in order to yield principles that
are applicable to other kindred situations that may
arise. That such a new observation is being considered
is indicated by the introductory words, "Again I saw."
Israel's troubled situation is the center about which
everything turns. Having gone out from it and traced
various problems, the author now returns to it — "I
returned" or "again." This construction is like the use
of the absolute infinitive in v. 1 (cf., *KS* 218b). With-

out letting higher points of view come into the foreground — for he says: "I saw under the sun" — the author makes an observation for which no particular spiritual insight is essential. The spiritual point of view will emerge more clearly later.

For an understanding of the observation that follows it is necessary to bear in mind only who would at the time have deserved to be termed "the swift," "the strong," etc. Without doubt the ruling nation of the day, the Persians, deserved to be described thus. This establishes a contrast which should be kept in mind throughout the rest of the chapter and furnishes the foundation which supports the interpretation that we propose to advance. The thought of this verse is then as follows: Not they who have power and resources and every conceivable advantage are the ones that must ultimately succeed; there is a Higher Destiny that still controls issues; "there's a Divinity that shapes our ends." This thought implies that they who are for the time being not "swift," "strong," "wise," "understanding," and "skillful," at least not in the judgment of men of that time, can, nevertheless, succeed according to the purposes of this same Higher Destiny. In other words, Israel's high prerogatives that had been committed to her by God are not cancelled and brought to nought.

The "time and chance" spoken of are not to be conceived as powers that reign apart from, or even above, God. They are things under God's immediate control. This is indicated by their being used with a singular verb (*yikreh*), which fact combines them into one compact idea. Since "time" is used in the sense of "judgment" or "time of judgment" (as in Isa. 13:22; Ezek. 7:7) is evident that this implies *God's* activity; and so all unscriptural ideas of an all-powerful fate are eliminated. So, too, the word "chance," *pega'*, as in I Kings 5:18 (Heb.) but v. 4 (Eng.), means only "occurrence" since it is derived from the verb which means "to meet." But it usually connotes evil, therefore in I Kings 5:4 it means *"evil* occurrence." God may let things transpire that overthrow those who have apparently had all resources and gifts at their disposal. He may let something meet them and cross their path, events that interrupt their prosperous course and alter it permanently.

This same thought is expressed in much the same form elsewhere in the Scriptures, most prominently in Ps. 33:16, 17: "There is no king saved by the multitude of a host, a mighty man is not delivered by his great power. A horse is a vain thing for safety, neither does he deliver any by his great power." But as in v. 18 of Ps. 33 the eyes are at once directed to Jehovah, so are they in all similar passages such as II Chron. 20: 15; Prov. 21:30, 31; I Sam. 17:47. Approaching our verse in the same manner, we should then say that it stresses *divine* governance and puts at naught all human resources that men conceive of as though they were a guarantee of success in human enterprises.

In the different instances cited the quality mentioned corresponds closely to the good things that it might produce such as "swift" vs. "race," etc. The term "wise" must, therefore, be used with reference to the wisdom that moves on a lower level inasmuch as its product would be only "bread."

Whereas our verse stresses the negative, Rom. 9: 16 stresses primarily the positive, but in another connection.

The preceding verse showed that human abilities do not guaranty success. Verse 12 shows that persons who possess these may be caught unsuspectingly and suddenly. The reference, though worded quite generally, is, as suggested above, without doubt also to the Persians. They are the ones who shall be snared unawares and so fall prey to another nation as

happened only too soon in the conquest of Alexander.
To be more exact, since "for" introduces the verse,
we have an explanation of v. 11. Since these proud
rulers shall be snared, therefore their power and
might shall not yield success to them. The word
"time" refers to the time of judgment as it did in
the preceding verse. — In the phrase *le'eth ra'ah,*
ra'ah is best taken as a noun — "the time of evil," and
so it is again the antecedent to which the subject
(fem.) of *hippol* refers.

The two similes of the "fishes" and the "birds" that
are caught aim to stress first how unexpectedly the
evil predicted is to come, for when such creatures are
taken they never anticipate it. The Persians surely
never anticipated defeat at the hands of the Greeks,
who were numerically far inferior to them. Second,
these similes show how small the nations are to be
esteemed over against the Almighty; for, in the last
analysis, it is He who takes the nations captivé though
He uses His agents to do so. But in taking them God
does this with such ease as a man might use who
catches fish with the net or birds with the snare. Another thought follows: as a man sets the snare or net
and lets the birds or the fish be caught, so God creates
the situation whereby the nations shall be taken, and
they are caught without further effort on His part.
Thoughts such as these may well have encouraged
Israel in the evil days she encountered.

6. Wisdom still the greatest of Israel's resources
(v. 13-18)

The author now turns the thoughts of all true
Israelites back to themselves. The proud masters of
Israel shall, indeed, suddenly become the prey of
others, but Israel shall still remain in possession of
its rare gift — *wisdom;* and the value of that gift is
as great as it always was though for the present it

may not be recognized, and its advantages may be largely nullified.

(13) **Also this have I seen as an example of wisdom under the sun, and it seemed great to me: (14) there was a small city and but few men in it, and there came against it a great king and encircled it and built great bulwarks against it. (15) Now he found in it a poor, wise man, and he delivered the city by his wisdom; yet no man had remembered that same poor man. (16) But I said, Wisdom is better than strength even though the wisdom of the poor man was despised, and his words were not heeded. (17) The words of wise men heard in quiet are better than the outcry of a prince among fools. (18) Wisdom is better than weapons of war, but one sinner destroys much good.**

The translations for the most part, except the A.R.V. which we follow, fail to do justice to the original. The A.V. and Luther, for example, render: "This wisdom have I seen," making *zoh* a demonstrative adjective, which, according to its position, it cannot be. The "this" points forward to v. 14; the position of "wisdom" in the sentence indicates that this is the object which is being announced as about to be considered or, as our translation indicates, this is "an example of wisdom." That "wisdom" should be modified by the phrase, "under the sun," means no more than that the instance under consideration is one in which wisdom concerned itself with matters under the sun. The author prefers to keep on the lower level of things in order that the generation to whom he is speaking may readily follow him, for it is not a generation that is distinguished for particular depth of insight or unusual loftiness of sentiment.

He adds: "and it seemed great unto me." What he states in v. 13-15 is a kind of parable: the relatively simple event that he had witnessed conveyed to him a deeper lesson that he wishes to share with his people. Unless with the author we delve more deeply into the matter and discern the deeper meaning of what he discusses we should hardly agree with the author that the matter he found was "great." We should, in fact, be dealing with a few commonplaces such as: a wise man delivered a city, yet wisdom is not esteemed as it ought to be, and its best results can be destroyed by sinners. Various adjectives might describe such a situation but not the term "great." But to see in the discussion a parable of what Israel, "the poor wise man," has in the possession of *wisdom* and to discern the possibilities that lie behind that gift for the nations and for all such as are ready to give ear to that wisdom — that is something that truly merits the term *great* even though for the present Israel's peculiar prerogative is not being appreciated by the nations around it.

The parable itself is this: "There was a small city and but few men within it." Athens under Themistocles can hardly be referred to, for Athens was no "small city." "Few men" refers to the number of those who could bear arms. "There came a great king against it and encircled it and built great bulwarks against it." It is unnecessary at this point to determine whether the Persian monarch is meant, or what particular situation the author may have in mind. For that matter, even if some interpreters suppose that the deliverer of the city was the author himself (*Cox*), nothing is gained for the interpretation by such a view. The situation is clear enough — "a small city" *vs.* "a great king." The "bulwarks" (*metsodhim*) are very likely "siege towers," which were used both to discover the vulnerable parts of the city and also to carry the besiegers up to the city walls and upon them when attacks were to be made.

"Now he found in it a poor wise man." *Umatsa'* had best be translated personally, for the subject of *matsa'* may well be the "great king," of whom it may very correctly be said "he found" even if he never sought, for "finding" is often used in the loose sense of "coming upon" or "encountering" (*KS* 323e). Though it might make very interesting reading to know how "this poor, wise man," a clever Archimedes, as it were, delivered the city, such a feature would not subserve the main purpose of this parable and is, therefore, disposed of very briefly. Scriptural parallels are II Sam. 20, where a wise woman saved Abel of Bethmaacah, and, perhaps, Judg. 9:53. *Galling* creates quite a different situation by translating "who could have delivered the city" instead of "and he delivered the city," yet he offers no reason for his rendering. If his translation were tenable it would have to be reckoned with.

Umillat hu' is a late construction for the earlier *waymallet*. The translation of the rest of the verse: "yet no man remembered the same poor man," is not the best rendering. For it makes the word "remember" point to the future and at once takes up an element that would hardly be the next in the sequence of events, for the deliverer of the city would certainly be the man of the hour for some time after the deliverance. Again, the quick forgetting of the poor wise man is not one of the features that the parable stresses. Therefore *zakhar* is best rendered as a pluperfect, "and no man *had remembered* that poor wise man," that means up till the time when the city was in grave danger. — In *'adham lo'* for *'ish lo'* we again have an example of the later language of the book.

To be perfectly clear as to the *tertium comparationis* of the parable let this be remembered: Only one point is to be made, viz., Israel is at present like unto that man who is *poor* and *wise*. She carries about with her great resources by virtue of her wisdom. She can help others by means of her wisdom, but, unfortunately, she is despised, and men will not take from her what she stands ready to give. This is the summary that v. 16 now makes of the matter.

"Then I said," *we'amarti 'ani,* is one of the formulas that are used for introducing observations or setting forth conclusions that are to be drawn. The conclusion itself is not difficult to arrive at: "strength" is the part of the rulers, the Persians; "wisdom" is the prerogative of Israel; "wisdom" is certainly the greater asset. But just as evident is the present situation that "wisdom is despised," or, what amounts to the same thing, since wisdom is always imparted to others by words, the poor man's "words are not heard," i.e., not listened to with respect in an attempt to learn.

But be that all as it may, for the attentive reader the glorious fact still remained to cheer his heart: Ours is the talent of wisdom. After hearing and understanding the parable, one cannot help but feel that the hero of the episode is the "poor wise man" who is all the more heroic because he is ready to do his part even though men will not honor him as he deserves to be honored.

Some commentators brush aside the thought of a parable and make no effort to refute that idea. The fondness of the Oriental for parabolic discourse alone should lead men to sense that "more is meant than meets the ear."

The two sides of the matter that v. 16 emphasized are to be stressed a bit more fully. First, in v. 17, the advantage of hearing what the wise man has to offer is presented. The word "heard," *nishma'im,* is closely connected with the same word used in the preceding verse and establishes a thought sequence about as follows: "It is true, the wise man's words are not *heard;* but if they are *heard* . . . ." However, a certain mental attitude is requisite for such proper hearing, namely, an inner "quietness," *nachath,* from *nuach, to rest, settle down, repose.* The tension caused by sinful and worldly pursuits, by the engrossment in material ambitions must be eased before wisdom can lodge in the heart.

It is better to interpret thus — all the more so since the word is spoken in a tone of instruction which would naturally teach how hearing is to be done — than to render: "the hearing of the words of the wise as they quietly speak," making *benachath* modify "the wise." For though a more perfect contrast is thus secured—the wise men in repose *vs.* a fool ruler crying out — the accents in the Hebrew are against such a construction, and the Hebrew order, if followed, gives a very harsh rendering: "The word of the wise at rest heard . . . "

We shall readily understand what the contrast involved is if we can determine who "the prince among fools" may be. If the "wise" are Israel, the "prince among fools" is naturally the ruling nation of the time, which, having refused wise counsel, is simply the most prominent among all those who have remained in their folly. Though this ruler may cry out harshly (*BDB ze-'akah = outcry, clamor*) with overbearing authority, and though all men may at that time be submitting to him, "words of the wise" are far to be preferred to his "clamor." The latter is simply to be borne because it must be. The former is rich with all manner of blessings. In the first half of this contrast the plural is used — "the wise men" — because there were many in Israel to whom a measure of this gift had been imparted, and the manifestations of wisdom were rich and manifold. Among the fools all utterances showed their poverty. All were of the same kind. All were characterized by the selfsame folly. In the second half

of the comparison the singular is, therefore, used —
"the ruler."

Williams limits the word "outcry or clamor" unduly
by saying that it is a "cry of pain or an appeal for
help." He then concludes that the *Targum* may be on
the right track when it interprets thus: "The words
of the prayer of the wise (spoken in silence) have
more acceptance before the Lord of the universe than
the cry of a wicked man who rules over fools, who cry
aloud and are not accepted." But the discussion has not
been on the subject of *prayer* or regarding who would
be heard if he prays. — The adjective "better" is implied
in the use of the comparative *min*, cf., *KS* 308c.

The first part of v. 18 continues this line of thought
while the second half amplifies what happens when,
as 16b says, wisdom is despised.

Who has the weapons of war? The conquering nation, Persia. What did the parable prove? That wisdom
is superior to martial equipment. This must be stressed,
for militaristic preparations, e.g., in the case of Xerxes
against Greece, certainly were made on a very grand
scale and could present a very imposing front. Many
might conclude: The advantage certainly lies with "the
weapons of war." Most assuredly not, says the Preacher. "Better is wisdom," is his firm contention, *"better"*
standing first by way of emphasis.

Though the author is ready to maintain his point,
and though he is perfectly clear regarding this issue,
he, nevertheless, does not close his eyes to facts and
with a half-sigh concludes this part of the discussion,
coming back to things as his people must daily find them:
"one sinner destroyeth much good." Here as in 5:10,
17 and 6:6 "good" (*tobhah*) has no moral connotation;
it merely designates "possessions," "goods." He means:
as long as the present maladjustment continues, "a sinner" (*choteh* with seghol—so almost regularly in
Eccles.) like the ruler at the helm in the empire can

destroy much that is good. In making this statement he apparently casts a passing glance at the very evident fact that the rule of monarchs who refuse to accept "wisdom" is always characterized by folly and leads to the overthrow of their kingdom. That is a part of the "much good" that they destroy.

In leaving this chapter we draw attention to the fact that our interpretation of the parable here involved yielded some very tangible and positive comfort to the distressed in Israel. Those interpreters who do not find a parable in this passage move about among shadowy figures and vague counsels that do not yield substantial guidance. *Delitzsch* gives as a heading for 9:13—10:3, "Experiences and Proverbs Touching Wisdom and the Contrasts to It." These verses surely have more to offer than such vague generalities.

CHAPTER X

7. The ultimate readjustment of disturbing discrepancies in God's government (10:1-11)

a) Folly will bear its usual fruit (v. 1-4)

When in concluding the preceding subject the Preacher indicated (v. 18b) that the absence of wisdom on the part of the non-Israelites could be productive of much harm he was already indicating the next line of thought that he proposed to develop. But he fits this line of thought into a connection which can make it particularly instructive for his contemporaries. For the thing that was continually disturbing the people of God was the incongruity between what God had destined them to be as His chosen people and what they outwardly appeared to be in those evil days—a downtrodden, insignificant, abject, and miserable race. The Preacher now shows that a readjustment is to be looked for, but that it shall come in such a way that folly will bear its usual fruit and ultimately destroy itself.

(1) **Deadly flies make the perfumer's ointment to stink and ferment; so a little folly destroys him that is in reputation for wisdom and honor.** (2) **The wise man's mind is toward his right hand, the fool's mind is toward his left.** (3) **And also when the fool walks in the way, his understanding fails him, and he tells all men that he is a fool.** (4) **If the anger of the ruler rises up against you, do not leave your place, for composure checks great sins.**

A number of grammatical difficulties are found in this section. "Deadly flies" is construed with a singular verb. Explanation: in the construct relationship "flies of death" the second term, "death," is the emphatic

one so that it is that noun rather than "flies" that controls the verb (*KS* 349g). Again, "dead flies" is not
a satisfactory rendering of *zebhubhe maweth,* for the
latter expression is to be understood after the analogy
of expressions like "instruments of death" (Ps. 7:13)
and "snares of death" (Ps. 18:5). Therefore "flies of
death" are flies that bring death, e.g., by their excrement or poisonous sting. "Poisonous flies" is a good
rendering. The point is then made still stronger. No
need of having a fly fall into the ointment and perish.
That might well cause putrefaction to set in. A mere
deposit of excrement can corrupt the costly oil. So a
small trace of folly may prove detrimental. See the New
Testament paralled in I Cor. 5:6. The use of the two
verbs "cause to stink" and "cause to ferment" without
a connective is an emphatic way of letting a second
term displace a first one which was not quite strong
enough. To have ointment stink indicates corruption;
to see the bubbles of ferment rise in it is indicative of
total corruption.

Without using a single word to indicate that the
second half of the verse is the application of the figurative thought of the first half, the author, as is occasionally done, sets the figure and the reality side by
side. To insert a "so" as our A.V. does is entirely
proper. To the "deadly flies" corresponds "a little
folly"; both start corruption by a trifling matter. To
the reputable man corresponds the goodly ointment.
The complete deterioration is the ultimate outcome.
This is not expressed in the original but is the emphatic
feature of the thought just because it was the point of
comparison (*tertium comparationis*) and was emphatically expressed by the two colorful verbs "stink" and
"ferment."

There is again more involved in this figurative saying than the platitudinous remark that folly may entirely corrupt the wise. Our exposition of the preceding

chapter showed how a very specific allusion—slightly veiled, it is true, by its figurative form—was being made to existing conditions. That is being done here. The Persian monarchs or the Persian monarchy are the ones who are indicated as being liable to suffer extreme corruption. The inspired writer must have detected the elements that were already at work in the Persian nobles that made them as time went on the most dissolute, effeminate, and incompetent princes—a veritable mass of putrefaction. Still, the early rulers of this monarchy had been men who "were in reputation as a result of wisdom and honor." Such a one was Cyrus. The *wisdom* referred to seems to be an allusion to a greater measure of the fear of God that this Gentile monarch possessed. A praiseworthy moral attitude was the outgrowth of this. The *honor* referred to is the outward reputation enjoyed by such as he was because of their solid achievements. Israel may well regard this word as a prophecy and wait for time to subtantiate it and to vindicate God's attitude toward Israel.

A word about our rendering of the second half of this verse. The King James version is still the best. The A.R.V. makes all depend on the unusual rendering of *yakar* as "weighty." This is, indeed, the meaning of the root in cognate languages, but unfortunately this meaning is never found in Hebrew, as *Taylor Lewis* points out. In Hebrew this word means "precious," "rare," "splendid." In this instance it is masculine, therefore "one that is in reputation." The *min* following is the "*min* causal"; therefore: "renowned *because of* wisdom." This yields a very clear thought and tallies admirably with the comparison that precedes and with the circumstances.

Since we believe that the author is writing coherent discourse and has logical sequence of thought we shall expect the thought of the first verse to remain in the forefront, viz., how low the now esteemed Persian

monarchy shall be brought by its folly, which is already
operative. We have, therefore, not only general observations that contrast folly and wisdom but thoughts
which bear very distinctly upon the historical situation.
The emphasis is, therefore, not chiefly on the "wise
man" and his tendencies. He is brought in only as a
foil to the "fool." The thought, by way of contrast,
runs about as follows: Had the ruling people been wise
they would have turned to the right, for the heart of
wise men is thus inclined; but being fools, they have
directed their attention toward that which is not right.
It will be observed that in the languages of the Scriptures the "right hand" suggests that which is honorable, mighty, associated with the oath, even with God
and His work, so that, as in other languages, "right
hand" becomes synonymous with that which is right,
good, honorable (cf., Luke 1:11). Of necessity, the left
hand becomes associated with that which is evil, per-
verse, sinister, morally repellant (cf., Matt. 25:41). To
such things the inclination of the fool turns. Such being his fundamental bent, Israel need not wonder at
the end he shall meet. It requires no deep foresight to
foretell it.

The term "heart," which we rendered "mind,"
refers to the inner nature of a man, chiefly its rational
powers; it is, therefore, like the German *Verstand*.
Nothing is gained by substituting for the Biblical ide-
ology the heathen conceptions that "right" is synonymous with good luck and "left" with bad luck. Biblical
writers did not believe in the goddess Fortune or good
luck.

In v. 3 the Preacher goes on to show how the tendency just described is becoming more and more apparent. Considered out of its connection, the verse
would present nothing more than a very true observation to the effect that folly betrays itself: if it resides
in a heart, it will not take long till its presence becomes

apparent. But considered as a part of a logical development of thought, the verse apparently stresses the fact that there is abundant evidence of the fool's being a fool, if the wise will but observe. Dropping all allusions and figures, we should state it thus: Persia's folly, which will ultimately prove her downfall, is displaying itself very plainly. We think, by way of explanation, of one foolish Persian quality that may have been in the author's mind as he wrote this: debauchery and all forms of dissolute living were certainly highly developed in Persia at this time as the Book of Esther plainly shows.

That the emphasis of the verse rests on the open display of destructive folly appears from the order of the words, which thrusts "in the way" emphatically forward. "In the way" signifies as much as "publicly" or "abroad"; the opposite is "at home" (Deut. 6:7). The verse might, therefore, be translated thus in order to convey the peculiar emphasis of the thought: "Also, as soon as he goes abroad, the fool's understanding fails him," etc. Because this emphasis is overlooked some commentators offer a peculiar construction of the close of the verse. They have the fool say in respect to every man: "Thou art a fool." This translation, which is grammatically possible, does not adequately present the purpose of the verse. Our translation is, however, equally permissible as *Deane* has shown who points to a similar construction in Ps. 9:20.

To all this a very practical application is attached in the following verse. At the same time a corrective against misapplication of what has just been set forth is given. Some in Israel, despising the ruling nation because it bore the germ of destruction within itself, might make light of the sovereign nation, especially when haughty authorities thought they had just cause for anger against Israel. Therefore v. 4 is added.

Israel's claims of superiority because of God's election, especially if such claims were misrepresented by her foes, might well rouse rulers to anger (*ruach* here means *anger, temper,* BDB). Consider the situations that arose in Ezra's and Nehemiah's time. Israel should in such a case not leave its "place," that is, it should not seek to extricate itself from the position of political subordination, which God has for the present ordained for it. Israel should not rise in rebellion. That would be the leaving of the place which God has assigned. Its attitude should be *marpe', composure, calmness.* No better rendering can be found than the German *Gelassenheit* (KW). The word means as much as *relaxation, keeping calm and unruffled.*

If Israel left its place it would become guilty of "great sins," for this would be a flying in the face of divine providence. The Old Testament as well as the New counsels submission to the "powers that be." Keeping composed "does not permit these great sins to be done." When one considers the history of Israel from this time to the destruction of Jerusalem, the need of this bit of counsel and its wisdom are only too apparent. Much of Israel's misery was occasioned by its rebellious spirit, by its unreadiness to bear the yoke God had suffered it to be burdened with.

Our rendering has kept the meaning of the Hiphil of *nuach,* viz., *tannach* and *yanniach* the same, as nearly as this is possible in English. The German *lassen* would cover both cases better and be more like the Hebrew.

b)　The discrepancy — Israel's humiliation (v. 5-7)

(5) **There is an evil which I have seen under the sun, like unto an oversight which proceeds from the presence of the Ruler. (6) Folly is set in high places while the rich dwell in lowliness. (7) I have**

seen slaves on horseback and princes walking afoot as slaves.

Though folly was going to bring the foolish low, for the present it was the chosen people who were brought low. This situation was so utterly divergent from what it ought to have been, it was so disturbing a discrepancy that it was almost always present to the mind of the people. Nor did it take them long to discern what the Preacher's figurative language meant. As long as the factors under heaven alone were considered—cf. "under the sun" again—there was only one conclusion that could be reached in reference to the matter, and that was, that it was an out-and-out "evil." One could never view the experience from any other aspect as long as higher considerations were ruled out. In fact, one would have to use even stronger terms: the Almighty was guilty of an "oversight" (*sheghaghah*). *Galling* translates the word rather effectively *verfehlte Anordnung,* that is to say, "a misdirected decree." But the Preacher indicates that it only *seems* like an error to such a one-sided view by using the particle *ke* ("as"). He does not charge God with an error; he merely suggests that the first impression lets it appear as an error. We have, therefore, not the so-called *kaph veritatis* here but the *kaph similitudinis.*

Nothing lies nearer, therefore, than to let the "Ruler" be considered to be God Himself. The context makes this interpretation feasible. The second argument in support of this view is the fact that a different word for ruler is used than that used in v. 4, where the earthly ruler is meant (*moshel*). Here we have *shallet,* a late, Aramaic term. In the third place, here we have the definite article, *the* Ruler. Fourth, the Book of Daniel shows that *shallet* may be referred to the Almighty, cf., Dan. 4:14, 22, 29; 5:21. In the face of these sound exegetical arguments it is strange to observe that commentators dismiss the thought that

God is meant without offering a single argument to refute it.

This is the matter that seems to be very disturbing. This verse gives one statement of the case: they that should be low are high, and they that should be high are low. Stronger is the statement of the case, which, instead of saying: The *fool* is set on high, says: *Folly* is elevated, though, of course, the fool is meant. This does not apply to any one person or set of persons but to all those who were strangers to the true fear of God and yet enjoyed pre-eminence of position as was true in regard to all persons of high station in Koheleth's day. They, however, who by birth and training were qualified for positions of great responsibility found themselves abased. The persons referred to are Israelites in so far as their nation achieved her spiritual destiny.

In the figure the term "rich" apparently refers to "persons of ancestral wealth," persons who had been bred so as to qualify for positions of rule. The Israelites were such persons in the realm of true riches. Having true riches, they understood values as others could not understand them. Having a true sense of values, they possessed that judgment which is requisite for administering offices that involve great responsibility. To make their outward position conform to their inward dignity, God had at various times promised material wealth as a favor to be granted to faithful Israel, cf., Deut. 15:4, 6; 28:11. That experience, then, which made the incongruity of position all the more glaring was the fact that "folly" was "set in high places." Observe that the plural, "places," is used because many instances of this sort were to be observed.

Verse 7 brings the second statement of the same case, namely, of the "great evil" that has disturbed the author. In the Orient, even to within comparatively modern times, distinctions such as allowing only per-

sons of some dignity to appear mounted were observed
with great strictness. On the other hand, in the rise
and the fall of monarchies unworthy persons often rose
to eminence, and very excellent characters were unduly
humbled. Though these things were to be observed, such
reverses of fortune were not the issues that had proved
very disturbing to Koheleth. He was rather affected by
those greater reverses that were suffered by the most
princely of nations, Israel, to whom it had been promised that other nations should become her "servants."
These promises were numerous and clear. Not external
superiority had been promised to Israel but true spiritual dominion since Jacob had prophesied that the
"willing obedience of the peoples" should be tendered
to the Messiah (Shiloh), Gen. 49:10. Note besides the
other Scripture passages that clearly convey the same
thought: Exod. 19:6; Deut. 33:29; Isa. 44:5; 45:14;
Deut. 28:13-43; Isa. 61:5, and most particularly, Dan.
7:27, among the prophecies of a later date. If in the
face of all these prophecies Israel had failed to grasp
that hers was an exalted destiny and had not yet understood that God had made other nations to be "servants" in reference to her, Israel would have been extremely obtuse. But knowing this fact as she did, it
would have been very unusual for her not to think of
it in this connection. Besides, other Scripture passages
had definitely applied the term "princess" to Israel
in comparison with other nations, cf., Lam. 1:1: "She
that was a princess among the provinces is become
tributary."

c) **The ultimate failure of great worldly enterprises
through lack of wisdom (v. 8-11)**

(8) **He that digs a pit may fall into it; and he
that breaks down a wall may be bitten by a serpent.
(9) He that quarries stones may be hurt by them;
he that cleaves wood is endangered thereby. (10)**

If the axe is dull, and a man does not sharpen its edge, then he must exert more strength; but wisdom prepares the way for success. (11) If the serpent bites because it is not charmed, then there is no advantage in having a charmer.

The plight of Israel was from every point of view so out of harmony with what she ought to have experienced that the explanation and the instruction given in vv. 1-4 could hardly be deemed adequate, especially since the memory had been painfully refreshed by the statement of this "evil" in vv. 5-7. A new approach is made in these verses, 8-11, and the possible outcome is indicated only mildly. But such a form of argumentation weighs heavily in the balances because of its suggestiveness.

These verses (8-11) are a unit and bear directly upon the historical situation. The diversity of views found among commentators is, therefore, rather surprising. One interpreter says with reference to these verses: "Cautions and consolations, which, because free and open speech was very dangerous under the Persian despotism, he wraps up in obscure maxims capable of double sense—nay, as the commentators have shown, capable of a good many more senses than two— to the true sense of which 'a foolish ruler' was by no means likely to penetrate, even if they fell into his hands" (*Cox*). It is true that caution suggested a slight veiling of the meaning because of Persian despotism. If two and more senses were found in these verses that would be due to the fact that the scope of the passage had not been discerned; consequently two or more meanings could be established, all of which were equally plausible and applicable.

This is the line of thought in summary: the Preacher first shows (v. 8) that all the *destructive* work that the ruling nation of the time was doing might well terminate harmfully for itself; he next shows that all *constructive* efforts might come to a similar end (v. 9) ; he shows lastly that, since folly prevailed, the success that wisdom could have procured will not be secured despite tremendous efforts (v. 10).

Hengstenberg, though he is right in the main, does not notice the neat order of the thoughts. *Delitzsch* has a series of detached gnomes and says that they "treat of distinction between wisdom and folly, that the wise man is everywhere conscious of his danger and guards against it" — not a very deep thought. *Hertzberg*, misled by a pet theory, does not see the obvious line of thought.

First of all, note the suggestive tone of the argument: "may fall," "may be bitten." For we must thus translate the imperfect. It is like the German "der *kann* hineinfallen." For surely nothing is more true than this, that he that diggeth a pit *may* fall into it. Nor is it more than a possibility that he that tears down a wall may be bitten by a serpent. Yet we know that the milder statement of a case is often more persuasive than is a positive, challenging form of statement.

Two forms of destructive labor are being considered. In connections such as these (cf., Ps. 7:15, 16; 57:6) "pits" refer to pits that are used to entrap prey. So the Persians were seeking to capture nation after nation, or better still, since this earlier stage of conquest was past, to ensnare one after another of those who were in any wise opposed to Persian dominion and pretensions. Just as a hunter, after making pits might accidentally step into one of his own, momentarily forgetting where they were located, so might the tyrannical ensnaring of the Persians result in their being entrapped themselves, for tyranny often defeats its own purposes by too great severity. — The word for "pit" (*gumats*) is late and Aramaic.

Another piece of the destructive work referred to is expressed by the words, "he that breaketh down a wall." The reference is to one who has made a conquest and then proceeds utterly to destroy what was conquered. How often conquering nations did this in order to discourage those conquered or to destroy their last stronghold! Such a course on the part of the conquerors is not without danger, for, as out of the crannies of a hedging wall around vineyards (*gadher*) a viper may suddenly strike him that disturbs her as he destroys the wall, so the undue severity of the conqueror may rouse the conquered to a fury of opposition that may prove fatal to the former.

This is, of course, a very correct observation. The conquerors of olden times never did wise constructive work, and their very efforts at killing all opposition frequently stirred opposition and entrapped them even as they hoped to entrap others.

The same is true with regard to the constructive efforts that were attempted (v. 9). When stones are quarried and trees felled, men are engaged in building something new. The contrast with v. 8 is very apparent. Even good, constructive effort in empire building is dangerous because too much unwise destructive effort preceded it. The author, however, deduces the thought of danger from the figure he employs. For it is true enough that to "quarry" stones or any "tearing up" of stones (if we desire to leave *massia'* in its most general sense) involves the danger of being injured by such stones. The suggestion of *Williams* offers another possibility. He refers to the Greek translation of Symmachus, "swinging stones in the air" by ropes and "sheaves," and so advances "the thought of a stone still in the quarry and in the act of being moved from its original site."

It is equally true that woodcutting is a highly dangerous occupation (*yissakhen* apparently means no

more than to be involved in danger, *KW*). Therefore,
looking at the case from the most favorable angle, even
if the reigning power attempts constructive work she
becomes involved in dangers that may prove fatal. It
seems that here the reality transcends in danger what
the figure suggested. There is a relative safety about
the tasks of stonecutting and woodcutting, but surely
empire building is fraught with numerous dangers.
Like a clever debater, the author understates the case,
knowing that the sympathetic listener will catch the
force the more and so will be the more strongly convinced because he will have reasoned out the danger
involved for himself.

Having touched only upon possible developments,
the Preacher plunges deep into the heart of the matter.
What is wrong with all that the powers that be are
doing? At heart it is this: they lack wisdom. And without wisdom, solid, constructive building is impossible.
It will, therefore, not do to be too deeply impressed by
what the Persian monarchy is achieving. She rather
deserves pity because she cannot last.

Verse 10. Commentators differ in regard to the
meaning of this verse. Some regard it as "one of the
most difficult of the book," others as the most difficult
of all. Unusual forms and *hapax legomena* characterize
the verse. We shall be obliged to justify our translation
and interpretation of it.

Let us first dispose of the problems of translation.
We take the Piel *kehah,* not in the sense of "make dull,"
but rather as "be dull." Since no other Piel of the verb
occurs, the Piel has more in common with the Kal than
with the Hiphil. Again, *hu'* indicates a change of subject; it, therefore, refers to him who wields the axe.
Furthermore, *kilkal* in the *Pilpal* — here used imper-
sonally, *KS* 352i — had best be taken as "whetting,"
"to move rapidly to and fro" (*BDB*). The last part of
the verse should be kept as the text reads, leaving the

absolute infinitive, and it makes very acceptable sense as some have rendered it: "But an advantage for giving success is wisdom" (*BDB*), though, perhaps, *KW* with the meaning *zurechtmachen* for *hakhsher* is still nearer the truth. We, therefore, render: "but wisdom prepares the way for success."

In any event, we need not remain absolutely in the dark as to the drift of the thought of the verse. The author apparently wishes to trace this ultimate failure of the ruling power to its ultimate cause. He likens the mode of operation followed by those who rule to working with a dull instrument. Neither are they who use it sharpening it. The logical thing to be done would be to sharpen it. As long as such sharpening is not done, a great amount of strength must be employed, but it will very likely be of little avail.

That is really a very good picture of the activity of the heathen powers. Enough efforts were certainly put forth to achieve success. Witness the elaborate and vast preparations of Xerxes against the Greeks. What was the trouble that such unheard-of preparations still fell short of success? Answer: dull instruments. How is that meant? If there is any sequence of thought in this verse, the closing part of the verse gives the clue to the first part. When it says, "an advantage for giving success is wisdom," it means: what will give a true edge to the purpose and means of the heathen and so make real success possible is *wisdom*. But, unfortunately, they have everything but that. Therefore, though they try very hard, all efforts are bound to result in failure. Folly has blunted all means and made success unattainable. Are the servants riding on horseback (v. 7) still to be looked at with envy? Not when you consider this outcome.

Before this outcome becomes reality, there will be plenty of occasions when this imbecile heathen power will become aware of its actual imbecility and will be

much vexed at that people that it feels is its superior
and must ultimately survive it, i.e., God's people, and
will occasionally vent its spite upon them and make
them suffer. For such experiences, too, there is a wise
course open to the possessors of wisdom, a course
which the Preacher suggests be followed since there
is little else that subjugated Israel can do.

This section, v. 8-11, does not want to be merely
an academic discussion of what Persian tyranny will
ultimately come to. The Preacher is always very practical. He suggests something that Israel might profitably
do in the meantime. He counsels patient endurance.
But there is more that can be done.

This line of thought is suggested the more strongly
by the similarity of the close of v. 10 and of v. 11, a
similarity which translations often overlook. We
might have indicated it by closing v. 10: "an advantage
(*yithron*) for giving success is wisdom"; and v. 11:
"there is no advantage (*yithron*) in the charmer." A
contrast is apparently intended. This fact gives the
best clue to the purpose of v. 11. Verse 10 showed that
wisdom could help; v. 11 shows that there is no profit
in possessing such wisdom if one permits damage to
be done that one could have forestalled by prompt action.

To be more specific: the "serpent" apparently stands
for the wicked who are rulers, for the wicked spiritual
rulers are called "serpents" also by Christ (Matt.
23:33), and wild beasts generally are likened to earthly
kingdoms and their rulers. So the wicked rulers will
bite Israel, bite painfully and with deadly effect, if
that which could serve to put them under a ban, like
the charm upon serpents, is neglected. What does
wisdom suggest as an advantage for rendering futile
the serpent's sting? Apparently *prayer*, earnest supplication made to God for His protection against the
dangerous venom of the vindictive beast. If it seems
rather farfetched to let charming typify prayer, note

that the very word for charming (*lachash*) is used for prayer in Isa. 26:16.

But it is not only prayer in a general way that the Preacher here counsels men to use but the prompt use of prayer as a safeguard against the wicked devices of evil rulers whereby they sting. To be capable of charming a snake but to neglect to use this power because of sloth, and then unfortunately to be bitten — what a pitiful situation! What is the use of the gift in such a case? Just so, to be able to ban and to bind heathen rulers in their spitefulness, and to be able to do this by earnest and believing prayer and to neglect to use the gift — what a pity! So the discussion has run out into an admonition to gird on the armor of prayer.

The unity of purpose of the interpretation that we are offering, especially of vv. 1-11, is its best defence. No other approach develops the unity of the chapter with a comparable measure of success. *Barton* calls the passage "largely interpolated"; *Galling* changes the text to secure certain results but treats the whole passage as consisting of more or less prosy and disconnected pronouncements.

8. A correct estimate of the rulers of the time
(v. 12-20)

a) The vanity of the endeavors of foolish rulers
(v. 12-15)

Here we may again find either "some maxims" (*Deane*) which are rather loosely bound together or a unified discourse — depending upon our approach. The following arguments suggest that our heading is correct in referring the section to the rulers of that time: a) the subject was certainly under consideration in v. 5-7; b) the close of the section, v. 16-20, manifestly treats this subject; c) v. 20 gives the most excellent explanations as to why the references to the rulers of the day could not be made more explicit —

spies reported seditious utterances; d) the unity of the whole chapter is too striking to be called artificial.

Our heading is certainly more to the point than is "Fools and Their Talk" (*Williams*). *Zoeckler* comes nearest to presenting a unified conception with his title for v. 11-20, "Concerning the Advantage of Silence and Persistent Diligence of the Wise Man over against the Garrulity and Slothfulness of the Fool." Yet he admits that he sees no connection between the first and the second half (16-19) of this section. Neither do others. They sometimes construct a bridge which is nothing more than an accidental point of contact between the two. Verse 20 should have convinced interpreters that rulers and government are under consideration.

Practical maxims concerning diligence, silence, and the like have been given with sufficient consideration of all sides of the subject in the Book of Proverbs. It is not the manner of the Scriptures to report more or less idly what has already received sufficiently thorough treatment elsewhere.

(12) **The words of a wise man's mouth are gracious, but the lips of a fool destroy him. (13) The beginning of the words of his mouth is folly, and the end of his talk is mischievous madness. (14) A fool multiplies words; yet man does not know what shall be; and who can tell him what will be after him? (15) The toiling of fools wearies everyone of them because he does not even know how to go to the city.**

Let the subject be borne in mind: The Vanity of the Endeavors of Foolish Rulers. The purpose of this verse will then appear clearly. As v. 13-15 also suggest, it is the fool who is under consideration. The contrast of this verse serves to make the fool's words stand out more clearly as what they actually are. The words coming from the wise man's mouth are also referred to by way of bridging over from the preceding section. There his words of prayer that he should use in supplication before God were considered. Surely, they are gracious words. But how harsh the contrast with that which emanates from the fool's lips! The fool is, as he was in vv. 1-4, primarily the Persian, especially the ruler and magistrate. There were many indications of what folly actually impelled fools, so many, in fact, that the superior wisdom of Israel could foresee that this fool's words (literally, "lips") must ultimately "destroy him" (literally, "swallow him up"). Israel knew of good and wise kings whose utterances had been excellent, life-giving wisdom. The grandiloquent, pompous, vain-glorious, and even blasphemous utterances of Persian kings and nobles could not but produce an inflated notion of what Persians were. Such utterances must ultimately bring about their own undoing. — The verb *tebhalle 'ennu* is feminine singular though the subject is plural; KS explains it as a "singular genetive" because the noun dependent on the subject is singular (349g). GK 145k gives a different explanation.

The Preacher continues the thought in v. 13. If the general force of this word were to be applied here, we should say that it is akin to Prov. 27:22. But since it refers to rulers in their folly it pictures the process of disintegration that worldly folly causes in those who are its exponents. They go from bad to worse. When they begin to speak, that which they utter is foolish; when the conclusion of their utterance is reached, it is no longer merely silly or idle. There is an element of the "evil" (*ra'ah*) in it, which is here rendered "mischievous." It further deserves a harder term than "folly." It is, therefore, called "madness." After the preceding discussion relative to the collapse of the worldly enterprises the reader of a verse such as this cannot help but feel that such growth in folly as is here referred to must end in the destruction of all who are actuated by a "folly" which grows more mad continually.

The picture is rounded out (v. 14) to show more fully the vanity of the endeavors of those who plan magnificent enterprises. For when it is said that "the fool multiplieth words," that does not refer only to his idle and loquacious prating. For the verse at once goes on to show that man cannot know what shall be. These two statements are plainly closely connected. Therefore the many words that the fool makes must be the statement of his plans for the future. Jas. 4:13 is a good case in point: "Come now, ye that say, Today or tomorrow we will go into this city, and spend a year there, and trade and get gain: whereas ye know not what shall be on the morrow." Similar are the enterprising plans of the rich fool, Luke 12:18-20. So the plans for future greatness on the part of these men require the multiplying of words merely to state them all.

A twofold reference is made to man's inability to prognosticate the future. On the one hand, man simply cannot "know what shall be": the knowledge of the future, generally speaking, is closed to him. Or, to take merely a very limited portion of the future, say those things that shall come to pass immediately after we are dead and gone, even they are entirely beyond our ken. That is the meaning of the second statement: "and who can tell him what will be after him?" For "after him" refers to the things after his death. It is like *me' acharaw* in Deut. 29:21. Since no one knows either the immediate future or the future generally speaking, plans for the future, especially grandiose plans of foolish rulers, are bound to be idle chatter, words multiplied.

This interpretation of this verse dates back to *Aben Ezra* and *Rashi*, the latter particularly deserving to be mentioned as quoted by Taylor Lewis: "In his simpleness the fool is full of words, deciding confidently and saying: 'Tomorrow I will do so and so, when he knoweth not what shall be on the morrow' — or when he would undertake a journey for gain." James 4 may refer to this passage. It does give an interpretation of it.

Referring to all these ambitious plans, v. 15 continues the thought by calling them "the toiling of fools." That is all it is. The plans are ambitious enough. What marvelous things Xerxes attempted in order to subdue Greece! — The verb (*teyagge 'ennu*) shows that *'amal* is here construed as a feminine (*KS*249m).

The last clause of the verse gives the reason that his toiling wearies the fool — "because he does not even know how to go to the city." Roads to the various cities were marked and easy to follow. The fool is so deficient in intelligence that he cannot even follow such a road. No wonder that his "toiling" wearies "every one of them!" The fools do not even employ ordinary common sense about everyday tasks. *Barton* cites as a parallel the expression, "He doesn't know enough to come in when it rains." If a man cannot even find his way to the city, what business has he to devise elaborate plans for the future in his boastful attempt to grow greater and greater?

So closes the paragraph. It shows us what little ground for confidence the foolish rulers of the dominant nation of the day had: they planned, but all their plans were futile because these fools could not foretell what course the future would take.

There was, however, another matter that made their future and their success very problematic, and that is to be discussed next: their reprehensible debauchery which caused the speedy downfall of the Persian monarchy and went on with its contagion to poison Greece and Rome, a debauchery that might well have caused a truly wise man of the Preacher's day to venture a pretty certain prophecy as to the end of the nation.

b) Their reprehensible debauchery (v. 16-20)

(16) **Woe to you, O land, whose king is a child, and whose princes feast in the morning!** (17) **Fortunate are you, O land, whose king is noble, and whose princes eat at the proper time, for strength and not for drunkenness.** (18) **Because of great sloth the rafters collapse; and because of lazy hands the house leaks.** (19) **Meals are prepared chiefly for gay times; wine gladdens life; money pays for everything.** (20) **Do not curse the king, not even in your thoughts; and do not curse a rich man, not even in your bedchamber; for a bird of the heavens may carry the sound, and a winged creature may tell something.**

In the preceding section the Persian rulers were described as "fools." Instances of their folly are now given. One is their pitiable immaturity. Though they occupy positions that would seem to require earnest-mindedness and set purpose they are so little aware of their responsibility that they, particularly their king, deserve to be called a "child," *na'ar*. The term has no reference to youthfulness in point of actual age in years; but since moral defects are enumerated throughout this section, mental and moral immaturity is referred to.

The second instance of folly, which is also the chief one in this word of censure, is the manner in which their immaturity primarily shows itself, namely, in debauchery: "the princes feast in the morning." In a list of sins a statement such as this must be an indictment. It cannot refer to a normal breakfast but has in mind a case where eating is made an issue early in the morning. Princes are thought of whose thinking centers in feasting at a time when sober cares of state should be engrossing their entire attention. All sober-minded men who view this situation cannot do otherwise than feel grave concern for a land whose rulers merit the criticism just pronounced. Foreseeing, therefore, the speedy ruin of their land, Koheleth cries out: "Woe unto thee, O land!" Thou shalt soon collapse in utter ruin. Parallel are the words of Isaiah 5:11 and 3:4, 12.

That the emphasis in *na'ar,* "young man," does not lie on youthfulness of years appears, e.g., from II Chron. 13:7, where it is used in reference to Rehoboam, who at the time of his accession had passed his fortieth year, cf., BDB, "with special stress on youthfulness."

Verse 17. How different everything in the land could be if the princes were of the type they ought to be! As far as disposition is concerned, the king should be "noble," literally, "son of nobles," that is to say, descended from them but primarily one who really merits the name. Yet the term seems to refer chiefly to outward station, for the Jews assign to the word "nobles" the meaning "freeborn." The meaning is the same, for the freeborn enjoy advantages of training that ought to make them truly noble. *Williams* points out that the expression *ben chorim* occurs only here but is common in inscriptions in northern Syria, "so that it is to be considered an Aramaism." He also states that it is here used in its "wider sense of a man of good birth." When princes turn to eating, such eating should be done "for strength" (*bighbhurah*), that is, in good appetite and as their strength demands, and not *bashshethi,* "for drunkenness."

Though the Preacher calls a land fortunate whose rulers manifest such princely virtues, we cannot help but detect that the verse must have been written with a sigh. Persia's chief sin is under consideration — debauchery; therefore such stress is laid upon what would oftentimes be considered a very commonplace virtue, temperance in food and drink.

Verse 18. The connection with what princes ought to be and do leads even those interpreters who otherwise find little connection of thought in this section to admit that this verse is to be applied to rulers. It cannot be interpreted otherwise. The two verses preceding indicated what vices mar the lives of the men who are in power. This verse shows how the state suffers in consequence. The state is the building (cf., the German, *Staatsgebaeude*) whose rafters collapse, and whose roof leaks. For as true as it is that a dwelling requires continual attention if it is to remain in good condition and be weather-proof, so the structure of the state requires the continual and strenuous endeavors of those who are entrusted with its government. But what marked the rulers of the land at this time? Not merely sloth but "great sloth"; *'atsaltayim* is a dual form: literally, "double slothfulness," cf., *KS* 257c. There have, perhaps, been few periods in history when affairs of state suffered more gross neglect than they did at this time.

It is also said that there were "lazy hands." Hands that should have been strenuously applied to particular tasks drooped idly at the side. It was as though in the building of the state prominent roof rafters were to be seen slipping out of place without anyone making an effort at readjustment, and roofs that should have been firmly plastered with a thick coating of clay were leaking so badly as to imperil the safety of the entire structure. True, the statement does not specifically assert that these things were happening. The verse simply lays down the principle of what results in specific instances. But this form of statement is in harmony with the tone of caution that marks all criticism of the times as is explained in verse 20. — N.B. *yimmakh* is Niphal imperfect from *makhakh*.

Verse 19. The thought reverts to the debauched manner of life of those degenerate nobles. They are again seen at their luxurious feasts. Shrill gales of silly laughter are to be heard when their convivial feasts are held. In fact, not having worked strenuously, they know no eating for hunger's sake. "For gay times" — placed first by way of emphasis — "they prepare their meal." We inserted "chiefly" to catch the emphasis of the emphatic position of the phrase, being first in the sentence. Others may prepare meals to meet the needs of the body, to these topers, however, the meal is an occasion for a jolly good time.

So, too, the good wine that is swilled is employed only to raise the measure of hilarity — "wine gladdens the life." Whatever other things their heart may desire, they have money in their pockets, and it must procure the other embellishments for the banquets, which were apparently very sumptuous. This is what is meant by "money pays for everything" or "money meets all demands" (*BDB*) literally "answereth all things."

This situation is naturally of such a kind as to provoke any man to cry out against the injustice of it all, to charge the offenders publicly with their misdeeds, and to make public denunciation of them. Yet such a course is not the part of wisdom. The situation would not be improved. The individual who protested would be imperilling his very life in the days when absolute monarchs ruled with the very highest degree of unlimited power. Therefore the caution of v. 20, which at the same time gives us the author's own explanation as to why he has spoken largely in figures and extended parables.

Verse 20. The rendering "curse" may be a bit too strong. *Tekallel* means "speak lightly of." It was not safe to make even a frivolous remark about such unworthy rulers. The author counsels the most extreme caution: do not permit yourself to harbor seditious *thoughts* (*madda 'akha*) about the king. For such thoughts, if they are allowed to sour the mind as they surely will, if they are brooded over, may unexpectedly betray a man into an ill-advised utterance, and his very life will be endangered in consequence.

Parallel is the thought: Not even your bedchamber is a safe place in which to speak lightly of a rich man. These rulers were apparently suspicious and kept spies for the very purpose of ferreting out all who made light of their superiors; and these spies were so numerous that double caution was the part of wisdom. For even as we speak of birds having told us something, so in what sounds like a proverbial expression of his day the Preacher says that incautious remarks will promptly be reported to the authorities that have been criticized, yea, "the winged creature" (*ba'al hakkenaphayim*) anything that is equipped with wings, fly or insect, may "tell something."

The Preacher proves himself a wise man by advising this caution. For to run your head blindly against a wall is not the part of wisdom. Denunciation was utterly futile. He is not a patriot or a man of God who rashly sacrifices his life to the tyranny of debauched rulers.

CHAPTER XI

D. Exhortation to Benevolence and Cheerful Activity (v. 1-8)

As we have observed throughout our study of this book, our author is dealing very directly with live issues of the everyday life of his people. He is no *Stubengelehrter* who theorizes about academic questions. Being a practical man and not a theorizer, he cannot content himself with the solution of problems in the abstract. Life offers concrete problems; life has work to be done. Therefore we find occasional admonitions strewn in here and there. These are again not incidental but deal with very live issues of the author's day, with work, for that matter, which always needs to be done.

Surely, in times such as those that confronted Koheleth men will be tempted particularly to sins of omission. Necessary benevolence, necessary works of charity will often be given short shrift just because the times seem to have crippled men's ability to reach out and to help others. Cheerful, aggressive work that looks to future results may often be unduly curtailed. Recognizing clearly what grave harm may be done, and how many necessary enterprises both in the life of the individual and in that of the church may be seriously crippled, Koheleth sends out a challenging summons: "Do not fall into slothful inactivity; be up and doing; work as vigorously as you might if the times were promising and the outlook hopeful."

(1) **Send forth your bread upon the waters, for you will find it again after many days. (2) Give a portion to seven, and even to eight; for you know**

not what evil shall be upon the earth. (3) If the
clouds be full of rain they will empty themselves
upon the earth; and if a tree fall to the south or to
the north, in the place where the tree falls, there
shall it be. (4) He that watches the wind will not
sow, and he that regards the clouds will not reap.
(5) Even as you do not know what the way of the
wind is, or how bones grow in the womb of a pregnant woman, so also you will not know the work of
God, who makes everything. (6) In the morning
sow your seed and till evening do not let your hand
rest; for you do not know which shall prosper,
whether this or that, or whether both shall be alike
good. (7) Also light is sweet, and it is good for the
eyes to behold the sun. (8) Yea, if a man live many
years, let him rejoice in them all, and let him remember that the days of darkness will be many.
Whatever may come is vanity.

Thus begins the exhortation to benevolence, which
continues to the end of the third verse. "Send forth"
is the only proper translation though *Galling* suggests
that you "cast your bread *into* the water," you may
perchance find it again at a later date.

It is only because the comparison is condensed
somewhat that interpreters have difficulty in getting
the trend of thought. Our cue must be the fact that
verses 1 and 2 are parallel. Each exhorts to benevolence. Verse 2 is the authoritative commentary on v. 1.
Being so sure that men would sense this, the author
abbreviated what, given in detail, would have run
about as follows: "Let the bread of charity go out as
ships do that venture to take their precious cargo over
the face of the waters." That is the equivalent of saying: Do your charity upon a venture; there will,
indeed, be a reward; let the reward encourage you;
but remember that, as vessels must oftentimes be
waited for long before the profit of the venture is re-

ceived, so you may be obliged to wait a good while before the reward of your investment comes back to you; but come back it will. The emphasis lies upon the certainty of reward as well as upon the fact that this certain reward will not be received at once: patient waiting is the right course to follow in this matter.

Since so much of the thought material of the book is taken from the days of Solomon, we shall do best to let the verse contain an allusion to the ventures of Solomon that were made by the fleet that sailed every three years from Eziongeber (cf., I Kings 10:22) and regularly came back, "bringing gold, and silver, ivory, and apes, and peacocks." A parallel thought is found in Prov. 31:14, where the worthy woman is likened unto "the merchant ships; she bringeth bread from afar." This comparison is more natural than is that which some interpreters find here, namely, the practice of the Egyptians of venturing out in boats before the waters had receded from their lands and sowing their seed broadcast upon the waters. It is a question whether an allusion to Egyptian customs lies as near in thought as does one to Solomon's time. Besides, we have no guaranty that the Israelites of this time were sufficiently familiar with Egyptian methods of agriculture to allow for a reference to them. Neither will it do to take the figure "from the corn trade of a seaport," a thing Israel never indulged in, and draw the conclusion that the verse means: "Seek thy support in the way of bold, confident adventure" (*Delitzsch*). That idea smacks too much of self-confidence whereas this book, like all other Biblical books, inculcates the principle of firm dependence upon divine blessing for ultimate success.

How ready men are to reduce their much-needed charity and benevolence in evil times is only too well known, and the propriety of this exhortation is immediately apparent. Less apparent is the author's purpose in stressing the motive that he does: "thou shalt find it again after many days." Some readers might take exception to the fact that this is an appeal to an apparently selfish motive. However, though motives are not always entirely altruistic they are, therefore, not necessarily evil. They can be classed as motives that lie on a lower plane. *Alleman* suggests that the advice, "cast thy bread upon the waters," "is not charity for selfish ends, but charity bestowed in confidence that there is a sure order in the world and a *God who doeth* (worketh) *all.*" If a man sees evil days coming and takes steps to provide for his well-being during these evil days, he is not guilty of wrong-doing. He has, as a matter of fact, done wisely. Such a motive can have a strong appeal. There may be higher motives. They, too, receive due emphasis on the pages of Holy Writ, but here the appeal is virtually equivalent to the thought: if you would curtail your charitable gift, for your *own sakes* do not; you cannot afford it at the present time.

Similar summons to do good are found elsewhere in the Scriptures with the promise of reward appended. Quite parallel are the following: Ps. 41:1, 2; Prov. 19: 17; I Tim. 6:18, 19; Luke 6:38; 16:9; Gal. 6:9. — The verb "find" has the meaning "recover," *Zoeckler*: *wiederfinden.*

The thought of the preceding verse is repeated and unfolded in v. 2. As is often done in the Scriptures and in all speech, classical and vernacular, the case is first stated in a figure to challenge attention — "Cast thy bread upon the waters," then a plain, literal statement is given to avoid all possibility of mis-understanding — "Give a portion." The expression, "to seven, yea, even to eight," is one that is patterned after several similar ones in the Hebrew and in other languages to express an indefinitely large number without asking one to be exact in his count. The thought is this: Let your gift be given to a good number of the needy, say seven, but do not stop short with that; if another person is found to be in need, try to help him, too, cf., e.g., Mic. 5:5. So also *Barton:* "It means here, Do not be punctilious about the exact number; incline to more rather than to less."

In like manner the motive that is stressed to induce men to engage in deeds of charity is very much akin to that found in the first verse: "thou knowest not what evil shall be upon the earth." If evil is going to befall, and you yourself shall no doubt share in it, be all the more zealous, as long as opportunity presents itself, to make provision against it by well-doing. For when you become involved in evil and stand in need of aid, your good deeds shall be requited unto you as a broader interpretation of v. 1 teaches. Here, too, it might be objected that the motive suggested is not entirely altruistic. But it does not need to be, for we are commanded only to love our neighbor as ourself, and proper care of self is not evil. This, which is the best kind of preparation for evil days inasmuch as it has *divine* promise of recompense and relief, is rather to be regarded as among the finest and most practical bits of counsel that the book has to offer.

Some commentators interpret v. 1 as referring to bold and energetic adventure that is undertaken by man for his own support. To harmonize v. 2 with this interpretation and to gain a sequence of thought, "give a portion unto seven" is said to mean, "divide your portion into seven parts," that is to say, the Preacher recommends "a division of property . . . that our all may not be lost at once." This interpretation gives an unusual meaning to the verb "give" (*nathan*) and cannot be supported by a reference to Josh. 18:5, where an entirely different verb is used, and where the plural "portions" is found. Besides, such counsel would scarcely be divinely inspired. It is a piece of shrewdness which may be practicable on certain occasions. So also *Hertz-berg* has two adversative statements which he gains by an unusual rendering of *ki*, but the *ki adversative* follows only negatives in a preceding clause (cf., BDB).

Zoeckler has the following title for 11:1 — 12:7: "The only True Way unto Happiness in this Life and in that to Come Consists in Benevolence, Fidelity in One's Calling, etc." He has evidently inserted a bit of his own thought into this formulation. The idea that this section offers "the only true way unto happiness" is a misunderstanding of the author's purpose. He simply counsels men for their own good to practice charity freely in evil days, also, as we shall see presently, to engage in cheerful activity by way of their calling.

The somewhat indirect reference to "evil that shall be upon the earth" is, however, too vague to satisfy and specific enough to lead his readers to expect a bit more of an explanation, therefore the Preacher touches upon this thought with just sufficient fulness to set the mind at ease as to what he meant.

The fathers found in verse 3 a statement of the irrevocable nature of the future state of man — a meaning that the verse might have, especially its second half, if it appeared in a different connection. Others find here a statement of a law of nature: certain results must of necessity follow if certain preliminary conditions are met. This thought is then applied in various ways. Since "the evil that shall be upon the earth" has just been referred to, it is best to regard this verse as a further reference to this evil. Since "clouds" are elsewhere in the Scriptures referred to as visible tokens of God's coming to judgment, cf., Isa. 19:1, Ps. 97:2; 18:11; Rev. 1:7, we have ample ground for here, too, thinking of God's judgments as we find these judgments to be the "evil" referred to at the close of the preceding verse. Equally true is the observation of

Hengstenberg that rain is referred to in the Scriptures in connection with God's judgments upon earth, cf., Isa. 4:6; Matt. 7:24; Eccles. 12:2.

The verse begins with this thought: When the time is ripe for God's judgment, that judgment empties itself as does a rain cloud that has come to the point of supersaturation of the atmosphere. This thought is made still plainer by a repetition which tells with almost unmistakable clearness just what judgment it is that should be likened to the bursting of a rain cloud. The thought sequence that lies in the picture is that of a storm which results in the definite overthrow of a mighty tree in the forest. So God's judgment, sweeping down upon the earth when the time is ripe, uproots a "tree." That tree may well be Israel's proud oppressor, Persia. To refer to monarchs and empires as "trees" is a common practice among the prophets and is most clearly exemplified in Daniel (see Dan. 4:20); cf. also, Isa. 10:18ff., and the reference to Assyria's mighty men in Ezek. 31:3ff.

The emphasis in the comparison is the thought that this tree, once overthrown, will remain overthrown. This nation can stage no comeback. That is the "evil" referred to in v. 2. This overthrow will, however, cause so mighty a convulsion among the nations, which are the powers that are tributary to Persia, that world-wide trouble will be growing out of it. Israel will suffer with the rest when thrones totter, conquests take place, and new governments are established. Therefore, let her get ready. Those interpreters who refer the clause "if wood falls" to divination (rhabdomancy) confuse the issue. — *Yehu* is a future from *hawah*, a contracted form. An *aleph* has been added to distinguish it from the contracted form of *Yahweh* (*Delitzsch*), or the *aleph* is added from the corresponding Aramaic verb (*KW*).

Since 9:11 we have been repeatedly referring to issues to which the text could be said to refer only if a deeper meaning, a kind of allegory, were implied. This type of interpretation is termed "allegorizing" by its opponents. Instances of such allegorizing are all those cases in which Israel was indicated behind the appellation such as "poor wise man" (9:15, 16), "princess" (10:7), and Persia behind terms such as "the swift," "the strong" (9:11), "servants" (10:7), "fool" (10:14), "tree" (11:3).

Though this type of interpretation is abhorred by many, let it be remembered that practically all expositors freely admit that there is an allegory when they come to 12:3-6. There all of them allegorize. Koheleth has without a doubt penned an allegory in chapter 12. Why should a similar one in 9:11-11:3 be unreasonable? Let it also be remembered that such an approach yields a harmonious interpretation that removes many of the difficulties of this section. Lastly, since all evidence points to the Persian period as the time of the composition of the book, why should not the references to the rulers (which references abound in this section) be distinctly designated as applying to the Persians?

Parallel with the exhortation to benevolence goes that to *cheerful activity* by way of one's calling. Koheleth is induced to draw men to this because days of adversity and suffering often beget a spirit of indifference to worthy enterprise or daily duties. Many disappointments kill initiative. For fear of another failure new projects are not even attempted. Such an attitude is not good; it is an evil to be overcome. Therefore we have the exhortation that follows in vv. 4-6.

This group of verses comes to a climax in v. 6 with an exhortation to sow. Verses 4 and 5 are preparatory. It, therefore, behooves us to establish in a preliminary way what "sowing" implies, for since it is spoken of all men alike it cannot be limited to the husbandman on the farm. It is not quite enough to say that sowing is here activity (*Hengstenberg*), nor to expand the definition thus: "sowing is an emblem of all activity in one's pursuit" (*Delitzsch*). For this term is taken from agricultural life and designates that portion of the farmer's work which looks to the future, expresses his hope of harvest, and expects to provide food and sustenance for days to come. Though all other work is auxiliary to this, this form of activity is mentioned because it stresses the hopeful outlook toward the future or, more particularly, the harvest. We, therefore, contend that it aims to describe all cheerful and hopeful activity by way of one's calling that has about it the air of hopeful enterprise, and so must include also all works of benevolence, as *Luther* also says: this pertains "in general to all human activity, but especially to charity." So these three verses glance back to the first three of the chapter but widen their purpose so as to include all work that looks to future results.

In regard to every kind of work that might be done with a look to the future men might grow pessimistic and lose all spirit of enterprise and do only what must be done to maintain life and to eke out a meagre existence. Any enterprise of greater moment that might seem in danger of miscarrying because of the perils and the uncertainties of the times is liable to be slighted because the dangers of failure seem so prominent. Reasonable caution with reference to undertakings on a major scale is naturally dictated by common sense. If men are going to be only cautious and undertake nothing they will be like unto the farmer that is about to sow but observes a strong wind that might blow away some of his seed and so puts off the sowing until a time when the wind is entirely suitable. Such a one may never get his sowing done.

He is also like unto one who, because there is no promise of an absolutely clear day or days for harvesting, watches the clouds until they seem to promise a succession of such days as he desires. Such a one may never harvest if he wants the surest guaranties of a successful outcome. So in all works of our calling, of charity, of the church, if the prospect is not entirely favorable, the waiting for perfect conditions will result in failure to get the necessary tasks done. A very suitable suggestion from every point of view!

It must be explained that our uncertainty in regard to how things will eventually turn out lies in the very nature of the case. When we behold that it is quite natural for us not to be able to foresee or understand even very common things that usually take care of themselves, we shall observe that the higher things will also turn out rightly under God's direction, even apart from our failure fully to apprehend them. Our part consists in merely doing our duty and letting God take care of the outcome.

One such simple phenomenon is the "way of the wind," that is, both "whence it cometh and whither it goeth" (John 3:8). No man can with any degree of certainty determine this simple occurrence although we have these winds every day. Despite all our ignorance of the matter the winds go their course as they are directed by the Higher Hand. So the trends and the currents of events go their way and are well directed by the Higher Power in spite of our ignorance.

In like manner we shall never be able to know how the "bones" appear or "grow in the womb of a pregnant woman." Parallels are Ps. 139:15; Job 10:11. Yet despite all our ignorance of the matter which, in spite of all tremendous advances in medical science, is perhaps almost as great and complete now as it was then, the foetus develops; bones are formed; children are born; the race perpetuates itself. Our ignorance does not prevent needful things from transpiring.

Our author's conclusion is a little more to the point when he says: "so also you will not know the work of God who doeth all." There are many works and results that God brings to pass even out of our humble efforts, even when the odds seemed strongly against success. For God still "doeth all" as and when He will. He is equally at work in evil and unpromising days. Our inability to see how certain tasks of ours can succeed should not deter us unduly in evil times. Our business, which we should faithfully perform, is according to v. 6: "Sow your seed," do that task which falls to your lot, that task which looks hopefully to a future yield of success under God's blessing.

Before examining the sixth verse it is necessary to examine some grammatical features of v. 5 that claim attention. The change in tense, so to say: "even as you *do not know* . . . so also *you will not know*," *lo'yodhea'* (participle) to *tedha'* (imperfect), roughly paraphrased, expresses this thought: as you are not now one who knows so in the future you will never find out —a nicety of the use of Hebrew tenses that it is almost impossible to reproduce in an English rendering.

Furthermore, *ruach* should here be rendered "wind" and not "spirit" (A.V.), for two reasons: a) in the preceding verse *ruach* without a doubt means "wind," and nothing indicates a shift of meaning in regard to this word; b) Jesus apparently cites this verse in John 3:8 and without a doubt refers to the wind in His citation.

We return to the exhortation, for the sake of which the framework of v. 4 and 5 was constructed. It exhorts to ceaseless and untiring activity of the kind defined above. It is really a stronger statement of the case than our versions give, for after "in the morning" the

Hebrew does not have as a correlative, *"in* the evening," but *"till* the evening" (*la'erebh*). Whereas the customary rendering says only: Be busy in the morning and in the evening, the Hebrew says: "Be busy early in the morning, and unto the evening let your hand keep at is task," or, negatively, "Do not let your hand rest." That means *unremitting activity.*

The reason assigned is an application of the principles which were emphasized in vv. 4 and 5. We cannot tell which of any two tasks that we take in hand shall succeed, "whether this or that." Let both be done. It may come to pass, under the providence of God, that "both shall be alike good." With such prospects and the certainty that God watches over all worth-while enterprises and brings to pass what deserves to succeed, the bane and the curse of hopelessness are lifted. The Preacher surely knows how to spur men on to honest efforts in days of discouragement.

He is going to carry his thought a bit farther and speak heartening words to those of his contemporaries who had gotten to the point where they were so weighed down by the hopelessness of the situation as to think that life was no longer worth living. In view of the point just established the author offers the very challenging affirmation: Even in these times it is a mighty fine thing to be alive.

Verse 7. The conjunction *û* before "sweet" merely marks a transition as it does in 3:16 and 12:9. To the preceding thoughts "also" these of v. 7 and 8 should be added. The emphasis of v. 7, which is secured by placing *mathok,* "sweet," first, shows that the author is not speaking about "light" but about the fact that light is *"sweet."* By a kind of metonymy which substitutes effect for cause light here designates life. For to have life enables a man to see the light. Inability to see the light is a token of death. By another figure, a metaphor, life is likened to a light that burns. That is the case in those instances where the expression "light of life" is used; cf., Ps. 56:13; Job 33:30; Ps. 36:9, 10. However, the former point of view is the one stressed in our passage as it is also in Job 3:16, 20 and Ps. 49: 19 (cf., *Buhl*). Parallel is the expression, "to behold the sun"; and that is said to be a "pleasant" thing. The author is really drawing a conclusion from his preceding contentions in this chapter. If a man has definite purposes in life — here "sowing" — life at once becomes a thing worth living for, "sweet" and "pleasant." All who have followed his substantial exhortation must agree with him.

Not only with the idea of living as such does the Preacher concern himself but with the prospect of living to a ripe old age. That, too, in the face of the evil of the day, and because "the light is sweet," should be regarded as a good gift of God, and in it a man should "rejoice." The *hortative* future is used because a man is really not so ready to adopt this attitude; but he *should*, and he is, therefore, admonished to make it his own. Furthermore, looking at life and at life's work as such, much as Jesus did when He said: He must work while it is day, "the night cometh when no man can work," the Preacher asks his hearers to remember that death comes, i.e., "the days of darkness," and these days "shall be many." As far as this life is concerned, it will then be impossible to taste of the days that are sweet and pleasant; or again, as far as this life is concerned, "all that cometh is vanity," for life's candle is snuffed out.

The author's point of view is not wrong, for he speaks of life as life and of the impossibility of sharing in it after it is terminated, and he surely does believe in a cheerful enjoyment of it. Yet it must be said that the fulness of the New Testament revelation has not yet dawned upon him. Otherwise he would have been more ready not to drop the subject at this point but to emphasize "the glory that shall be revealed in us," and what a desirable thing it is to "depart and be with Christ." But even so he has made a strong case against despair, complaint, bitterness, and disgust with life.

A few grammatical items: *ki 'im* are not to be combined as they so often are and then equal "but." They are two separate words as they are in Exod. 8:17. *Ki* is, however, best rendered "yea." "For" establishes a connection that it would otherwise be impossible to trace. *Shebba'* refers to the future, not to the past, as Luther renders it, cf., the same participle with a distinctly future meaning in Isa. 41:22. Correct is LXX: πᾶν τὸ ἐρχόμενον. The *ki* before *harbeh* is the *quod explicative*, "*that* they shall be many," rather than "because."

E. An Exhortation to Youth to Enjoy the Days of Youth (11:9-12:7)

The whole book has rhetorical finish: there is a more or less formal introduction; there is a body; we are here drawing near to the conclusion. Some interpreters have the conclusion begin at this point. We prefer to regard this section as a part of the body of the book, but we must notice that it serves the purpose of being at least a conclusion of the body.

There is a marked contrast between the introduction and this passage, which, in the opinion of some, begins the conclusion. The former is the quintessence of a soberness, which it seeks to inculcate by demonstrating the true vanity of all things; the latter is the strongest admonition to cultivate a spirit of true joyfulness. The two together are only the two sides of life as it is: it has its sober features; it is not to be devoid of joy. Between these two lie such special problems as warranted and necessitated the writing of this very useful book.

This exhortation is addressed to youth, not as though the whole book had been written primarily for the young people of the day, but because, if a true spirit of cheerfulness is to be cultivated, youth is the most suitable time for that. Men ought to begin to fear God in their youth, for the cultivation of this virtue requires time. Those who have passed the days of youth and find that this exhortation is addressed to this particular class can then be made to feel all the more acutely how much it behooves them to make more strenuous attempts to cultivate what they have been rather late beginning. Should one, however, have passed so far into the period of old age, which is here so graphically described, as to be unable to practice cheerfulness he could, nevertheless, give heed to that which is the "end of the matter" — the fear of God — and so gain a source of joy which only those know who truly fear God.

In the section 11:9-12:1a we have the exhortation as such.

(9) Rejoice, O young man, in your youth, and let your heart be glad while you are young, and do what your heart desires and what pleases your eyes; but know that for all these things God will bring you into judgment. (10) Put away vexation from your heart and remove evil from your flesh, for youth and the prime of life are vanity. (12:1) And remember your Creator while you are young.

We must first notice how these verses are related to the preceding statements. In v. 8 there was a statement that bade men to rejoice. But in the connection in which it appears it rather bade a man to take joy in necessary and proper activity. The thought now broadens out to the point where it bids a man in a general way to cultivate the spirit of true cheerfulness.

These three verses form a rather compact unit. The first (9) suggests rejoicing in all good things that

may give the heart true cheer. The second (10) bids
a man to put aside all those things that might interfere
with such legitimate joy. The third (12:1a) provides
the deep root which alone can make such true joy
possible, for without having gone to the Creator, the
source of life and joy, the best that man can arrive at
is a shallow optimism, a kind of Pollyanna happiness,
which tries to appear cheerful under all circumstances.
But where there is a definite, positive remembrance of
God, there the foundation of true joy is laid. This last
thought, stated more negatively, is prepared for by
v. 9 ("and know, etc.").

When this admonition to rejoice is thus regarded
as a unit it corrects all such misunderstanding as is,
e.g., expressed in Codex B of the Septuagint, which
regarded the word as dangerous which says: "walk in
the ways of thy heart," etc., and inserted a negative μή.
The *Targum* paraphrases negatively for fear of conflicting with the good word found in Num. 15:39 (where
the connection is entirely different) which says: "Be
prudent with reference to the sight of thine eyes."

The unified thought of the three verses is, therefore, the equivalent of an injunction which bids men
to cultivate a true joy that is tempered by the fear of
God. There can be nothing questionable about such an
injunction. To convey the idea that the thoughts of
these verses are a unified whole, several conjunctive
"and's" combine them; though the "and" before
"know" may be rendered by an adversative "but."
The "and" in 12:1, "*and* remember," should not be
rendered "now" — a translation which has induced
many persons to put undue stress upon the "now." It
should not be translated "also" (A.R.V.) but just
"and," to show how the component parts of this section
belong together.

To get the true import of the admonition "rejoice
in your youth," it should be remembered that it means:

"rejoice during your youth." For the author does not want young men to rejoice *that* they are young but rather to begin cultivating the virtue of joy *while* they are young. Otherwise he would be encouraging them to a practice that could last only as long as fleeting youth lasts. That the interpretation we suggest is correct is shown by the expression, which is entirely parallel, "Let your heart be glad while you are young." This last statement bids a man to let this practice be one that has its seat in the very center of his being, "the heart." The thing to be cultivated is not a shallow surface optimism but a deep heart joy. Therefore we have *Beth temporis* rather than *Beth sphaerae*.

This type of joy is to be explained so that men may recognize what a latitude of movement it offers. Therefore, "walk in the ways of thy heart" or as we have translated above: "Do what your heart desires." Remembering what we said above, we interpret this to mean: Let the heart that is rooted in the fear of God walk in whatever ways it may desire, for it will assuredly desire what is right. But the form of the statement emphasizes, not the restrictions involved, but the broad areas which are thrown open for our enjoyment. The sentiment of the next clause manifests the same spirit: "walk in the sight of thine eyes," which we translated above: "do what pleases your eyes," i.e., in whatever your eyes take pleasure in beholding as desirable. The Hebrew really makes this a broader statement than our version can give, for it has the plural "sights of thine eyes." — The *Keri* is unnecessary.

The "know thou" that follows is certainly to be more than a dead awareness. It must mean a knowledge that possesses and controls the heart. It implies that a man must actually reckon with this fact. Besides, there was no note of irony in the preceding part of the verse, which is then roughly brushed aside by this word.

The command implies simply: Do all your enjoying in such a way that you regulate it by the thought of the last judgment. For that the *last* judgment is referred to and not such visitations as may come when a man is made to bear the effects of his own dissolute living already in this life is distinctly indicated by the article: "God will bring you into *the* judgment" (*bammishpat*); not into various judgments, but into the one great judgment.

This thought is rejected by criticism because it definitely contains higher values, which are said to be wanting in the book. It is, therefore, called an addition by a glossator. They who have noted that the book is pitched on the usual high level of revealed truth find thoughts like these in harmony with the whole tenor of the work.

The negative side of the matter is stated in v. 10. The most noxious worm that gnaws at the root of joy in evil times is "vexation," "fretfulness" (*ka'as*) over existing circumstances. You may have every reason to believe that things should go better, especially with the people of God. The disparity between what they are and what they ought to be is so great that the disposition of many a man is soured. The state of fretfulness, unpleasant as it may seem to others, appeals to him as a virtue. The Preacher has the right view of things. He says: "Put away vexation from your heart," for he recognizes that it has fastened itself like a cancer upon the very heart of man. He knows, besides, that the cultivation of such a frame of mind is of absolutely no use. Therefore, away with it! Besides, there may be bodily ills and discomforts (*ra'ah* = "evil") that could be removed by affording the body certain almost necessary comforts. To make yourself suffer bodily ills because you are out of sorts with the times and like to appear as a sort of martyr is also an attitude that has nothing to recommend it. Therefore "remove" (*ha 'abher* = 'make to pass over') evil from your flesh."

The argument for both these courses is a purely practical one: "youth and the prime of life are vanity," which is as much as to say: The freshness of youth with its unimpaired vigor of the body, which makes joy taste all the sweeter, is but of short duration. When bodily decay sets in, enjoyment is difficult. This accounts for the peculiar synonym of youth, "days of black hair," which we rendered, "the prime of life." *Shacharuth* is often rendered "the dawn of life" (A.R.V.). There are, however, two reasons for the literal rendering "days of black hair," though there are two like stems, from either of which this word might be derived. The first reason is that the Jews, who were good perpetuators of tradition in days of old, preferred the *shachar* which means "to be black." The second is that "dawn of life" would be a period that lies prior to the time involved in the exhortation. For those addressed are beyond their "dawn of life," i.e., infancy and childhood, and the fact that these are vanity, therefore, has no bearing upon the case as far as they are concerned.

CHAPTER XII

12:1a gives the absolutely essential foundation for true joy: "And remember your Creator while you are young." To "remember" certainly implies more than to recall that there is a Creator. It surely means to let that remembrance shape conduct, for He is to be remembered as "Creator." As such, being the Author of our being, He has complete and absolute claims upon us. These we should acknowledge by our surrender to Him. But there is no time when this can be done to better advantage than "while you are young." Then self-surrender has not become difficult as a result of evil ways that have become habitual. The heart is less calloused to holy things. Besides, there is something mean about giving the Creator the remnants of life after its youth has been wasted upon the creature.

No man seems to have caught quite as well as did Luther the propriety of bidding youth be joyful, for over against the monastic tendencies of his day he writes in reference to this verse: to attempt to forbid joy to the youth "is nothing other than to make young folks to be dead logs and (as that most monkish of monks, Anselm, said) to try to plant a tree in a small flower pot . . . . There is nothing more dangerous for youth than loneliness. . . . Youth needs joy just as much as it needs to eat and to drink."

Bore'ekha is the plural form *bore'im* plus a suffix and means literally "Creators," a plural form that is like the plurals that are derived after the analogy of *'elohim* in Josh. 24:10 and Prov. 9:10, where *kedhoshim* is used.

The more extreme criticism does not approve of the reference to the Creator here, being of the opinion that neither the thought nor the expression fit into the context (e.g., *Galling*). One might expect such a view as far as the critical approach is concerned. Since it is of the opinion that the entire book moves on a low level of thought, every touch of higher values must of necessity be deleted. By substituting *bor* for *bore'* ("pit" for "Creator") criticism reaches a new low, for *bor* is supposed to be a reference to one's wife in clumsy allusion to Prov. 5:15.

A Highly Poetic Picture of the Debilities of Old Age (1b-5)

(1) . . . before the evil days come, and the years draw near when you shall say: There is no pleasure in them for me. (2) Before the sun grows dark, and the light of the moon and the stars; and the clouds return after the rain. (3) At the time when the guardians of the house tremble, and the strong men are bowed; and the grinding-women cease because they are few, and they that look out of the window are darkened. (4) And the doors leading out into the streets are shut; in that the sound of the grinding is low; and one rises when the voice of the bird is heard, and all tones are indistinct. (5) Also one is afraid of that which is high, and the road has its terrors; and the almond tree blossoms; and the locust drags himself along as a burden; and desire fails; because man is going to his eternal home, and the mourners walk about in the street.

This section shows the manner of things men have to suffer after youth is past. The thought is apparently that, because of his multifarious infirmities, man will then be so burdened as to have many difficulties remembering his Creator. He will have too much to do with his own weaknesses.

The author's description presents many pictures. Just because we might have expected less picturesque terms is no reason for offering the criticism that the colors are laid on too heavily, which is the substance of *Zoeckler's* criticism when he calls these pictures *schwuelstig,* "bombastic" or "overdrawn." The Preacher is driving his point home with emphasis. After having treated this point with Bible classes, I have observed that persons who had been unfamiliar with the passage remembered it for a long while thereafter. So also by its colorful and artistic detail the sketch impinges itself upon the consciousness of youth, who really have not taken such serious account of the infirmities of age as they should. In other words, the author does not, through inadvertency, lose himself in a welter of detail and so give disproportionate treatment to a minor point. He shows a proof of his rare skill in this that he knows how to make careless youth reflect upon what they usually overlook until it has come upon them. Besides, the highly poetic pictures challenge attention, and their enigmatic form is not so difficult of solution as to discourage investigation but is sufficiently skillful and artistic to make a man desirous of arriving at an interpretation.

The exposition of this section found in many commentaries is not very satisfactory. Some interpreters seem to have been intent upon displaying their ingenuity rather than upon ascertaining the author's thought. The caution which should always be employed in expounding figures and parables so as not to pass beyond the thought intended is especially necessary in connection with this passage. *Hertzberg* feels constrained to remark in connection with 5a that it "has given occasion to the wildest gambols of fanciful interpretation" (*den tollsten Bockspruengen der Auslegung*). We shall make but sparing reference to the vast array of possible and impossible interpretations that commentaries have to offer in this connection.

One very valuable thought to be borne in mind in reference to the verses 1b-5 is this: this description of the debilities of old age, without a doubt, proceeds on *general* terms to the end of v. 2; then begin the specific metaphors that unfold the substance of 1b, 2; these specific figures continue till the causal clause of v. 5 is reached, "because man, etc." At that point the figurative element is momentarily abandoned; the figures of vv. 6, 7, which give a poetic picture of death, again speak in general terms. It is especially this general character of v. 2 that has been overlooked. *Gerhard* felt the truth when he said in his *Loci* (VIII, 26, p47ff) in reference to this verse: "In this verse the unpleasant things and burdens of old age are described in a general way (γενικῶς) which in the following verses are to be explained more particularly (εἰδικῶς)."

"Evil days" are, of course, times of affliction. Years of which men say: "There is no pleasure in them for me" are, as the following words indicate, those when age with its disabilities has extracted all pleasure they might have afforded. Not without importance is the distinction between "days" and "years." Shorter periods come, during which specific afflictions are dominant — "evil *days*." Longer periods are encountered, which are devoid of the usual enjoyments — *"years* in which we take no pleasure." — The somewhat circumstantial conjunction *'ad 'asher lo'*, "until that not" = *before*.

The fact that this conjunction which introduces the very *general* description of old age (v. 1) introduces also v. 2 should alone be a sufficiently clear indication that this verse continues the *general* tone. The reappearance of the conjunction in v. 6, in our opinion, indicates the same general tone.

In the Scriptures "light" is quite generally a symbol of joy and, when it is sent by God, a token of favor. Just as clearly the Scriptures let darkness be synonymous with judgment and punishment, cf., Joel 3:4; 2:

10; Amos 8:9; Isa. 13:10; 5:3; Jer. 4:33; Ezek. 32:7; Rev. 6:12. Parallel is the thought that clouds are "images of trouble," cf., Ezek. 13:11-13; 38:22. The "sun," the most powerful giver of light, and "light," the most general term for this element, and "moon," the sun's nearest rival, and "the stars," the bearers of the faintest light — all these are used to designate every kind and class of joy, great and small. All joys are dimmed very materially in old age. In fact, one trouble is replaced by another even as in the rainy season the cessation of one "shower" (*geshem*) marks the beginning of the next.

Since the Scriptural usage of these terms suggests this interpretation, and since the thoughts that we have just discovered in this verse are very tangible, clear, and only too true to life, it seems rather useless to seek for deeper meanings in this verse. We shall mention but one of the attempts to go beyond what is intended by the writer and have selected as an example the most sober interpretation of all that have been offered. *Delitzsch* has the sun = the spirit of man; light = clear thought; the moon = the soul; stars = the five senses. This interpretation is strikingly clever. The Bible student is, however, at once moved to ask: Is there Scripture ground in the passage or elsewhere for such an interpretation? Careful examination will show that *clear* Scripture passages cannot be found for even the first point, viz., that the sun = the spirit of man. Consequently he must conclude that such an interpretation is unacceptable. In fact, *Delitzsch* himself voices uncertainty in regard to his view when he says: "However one may judge of the figurative language of v. 2, v. 3 *begins* the allegorical description of hoary old age after its individual bodily symptoms."

As hoary age is described according to its individual bodily symptoms, v. 3 and part of v. 4, in a metaphor, liken man to a house, a thought that is not uncommon

in the Scriptures, cf., Isa. 38:12; Job 4:19; II Cor. 5:
1, 2; II Pet. 1:13ff. That group of commentators who
say in reference to vv. 2-5 that they "set forth the
threatening approach of death under the image of a
tempest which, gathering over an Eastern city during
the day, breaks upon it toward evening" (*Cox*), have
only one support for their view in the text, namely,
the word "rain." But "rain" (*gĕshĕm*) never means
"storm."

Verse 3. The opening phrase, "in the day," which
connects this verse with the preceding and introduces
all the following items to the end of v. 5, here naturally
means "at the time"; *Luther* translates correctly *zur
Zeit.* "The guardians" or "keepers of the house" are
the arms, which are without a doubt that part of the
body which can accomplish most by way of protection.
They tremble with the approach of the infirmity of
age as is almost universally the case with very old
people. "The strong men" (*'anshe hechayil*) are the
legs, limbs that well deserve this name because the
biggest muscles of the body control their motions. For
that reason, too, the Scriptures speak of the legs of
man by way of metonomy for "strength," cf., Ps. 147:
10, also Song 5:15, where legs are likened to "pillars
of marble upon sockets of fine gold." It is a common
observation that with advancing age legs lose their
firm strength and their straightness and "are bowed."

The "grinding-women" are the teeth. They are
so called because theirs is the business of grinding
the food, for which reason they are in the Greek called
μύλαι, and our term "molars" conveys the same thought.
The feminine "grinding-*women*" (*tochanoth*, feminine
plural of the participle) is used because the work of
grinding was one of the daily tasks of the women.
Since many teeth are lost as years go by (*batelu* — a
late word that is found only here = "cease") the
grinding functions cannot be performed so well by

the isolated teeth that remain. "They that look out of the window" are beyond the shadow of a doubt the eyes. Their infirmity is the fact that they are "dark," the clear vision of youth is sadly impaired. The eyes are said to "be darkened" because the clear images that should be reflected upon man's perception by them have grown indistinct or dark.

On these points of v. 3 there is practical unanimity among commentators. With v. 4 there begins a rather wide divergence of opinion.

If the clause, "the doors leading out into the street are shut," were considered independently, the simplest meaning would very likely be that man's mouth shall be shut, either because the lips are drawn down over the toothless gums, or because of a certain moroseness and taciturnity that are incident upon old age. There are several objections to this interpretation: lips are no more apt to be shut in old age than they were before; second, if there is a taciturnity of old age, there is also the proverbial *garrulitas senilis*. Another objection to this view is the fact that in the Hebrew the circumstantial clause is construed as a phrase by the use of the preposition *be* plus the infinitive *shephal* which equals, "in that the sound of the grinding is low." This assigns the circumstances (not *cause* as *Koenig* claims, K.S., 403a) that attend the shutting of the doors. Doors are means of communicating with the outside world. The mouth and its teeth have been referred to (3c). Therefore the author is at this point referring to the *ears*. They are shut to the outer world as is attested by the fact that that common sound of the grinding of grain, which was heard daily about the Oriental home, is scarcely perceived by the unfortunate old man.

There follow the words: "and one rises up when the voice of the bird is heard." We have rendered *yakum*, whose subject is not expressed and is therefore indefinite, by the insertion of the impersonal subject, "one" or "the man"; for though "*a* man" would be the strict English equivalent, yet the old man, generally speaking, is the subject; therefore, "*the* man." The *le* in *leqol* is *lamed temporis* (cf., KS 331f). When the voice of the bird is heard in the early morning, the old persons, who are unable to sleep any longer, arise. The birds have not disturbed them; the time of the birds' song and their early rising happen to coincide. It does not seem reasonable to have the old man, whose hearing is much impaired, so much disturbed by the singing of birds as to be unable to sleep longer.

"All tones are indistinct" reads thus in the Hebrew: "All the daughters of music are brought low." This means: All singing as well as all appreciation of singing is a thing of the past. By a peculiar use of the word "daughter" (*bath*) "in phrases denoting character, quality, etc.," the combination "daughters of music" means as much as "songs, melodious notes" (*BDB*) or "tones" (*KW*). For this use of *bath* see also *GK*128v and *KS*306m. These are "brought low" in so far as personal efforts at rendering music are concerned (so the *Targum*). They are "brought low" in so far as appreciation of the musical efforts of others are concerned, cf., the case of Barsillai, II Sam. 19:35.

So as not to strain our attention unduly the Preacher for a moment (v. 5) leaves his metaphoric approach and speaks without a figure. Some commentators have not observed this and have interpreted literal speech in a figurative way. Koheleth simply states the oft-observed truth that an old person, whose limbs are stiff, and whose muscles have lost flexibility, does certainly dread going up that which is high, be it a staircase, the slope of a hill — of which there are very many in Palestine — or anything that demands efforts of climbing. For there is always the fear of a fall, or the difficulty of ascent, or the possible breaking of one of those stiff limbs. More than that: even the ordinary road (*hadderekh*) brings "terrors," for there is the continual danger of stumbling even over trifling obstacles.

A few colorful and expressive metaphors are added as last strokes of the brush, and the picture is complete. "The almond tree blossoms." This refers to the white hair which adorns the head of an old person but is at the same time a sign of physical decay. "An almond tree in full bloom upon a distant hillside has a certain likeness to a head of white hair." The fact that the blossoms of this tree are somewhat pinkish at first does not render this interpretation meaningless because, as these blossoms become ready to drop, they turn white. — *Weyane'ts*, from the root *natsats*, is a different mode of writing the form *yanetz*, imperfect with *aleph* like *ka'm* for *kam*, Hos. 10:4. — "The locust drags himself along as a burden." This rendering of the hithpael *yistabbel* is, no doubt, the best of all that have been offered (*BDB*). The crippled, dragging gait of the locust when it walks is an image of the ungainly and stiff gait that is characteristic of advanced age.

"And desire shall fail." Though translators and commentators almost without exception translate *'ab-hiyyonah* "caperberry," except the A.R.V. which retains the "desire" of the A.V., and Luther, *Lust;* one cannot help but observe that this ἅπαξ λεγόμενον is related to the root *'abhah*, "desire," though the noun formation is indeed without a parallel — an objection which holds good even if another meaning is given to the word. Besides, the oldest Jewish tradition for a long time offered only the translation "desire." In the face of this the rendering "caperberry," which originated with the Septuagint, looks like one of those many guesses to which these ancient translators resorted. At least nothing to substantiate it has ever been produced. If this rendering "caperberry" is retained, and the explanation is given: Since this berry was used as a stimulant of appetite, its failure to have any effect points to the failure of all physical appetites and desires, we should at best have arrived at the meaning "desire" by a more roundabout route. The simple meaning is: all desires, physical and mental, die down (*tapher*, "break"); appetite fails; and all this occurs because the bodily functions and needs are failing, and life is beginning to ebb low.

The explanation that follows applies to the entire preceding sketch, "because man is going to his eternal home." These various ills are a part of the process of his going. The participle *holekh* expresses this thought very fittingly, for the going is a continuous act of dissolution, which may involve many years in the case of some people. In determining what "the eternal home" (*beth 'olam*) means it is not accurate enough to say that it is the grave and then to cite many very apt parallels from antiquity, where the very same expression is used. Though this is commonly done, yet, as *Taylor Lewis* has pointed out, this first assigns a man to a place that is to be his *permanent* habitation ("eternal") and then presently (v. 7) informs us that at least a part of his being does not stay there but goes back to God who gave it. A most peculiar kind of *eternal* home! It will then, as far as this passage is concerned, be necessary for us to claim that the term "eternal home" refers to a state of being. As *Lewis* puts it: "This state of being is so called in distinction from the present upon the earth." But the expression certainly asserts that this state is "eternal," and that, therefore, the going there is so solemn a matter. For the present the author is saying nothing about the nature of this state of being. That lies beyond his present purpose.

The sketch closes with the words: "And the mourners walk about in the streets." Since it was customary in those days and those lands to hire professional mourners to make a loud lamentation, they, the "wailers" (*BDB*), are the ones referred to. "Mourners" is practically a technical name for these. The nearest of kin are not so designated; nor would they be walking about in the streets. This closing touch of the sketch takes us to the solemn hour when death is imminent, and the wailers, in anticipation of being hired for the funeral, are therefore holding themselves in readiness and are pacing back and forth in the street before the house.

As we in thought review the whole portrait as it was drawn, we feel that it is well calculated to give pause to a young and, perhaps, somewhat too light-headed youth, who has never viewed the future in such a way as to include old age and its termination. There is no more sober passage in any literature that drives home this fact with the same force and compels us to consider the need of "remembering our Creator in the days of our youth."

Since the author has come to the very subject of death, that, too, can be utilized for his purpose. He, therefore, goes on to give an *equally poetic picture of death,* vv. 6, 7.

(6) Before the silver cord is removed, and the golden bowl is broken; and the pitcher is shattered at the spring, and the wheel breaks down into the cistern; (7) and the dust returns to the earth as it was, and the spirit returns to God who gave it.

The conjunction "before" connects this verse and the next verse with v. 1, "Remember thy Creator, before," etc. Our author is not losing sight of his purpose in the multitude of poetic images that he has used. Here, too, we believe, there is danger when interpreting to make the *general* pictures, which depict the breakdown of the human organism, too specific by attempting to fix the meaning of "cord, bowl, wheel,

pitcher, fountain, and cistern." The number of interpretations attempted is excessively great and completely bewildering. No two commentators agree. They
are attempting what the author never wanted them
to try. Let all be content to call these pictures what
they, no doubt, intend to be: several different poetic
sketches of death — no more. Do not attempt to discover the specific meaning of "silver cord," "bowl,"
etc. They have no specific meaning; they are only a
part of the background of the picture.

The first two figures belong together in the nature
of the case. The golden lamp-bowl is attached to the
silver cord. When the cord is "removed," that is, cut
or broken, the lamp crashes to the ground and is
ruined. So death cuts off the golden bowl of life and
has the crash of death as a result. The whole figure
represents the loss of man's *life*. Therefore the author
speaks of the *silver* cord that supports the *golden* bowl.
Both are precious metals even as life is a precious
possession.

A few grammatical problems need to be disposed
of. *Yirchak*, the verb, should be pointed as a kal imperfect. The vowel points of the text are, as usual,
designed for the marginal *Keri*. The *Kethibh* (the
traditional text) may well stand. The kal would here
mean "be far away," a verb that is purposely vague
and not specific as are some of the emendations suggested because there is something vague and mysterious
about this process of being cut off by death. Compare
the present-day remark, "If something should happen
. . . " In reality, no man knows exactly what has
happened. The verb *taruts* is an unusual derivative
from *ratsats*, "to break," which makes kal imperfects
as though the form were *ruts*, cf., II Kings 23:12.

The objection that a golden bowl would not break
has little validity. If it is dropped from a good height
onto a marble floor, its momentum in falling would be

increased by the weight of oil it contained, and it would at least be ruined if not actually broken. *Williams* compares very aptly "a [single] lamp hammered out of a piece of gold . . . which hung by a chain of gold" in the Jewish temple at Leontopolis in Egypt about 154 B.C., as described by Josephus (*B.J.* vii, 10, 3).

The next picture presents the same thought but the author has changed the figure. Man's life is now represented as a "pitcher." Whereas the preceding composite picture represents life as a precious thing, this figure represents it as fragile, as fragile as the earthen pitcher (*kadh*) which, if but suffered to strike once against the stones at the side of the spring from which it was wont to draw water, falls to the ground, a mass of potsherds. The comparison has another propriety: both are vessels of clay and skillfully wrought. A touch of sadness is characteristic of all these pictures.

So, too, is the last of all: before "the wheel break down into the cistern." Cisterns would sometimes have a wheel affixed above them so that by means of the rope running over the wheel added leverage was obtained which would make the drawing of water easier. Life and the human body have many features of the letting down and the drawing up in them. There are systole and diastole; there are inspiration and expiration, etc. This continual process finally suffers a collapse, a breakdown, which is rendered even more graphic by a certain grammatical construction. We do not prefer the reading *galgal 'el habbor* (*galgal* without the article). For in that case "wheel" would be in the construct relationship, and we should have to translate, "the wheel at the cistern is broken" as our versions generally render it. The article before "wheel" separates it from the following phrase, which must then be connected more closely with the verb so that the preposition *'el* gains force, and we must render: "The wheel breaks down into the cistern," which wording gives us a picture of the ruined apparatus plus the wheel as they have crashed down into the old cistern. So man breaks down and falls into a pit also.

Verse 7. It was the breakdown of man that was stressed in the preceding verses. That being the point to be emphasized, it is now stated in plain, literal terms that are reminiscent of Gen. 3:19, "the dust returns to the earth as it was." By citing the Genesis passage the author practically says that the doom there foretold is finally realized. Sad as it is from one point of view, from another it is to be expected; for man's body is simply going back to the earth "as it was." This is really a most powerful motive to urge men to remember their Creator, for there comes a time when such remembering shall be impossible. But there is a still more powerful motive that the author has reserved to the last, and that is: "the spirit returns to God who gave it." If this remark is viewed in the light of the preceding utterances on the part of the Preacher, this statement must be a reference to the final judgment in God's presence, of which he has spoken before, cf., 3:17; 8:5, 6. The time to remember the Creator is before the hour has come to go to Him as Judge for the final reckoning. God is, of course, at liberty to make a spirit return unto Him because He is the one "who gave it." It is His creature and subject to *His* call. God's sovereignty is strongly stressed in this clause.

In this connection the thought can hardly be a reference to a peaceful homecoming to God, for it is the climax of the serious issues that shall befall man, a climax that has been prepared for since v. 1. The serious issues that should startle a man into making his peace with God *now* have been heaped up in a well-ordered arrangement. To introduce a thought of *com-*

fort at this point would be a serious blemish and defeat the author's purpose.

Some commentators find in this passage an indication of a re-absorption into God — a view that Old Testament writers cannot hold. Others claim that the idea of a personal continuance of existence is not indicated in this statement. Such views are manifestly unsatisfactory. This verse refers to a coming into judgment, and the very thought of judgment denotes a personal responsibility of the spirit that returns to God. Why should that spirit have lost its personality? We shall not on the basis of this passage attempt to build up a full doctrine of the Old Testament concerning life eternal. This doctrine was simply not yet revealed in all its fulness to the Old Testament saints. But, on the other hand, to leave this statement in a haze of uncertainty surely does scant justice to it. It tells every attentive reader: You personally will at your death appear before the judgment seat of God, therefore get ready.

When we say that the doctrine of the hereafter was not revealed in all its fulness in the Old Testament we do not imply that there was any defect or error in the statement of it, or that the Old Testament statement of it was so rudimentary as to give rise to all manner of misconceptions. The same truths that the New Testament presents are offered by the Old. But the Old does not know all details of these truths as yet.

Having let the whole passage pass in review before our eyes, we are in a better position to evaluate certain objections that are raised to this interpretation, or more particularly to its approach to the problem. Some interpreters claim that the individual whose end is depicted is not man in general but a particular type of man, the sensualist whose debaucheries have weakened his whole system and caused its collapse. But over against this it will be observed that the description is so entirely general in tone that no man would imagine for a moment that the sensualist's end is depicted.

Those interpreters who defend this view also suggest a second interpretation, namely, if it is not specially the sensualist whose senile decay is portrayed it is at least that of the *sinner*, generally speaking. This means: The righteous do not experience this decay of age, for it is written of them: "they shall flourish as a palm tree; they shall bring forth fruit in old age," Ps. 92:12, 13; and again: "They that trust in the Lord shall renew their strength." Though such promises were fulfilled also with reference to the physical side of the life of some men of God such as Moses and Caleb, these promises as such offer no immunity from the ravages of age. Most of the outstanding saints of God grew old as other men do, even with reference to the body; witness Isaac and Jacob and David. Our observation also shows us that God's saints, as a rule, have a generous measure of the infirmities of old age.

This much is, however, true: the dismal scene depicted in v. 1-7 is the only prospect an ungodly old age has to look forward to. They who have "remembered their Creator in the days of their youth" have treasures and resources to fall back upon which help them to be more than conquerors over these ailments; they are able even out of weakness to grow strong with a strength from on high.

IV. EPILOGUE (12:8-14)

We must first consider the claim that this Epilogue was not written by Koheleth himself. As *Delitzsch* states it: "The supposition that this section is from another hand is more natural than the contrary." We shall not attempt to refute *Hertzberg,* who assumes that three distinct men, not one of whom was Koheleth, successively made closing notations till the Epilogue was complete. We maintain that it is fully as easy to accept this Epilogue as being a component part of the book and as being carefully designed by the author to meet a felt need.Multiplicity of authorship should not be assumed unless strong evidence points to it. For, in the first place, the fact that the author speaks of himself in the third person is no more indication of the activity of another than it is in the case of the writings of St. John or in the secular field of Cæsar and Xenophon.

One might take exception to the statement, "Koheleth was wise" (v. 9) as being unsuited and as lacking in modesty. Two points may, however, be urged in its defense. First, this statement appears in the third person rather than in the first. That fact makes it milder. Second, "wise" (*chakham*) had a more technical meaning in Biblical usage than appears at first glance. Even as there was a "wisdom" literature among the Jews, so those who cultivated it were called "wise." So this becomes a technical designation which marks an individual as belonging to a certain class of literary men. In Biblical usage the expression referred to contains nothing more offensive than does the present-day statement: "I am a playwright or an author."

There is a New Testament parallel of an appendix written by another hand, namely, the conclusion of St. John's Gospel (21:24f.) which many conservative scholars regard as the work of the elders of the church at Ephesus. Such an appendix may be added quite appropriately. From this point of view the claim that Koheleth did not write 12:8-14 is not too serious. It must, however, be maintained that the appendix, if it is by another hand, is not intended to be a corrective of inadequate and incorrect statements found in the book. There is no evidence that a glossator is here trying to make a deficient work acceptable and orthodox.

As to language, the Epilogue is so obviously late Hebrew that no one could dispute that fact. But to claim that it differs from Biblical Hebrew more than the rest of the book does is a subjective opinion.

It should not be forgotten, furthermore, that though the preceding section for good reasons dwelt upon the thought of the *close of life*, that does not necessarily constitute a good *close of a book*. For the close of life was merely used as an argument for securing the right relation to the Creator betimes, and this again as a foundation upon which to build an attitude of joy in facing life. One of the many contentions that had to be made over against an abuse of the claim, "all is vanity," was the contention: "Rejoice," and, "Let your heart be glad." This one contention only is brought to a good conclusion by the section 11:9-12:7. The chief issues of the book have thereby not as yet been brought to a good and effective conclusion. The book needs some concluding statement.

Two things appear in this, which we regard as the author's own Epilogue, first an authentication of himself, v. 8-11; then a recommendation of his message, v. 12-14, both stated with becoming modesty.

When we remember that a claim to inspiration is advanced by the author himself we need not wonder that inspiration taught him to furnish an authentication of himself. The Spirit of inspiration is also the Spirit of prophecy, and God's providence foresaw how misunderstanding would in days to come derive teachings from this book that it never contained and so discredit an inspired work. It is not impossible or difficult of belief that God's Spirit should in view of this fact furnish the book with a recommendation of the author that was calculated to correct any errors of interpretation into which men might fall.

Furthermore, it is the part of the skillful teacher— and a teacher this man certainly aims to be — to state his chief point with unmistakable clearness by way of review so that no reader might fail to see the major issues. The recommendation of his message that the author gives in v. 12-14 does just this with consummate skill. We venture the suggestion that this conclusion is both very skilfully and effectively put and also very helpful. Since it does such admirable justice to the book, as we shall see presently, pray, who would be in a better position so skillfully to round off his book in this summary than is Koheleth himself? We believe that internal evidence speaks loudly in favor of Koheleth as being the author of the last portion of the book as certainly as he was the author of all that preceded.

A. The author's authentication of himself (v. 8-11)

(8) **Vanity of vanities, says the Preacher, all is vanity.** (9) **Aside from the fact that the Preacher was wise, he also taught the people knowledge continually; and he pondered and searched out diligently, then skillfully set down his many proverbs.** (10) **The Preacher sought to find pleasant words, and uprightly did he write words of truth.** (11) **The words of the wise are like goads; the collected words are as fastened nails; they are given by one Shepherd.**

We must first justify the fact that we have regarded v. 8 as a part of this Epilogue whereas almost all commentators at present have it conclude the preceding paragraph. Our chief reason is a grammatical one: v. 9 begins with the conjunction "and"; v. 8 begins without a conjunction. Verve 8 evidently begins what v. 9 continues. We hold this view in spite of the fact that, as some commentators point out, the presence of the "and" alone is not determinative because there is such a thing as a *transitional "and."* But the situation is different here. The "and" begins v. 9, but *at the same time* v. 8 begins without a conjunction. In such a case it cannot be said that such an "and" is the transitional one. Otherwise conjunctions become practically meaningless.

There is surely a connection in thought, by way of transition, with the preceding section. This is not so close, however, as to allow the words, "all is vanity," to close the preceding section. For the author was there showing how the Creator ought to be remembered before age came and made it impossible to do so. The description of old age and of death is furnished, not to demonstrate what a vain thing life is, but to show the need of making haste to remember the Creator. To let the closing thought be, "all is vanity," is illogical. But after the preceding section has been concluded, the author may look back upon his picturesque sketch of old age and of death and remark: By the way, that could also be used as a demonstration of my chief contention that all is vanity. In about that sense does he write v. 8 at this point: "Vanity of vanities, saith the Preacher; all is vanity."

Verse 9. We cannot charge the good Preacher with a lack of modesty because he sets forth these claims. He merely claims those qualities that people would have had a right to demand of one who aspired in so authoritative a way to direct his contemporaries in regard to very vital issues. He lays claim to being "wise" (*chakham*). This term, in addition to its technical meaning set forth above, implies that wisdom which is from on high, taught of God, and rooted in the fear of God. To claim this much is not more than if a regenerate man in our day claims to have God's Holy Spirit. It is expected of certain men that they will be able to make such a claim. Having this quality, the Preacher would have the requisite knowledge and judgment that the writing of such a work as this required.

Aside from that fact (*yother she*) the Preacher had publicly given proof of his willingness and his ability to function as a leader of godly thought in that he had "continually taught the people knowledge" in his day. Those who were taught had apparently recognized that he had divine authority behind what he said. Right "knowledge" (*da'ath*) was what his contemporaries needed. He was able to set it forth in such a way that his hearers actually profited thereby. "He taught . . . continually" refers not only to the teaching activity manifested in this book as such but to much teaching that was done before and after this book was written.

This "knowledge" that he had imparted in his public ministry the Preacher now cast into good proverb form. For the people of the East and the Hebrews in particular — as all their post-Biblical literature abundantly indicates — do love good proverbs that are skillfully arranged and artistically grouped. The Preacher, therefore, shows us what extreme care he used in casting his knowledge into proper form. He first "pondered," that is, weighed carefully everything that was to be presented; for this is the best meaning to give to this rare word whose root is *'azan,* from which there is derived *mo'znayim,* "balances"; *KW* says: *erwaegen.* The next step was: "he searched out diligently." This implies an attempt to delve even deeper into the issues than his previous instruction had led him to do (*KW* says: *Untersuchung anstellen*). These last two verbs were connected by "and." The next one is distinguished by being without a conjunction. We have sought to give the emphasis of this construction by inserting a "then"; "then did he skillfully set down his many proverbs." This refers to the type of artistic and poetic arrangement of words that deserves to be called "proverbs," *meshalim,* a term which allows for a wide variety of uses. It is much broader than our word "proverbs" would suggest. It is too strong a claim that this last word furnishes proof for the fact that the arrangement of the book is entirely poetic as to structure — *Hertzberg.*

This book grew out of his teaching experience and out of the further efforts that he made to present his precepts in the most effective way. For he sought to couch them in "pleasant words." We are reminded of the "words of grace" that the Savior Himself employed (Luke 4:22), for here, too, we have the expression *dibhre chephets*, i.e., "words of delight." He did not hastily record what he sought to impart but "sought to find" this type of words. The use of these words implies a careful search after the most acceptable terms for conveying his message.

"And he wrote words of truth"; literally: "and it was written in uprightness." The word *yosher*, "uprightness," is an accusative of manner. The word implies that perfect sincerity characterized all his efforts. He personally believed and meant all that he wrote. The arguments set forth were in every case his inmost conviction. But they were more than subjectively "straight" (that is the meaning of the root *yashar*) they were also objectively true. He, therefore, adds the apposition, "words of truth" (*'emeth*).

Surely, a man who can sincerely claim to have done all that he has stated deserves to be regarded as a conscientious author. Both form and content, he assures us, received all possible attention. It must also be noted that in vv. 9 and 10 a series of piel forms is used, all intensives, which imply a heightened and more intensive degree of activity, which fact we have tried to embody in our translation by appropriate adverbs — "diligently," "skillfully." Incidentally, we catch one of the few glimpses behind the scenes in the process of the inspiration which we claim for the Scriptures. For our author, who shall presently class himself with the inspired writers, did not because he was inspired neglect such human efforts as a successful writer ought to make in order to bring his work up to the very highest degree of perfection.

Verse 11. The Preacher stresses a twofold use of
words such as those which he has so skillfully arranged
in his book: they serve as "goads" and as fastened
"nails." The goads are goads in a general sense. The
purpose of goads is to prod the sluggish to action.
Good proverbs do that. They bear in them power to
give a mental and a spiritual stimulus, for they can
become "sharper than any two-edged sword." Besides
they serve as "nails fastened." For as nails fastened
give a definite point on which all manner of things
may be hung, so stable words of the wise give a man
something to hold and to tie to. They furnish a kind
of mental anchorage. These two excellent uses of his
words, the prodding and the establishing, ought further
to recommend them to all earnest-minded men.

Though this use is the chief point in the verse to
be emphasized, yet, knowing other inspired writings
as he does, the author would hardly claim for his own
book exclusively what they all so prominently manifest
(cf., II Tim. 3:16). Therefore, referring to all these, he
says: "the words [plural] of the wise." Nor can we
refer this claim indiscriminately to all good writings,
inspired and uninspired, as long as they only breathe
the wisdom from on high. For the concluding words
of the verse show that he has in mind only the *Sacred
Scriptures*, for he derives their peculiar power from
the fact that "they are given of one Shepherd." This
can be a reference only to Jahweh, the Shepherd of
Israel (Ps. 80:1), who shepherds His people by giving
them the pasturage of the Word on which they can at all
times richly feed. From that point of view the choice
of the name "shepherd" (*ro'eh*) is most appropriate.
Nor was there anything new about the term. Observe
its use in all periods of Israel's history: Gen. 48:15;
49:24; Ps. 23:1; Isa. 40:11; Jer. 31:10; Ezek. 34:11,
12. At this point many commentators are ready to
concede that the reference must be to Yahweh, e.g.,

Williams says: "If as is probable, the words of the wise are said to come from Him, there is no doubt who He is." — Note that *mih* before *ro'eh* may be the *min* of source or of agent (*KS* 107).

Observe what a correct and clear conception of the inspiration of the sacred writings prevailed in Israel at this time, especially of the fact that it was a unified work done by the Lord for the good of His people. Observe also that the Preacher is aware of the fact that God has been pleased to use him to share in this work. His writings rank on a par with the rest. Should men, misreading his message, feel their misgivings about his book, let them run up against this claim, mildly yet positively put, and when they feel its sincerity, let them go back to the book, determined to correct their misapprehension.

Our rendering, "the collected sayings," calls for some explanation. It is not entirely satisfactory, but it stresses the chief point. It takes the place of the expression, "the masters of assemblies" (A.V.). The reader who is not acquainted with the original may well wonder how such divergent renderings can originate. The Hebrew has *ba'ale 'asuppoth*, which rendered literally would be, "masters of the collections." However, the word *ba'al*, from which the plural construct *ba'ale* is derived, is an unusual word in the Hebrew, it is used as a "noun of relation" (*BDB*). A "*baal* of dreams" (Gen 37:19) is a "dreamer." Notice that in this particular example the translation "master" cannot be used. The expression simply describes a man who has the *quality* or *attribute* of being given to dreams. Using this instance as a parallel, we take our expression above as indicating a *quality* or *attribute* of "the words of the wise": they are "collected ones," or as we have rendered: "collected sayings."

What makes the rendering "masters of assemblies" doubtful is the parallelism of the verse at this point, which can be best demonstrated by the following arrangement:

Subject	Copula	Predicate
a) "the words of the wise"	"are"	"as goads"
b) "the collected ones"	"are"	"as fastened nails"

The two clauses run parallel in all their parts and in their meaning. In this scheme of things "masters of assemblies" have no place. They cannot be introduced without bringing in an element that will not fit into the picture. The *words* themselves are under consideration, not "leaders of synagogues," as some commentators have translated this expression. From this parallelism it follows that the word "collected ones" must mean "collected sayings" in order to agree with "the words of the wise." *KS* 306g offers the translation *Glieder einer Sammlung*, which might be rendered "the constituent parts of a collection" — practically the same as our rendering above.

B)   **The author's recommendation of his message**
(v. 12-14)

There are several important things that the Preacher has yet to say about his message. The first has to do with the use of his book over against the ephemeral productions or the secular works of his day. To be able to recommend his own work as strongly as he does requires on the part of the author a distinct consciousness of the inspiration of the book. But if he is convinced that this is an inspired book he dare not speak of it in terms that put forth its claims mildly and hesitatingly.

(12) **And as to what is more than these, be admonished, my son, of the making of many books there is no end, and much study is weariness of the flesh. (13) Let us hear the conclusion of the discourse, the whole thing: Fear God and keep His commandments, for this concerns all men. (14) For**

God will bring every work into the judgment over every concealed thing, whether it be good or evil.

The first words, *weyother mehemmah*, are not only a general "furthermore." Nor is the *mehemmah* to be joined with the following: "By these be admonished" (A.V.); for the time element in similar phrases has *yother* joined with *min* (cf., Esther 6:6). The pronoun *hemmah*, "these," refers to the inspired writings that were just mentioned. "As to what is more than these" refers to other writings apart from the inspired writings. In regard to these every reader, who is to regard himself as a "son" of the good Preacher (cf., "son" in Prov. 1:8, 10, 15; 2:1, etc.) is to "let himself be admonished."

It must have been an age of great literary activity both among Jews and Gentiles: "of making many books there is no end." Koheleth cannot claim for these works such high attributes as "words of the wise" or "given of one Shepherd." They are only a part of the mass of literary productions that were currently on the market. What a censure of all these productions and their value when the Preacher finds only this to say in reference to them: to study them eagerly brings you only "weariness of the flesh"! For he cannot be speaking of study in general or include in such study the efforts made to meditate day and night in the law of the Lord. For the Scriptures regard that effort as stimulating and refreshing to the point even where the incidental weariness of the flesh that results is not worthy of mention over against the refreshment of the heart and the body that have been received. The three parts of v. 12 are very closely related to one another.

"Study" (*lahagh*) from an Arabic root meaning "to apply oneself assiduously" and used only here can according to the connection mean only "study," but a study that is done in eager application to the subject in hand; not "preaching" (*Luther*) which does not fit into the thought sequence nor agree with the root meaning of the word.

So the author has put an estimate upon his work over against contemporary productions, an estimate that is very definite and clear-cut and condemnatory, it is true, but not arrogant. In fact, it is very modestly stated. This was one way of recommending his message. Another is to give the substance and chief point of it. This he does in v. 13.

We have more than just the "end" of the matter in these words: we have a "sum" (BDB) or a "conclusion" (*suph*) that does both: it summarizes the contents; it skillfully concludes the matter. Since all this is more than the "end" (A.R.V.), the better rendering is that of the A.V.: "Let us hear the conclusion." The thought that we have a summary is emphasized by the appositional statement, "the whole thing" (*hakkol*). Such a concluding summary is not a philosophical theory finally arrived at but a piece of practical wisdom to which a man ought to hearken. Koheleth is himself ready to give heed and therefore includes himself in the exhortation, "Let *us* hear." — To translate *nishma'* "all has been heard" is rather lame. It is, of course, the pausal form.

Here, then, is the place to look for the author's own statement of the theme of his book, for the summarizing conclusion must at the same time give the theme in one form or another. "All is vanity" cannot, therefore, be called the theme. It is merely one of the major items that has to be impressed upon his generation. Besides, if what the thirteenth verse states is the all-important thought to be carried away from a study of the book, as the substance of it, we see how unsatisfactory is the reasoning of all interpreters who find the author guilty of questionable ethics, eudaemonism, pessimism, and the like. This is, so to speak, the substance of his contentions, the light by which all things else should be judged.

This summary is bipartite, very brief, very readily understood, and has been met with repeatedly in one form or another throughout the book: "Fear God and keep His commandments." The order of the original is: "God thou shalt fear." Not fate, not mischance, not calamities, not men, not rulers — *God*. That is a good thought for evil days. All other things are subservient to Him. The "fear" is, of course, that reverent awe which grows out of the faith which the frail creature should have toward the holy God. Or better, to use the author's own commentary, it consists in "keeping His commandments." It is such respect for Him that His revealed will, which He has made known to us, is unquestioningly obeyed. Any fear of God that neglects this simple evidence of sincerity is not fear of God but an idle sham. Without a doubt this is the kernel of true wisdom for any situation.

As this truth is final in its scope and an actual summary of what man should bear in mind, so it is universal in its application: "This is the duty of all men," as *J. M. Powis Smith* also translates: "This concerns all mankind." For in some such fashion this statement must be rendered, for *kol-ha'adham* = "the whole of mankind" (*BDB*), cf., Num. 12:3; 16:29; Judg. 16:17, etc. Such is also Luther's rendering: *denn das gehoert allen Menschen zu*. The Hebrew is curt: "For this, all men." The rendering: "This is the whole duty of man" (A.R.V.) is unsatisfactory. By advancing this as a cause for obedience the author has practically said: How can anyone overlook so obvious a thing as this practical suggestion, seeing that it is the duty of all alike!

Verse 14. A further reason is assigned as to why men should "fear" and obey the summary expressed in v. 13. Koheleth does not want it to be trifled with.

The fear of God and the keeping of His commandments should be practiced as though being done by men who expect to face God "in the judgment over every concealed thing." By this unusual term is the judgment here described, for that is the feature of it that is here under consideration: it will bring to light "the hidden things of darkness" (I Cor. 4:5), and, therefore, all the insincerity that might have characterized the careless man's fear of God. Koheleth does not want anyone to trifle with the fear of God that he has in mind. This is certainly an emphatic and a skillful way of driving home his chief point. *Williams* makes a good observation: "Observe the strength of the reason, much more virile than the appeal to God's love as presented by too many Christian preachers."

The Masoretes failed to learn from this wise teacher when they appended the note after the conclusion of the text that v. 13 is to be reread after v. 14 lest the book seem to come to a conclusion on too ominous a note, which is practically the same procedure they followed at the conclusion of the text of Malachi.

Verse 14 may well be regarded as an excellent example of when the words of the wise man are truly "goads" and "nails."

SOLI DEO GLORIA

Index of Subjects

Activity 261ff
age (old) 274ff
allegorizing 261
anger 149
archaeology 32
author of Eccl. 14ff

Babylonian influence 31
benevolence 254ff
books 298f

Chance 96
cheerfulness 214
church 81
comfort 214

Death 148, 283ff
debauchery 249ff
destiny 249ff
dreams 120

Egyptian influence 32
epilogue 288ff
eternity 91

Fatalism 67, 229ff
fate 67
feasting 148
folly 60, 229ff
fool 106
formalism 117

Gain 43
Gilgamesh epic 216
Greek influence 31

Heart 52
hidden God 80
high station 111
horticultural experiments 61

Injustice 193
inscrutability of God 200ff
integrity of text 23ff
Israel 141, 168f, 236

Judgment 287

Koheleth 7

Language of the book 13

light 276

Man 142
memento mori 145
mirth 59
miser 109
money 125

Nothing new 48f

Opportunism 165
oppression 103ff, 191ff
outline of Eccl. 24ff

Patience 154
Persia 227, 230, 232, 240ff,
    245ff, 259
Persians 134f, 153f, 189
periodicity 85
perversion of justice 93ff
pessimism 29f
philosophy (heathen) 173f
prayer 119, 244
"Preacher" 38, 292ff
purpose of Ecclesiastes 17ff

Rebuke 151
resurrection 98
riches 107ff, 125ff, 139ff, 142ff
righteousness 162f
rulers (foolish) 244ff

Self-restraint 166ff
sensual enjoyment 58
Solomon 10, 51, 55, 58, 63, 256
sorrow 145ff
soul 137f, 140
sovereignty of God 186
spirit 155
style of Ecclesiastes 21ff
suffering 145ff, 156ff
summum bonum 20

Treasures 62

"Under the sun" 28, 42, 60

Vanity 40ff
vanity of all things 50ff
vows 120

Waw consecutive 56
wine 60f
wisdom 51, 65ff, 156ff, 179ff, 221ff

work 70ff
worship 116ff

Youth 267ff

Index of Authors

Aalders 35
Aben Ezra 247
Albright 32
Alleman 79, 257

Barton 35, 43, 52, 56, 99, 103, 125, 138, 149, 150, 152, 153, 162, 165, 167, 169, 171, 177, 178, 180, 216, 244, 248
Bradley 34

Cox 17, 34, 223, 238, 278

Deane 24, 34, 233, 244
Delitzsch 14, 22, 31, 34, 91, 98, 99, 119, 134, 136, 137, 140, 147(2), 153 (2), 162, 165, 166, 204, 206, 215, 228, 239, 256, 260, 262, 277, 288

Ewald 207

Fausset 34

Galling 24, 32, 35, 43, 80, 90, 125, 137(3), 151, 160, 162, 164, 174, 224, 235, 244, 255, 274
Gerhard 276
Ginsburg 12, 75, 150, 165, 215, 217

Hartmann 19
Heine 19
Hertzberg 22, 30, 35, 45, 49, 62, 68, 75, 82, 90, 96, 98, 119, 139, 144, 145, 153, 239, 259, 275, 288, 293
Hengstenberg 33, 46, 66, 82, 98, 134, 149, 153, 173, 174, 197, 209, 239, 260, 262

Hitzig 207

Jastrow 35
Jerome 38

Koenig 14, 22, 38, 130, 279
Lewis 16, 98, 231, 248, 282
Luther 7, 33, 38, 53, 65, 83, 91, 92, 122, 131, 133, 138, 149, 160, 197, 207, 215, 222, 262, 267, 278, 281, 298, 300

MacDonald 36
McNeil 178
Michaelis 173

Oehler 20

Pfeiffer 22

Rashi 247
Reynolds 33
Robinson 80
Rupprecht 16

Siegfried 23, 35, 178
Smith, J. M. P. 300

Targum 180, 227, 269

Vaihinger 150
Vilmar 31
Volck 30, 34, 147, 206

Wildeboer 35
Williams 35, 60, 92(2), 102, 112(2), 146(2), 148, 152, 164, 180, 192, 199, 211, 227, 240, 245, 250, 285, 296, 301

Zoeckler 22, 33, 98, 101, 122, 140, 161, 203, 210, 245, 257, 259, 275